MAP 1. THE SELJUK SULTANATE OF ANATOLIA (RUM)

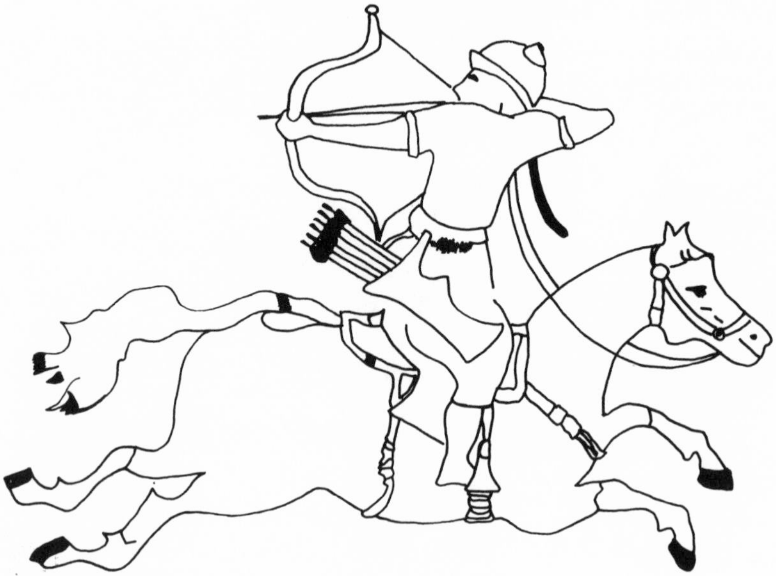

A History of the SELJUKS

İbrahim Kafesoğlu's Interpretation and the Resulting Controversy

Translated, Edited and with an Introduction by GARY LEISER

Southern Illinois University Press
Carbondale and Edwardsville

Printed in the United States of America
Designed by Cindy Small
Production supervised by Natalia Nadraga

Library of Congress Cataloging-in-Publication Data

Kafesoğlu, İbrahim.
A history of the Seljuks.

Translation of the article Selçuklular from the
İslâm ansiklopedisi.
Bibliography: p.
Includes index.
1. Seljuks. 2. Islamic Empire—History—750–1258.
3. Kafesoğlu, İbrahim, 1914–1984. 4. Turan, Osman, 1914–1978. 5. Ateş, Ahmed, 1917–1966. I. Leiser, Gary, 1946–
II. Title.
DS27.K28 1988 956.1′01 87-26377
ISBN 0-8093-1414-2

Contents

Preface

A student of Seljuk history faces several major obstacles. His primary sources are widely scattered and, in some cases, still unpublished. They are in many, very different, medieval languages. Moreover, for the most part, they are not in Turkish nor written by Turks. His secondary sources, that is, modern works on the Seljuks, are chiefly in Western languages in addition to Turkish. Western specialists in medieval Islamic history, which includes the Seljuk period, generally know one or more of the languages of the primary sources, but rarely understand modern Turkish. Consequently, these specialists usually ignore the work that has been done by Turkish scholars, some of which is very important, or sometimes include it in their references or bibliographies without fully understanding it. This lack of awareness of Turkish scholarship is understandably even more pronounced among Western Byzantinists and historians of the Crusades.

The work presented in this book, İbrahim Kafesoğlu's article on the Seljuks in the *İslâm Ansiklopedisi* (hereinafter abbreviated as *İA*), has been translated with this in mind. Not only is it a significant Turkish contribution to Seljuk historiography, but it is also among the most recent surveys of the entire Seljuk period in any language, even though it was published between 1964 and 1965. For English speakers who are unfamiliar with Turkish, a translation of this article has several immediate advantages. First, it provides a compact survey of Seljuk history and civilization where none currently exists in English. Second, it brings interested scholars relatively up to date on what their Turkish counterparts have done in this field. And third, it offers a Turkish interpretation of this subject, one that is not commonly known in the West. Moreover, the appearance of Kafesoğlu's article led to a very tumultuous controversy between himself and Osman Turan, another of Turkey's leading authorities on the Seljuks. Turan's critique of

Kafesoğlu's work and the counter-critiques by Kafesoğlu and Ahmed Ateş, the director of the editorial committee of the *İA,* bring out, among other things, certain salient features of contemporary, Turkish Seljuk historiography. The critique and counter-critiques have therefore been included in this book as well.

Altogether it is hoped that this combined material will serve, to some degree, as a guide to Turkish Seljuk historiography and encourage Western scholars to take greater account of it. At the same time, this book may also be of some assistance to the layman who wants a general introduction to the field. It should be mentioned, though, that no attempt has been made by the translator to evaluate Kafesoğlu's article or to pass judgment on the controversy that it produced. In this respect, the intention is only to provide translations that will be grist for scholarly mills. Furthermore, it must be stated that, in light of recent research on the Seljuks, Kafesoğlu had intended to make certain corrections and revisions in his article for the English translation, but unfortunately he recently passed away before being able to do so.

Finally, it is with great pleasure that I thank several people who eased my work of translation. Mr. Hüsameddin Güz, with unflagging patience, not only answered all my questions about many, very complex Turkish sentences, but also painstakingly compared Kafesoğlu's Turkish text with the English and saved me from a number of errors. Dr. Toni Cross, the director of the Ankara branch of the American Research Institute in Turkey, provided very helpful criticism to improve the flow of the English text. Joyce Atwood of Southern Illinois University Press admirably copyedited the entire, very complex work. And my wife, Patricia, possessed the word-processing wizardry to manipulate texts and design certain Turkish letters, as well as a transliteration system for the Arabic alphabet, which made possible a more speedy and accurate translation.

Abbreviations

ANSNS	American Numismatic Society, New Series
AÜİF Dergisi	*Ankara Üniversitesi İlâhiyat Fakültesi Dergisi* [The journal of the Faculty of Divinity of Ankara University]
AÜSBF Dergisi	*Ankara Üniversitesi Siyasal Bilgiler Fakültesi Dergisi* [The journal of the Social Science Faculty of Ankara University]
BSOAS	*Bulletin of the School of Oriental and African Studies*
DTCF Dergisi	*Dil ve Tarih-Coğrafya Fakültesi Dergisi* [The journal of the Faculty of Language, History, and Geography of Ankara University]
EI	*Encyclopaedia of Islam*
GMS	*Gibb Memorial Series*
İA	*İslâm Ansiklopedisi*
İÜİF Mecmuası	*İstanbul Üniversitesi İktisat Fakültesi Mecmuası* [The journal of the Faculty of Economics of Istanbul University]
JA	*Journal Asiatique*
KCA	*Körösi Csoma Archivum* [The journal of Alexis Sandor Körösi Csoma Archives]
MTM	*Millî Tetebbûlar Mecmuası* [The journal of national research]
RO	*Rocznik Orientalistyczny*
ŞM	*Şarkiyat Mecmuası* [The journal of oriental studies]
TDK	Türk Dil Kurumu [Turkish Language Association]
THİT Mecmuası	*Türk Hukuk ve İktisat Tarihi Mecmuası* [The journal of Turkish legal and economic history]

TM	*Türkiyat Mecmuası* [The journal of Turkish studies]
TOEM	*Tarîkh-i ʿOsmânî Encümeni Mecmuası* [The journal of the committee for Ottoman history]
TTK	Türk Tarih Kurumu [Turkish Historical Association]
VD	*Vakıflar Dergisi* [The journal of *waqfs*]

Part One

Seljuk Historiography

1
Work in the West

There is no question that the coming of the Seljuk Turks to the Middle East opened a new era in the history of the Muslim world. Under their rule, the heartlands of the Middle East experienced a profound political, religious, and cultural transformation. When the Seljuks appeared on the scene in the eleventh century, they found a Muslim world in complete political disarray. From Egypt to Central Asia, the entire region was a mosaic of large and small states whose political rivalries were often accentuated by religious differences. Indeed, there were rival caliphs in Baghdad and Cairo, and a third caliphate was about to expire in Cordova. Moreover, to the great consternation of Sunnī Muslims, the caliph in Cairo was a Shīʿī and bent on imposing his authority and version of Islam on them all. In Baghdad, the legitimate successor to Muḥammad was little more than a puppet in the hands of another Shīʿī dynasty. It seemed to many Sunnīs that true, orthodox Islam would soon be displaced by heresy.

In addition to political and religious disunity, Islamic culture had begun to decline. Political and religious disunity, of course, limited various economic and social resources thus making a general cultural decline inevitable. By the beginning of the eleventh century, the "golden age of classical Islamic civilization" had passed. The high culture of this golden age started to give way to local and more provincial traditions. Arabic literature began to lose its vitality and become increasingly imitative. Art and architecture too became rather static with few perceptible innovations. Even in the "hard sciences" like medicine and mathematics there was less speculation and research as more men of learning were content to follow their predecessors. Altogether, most of Muslim society seemed to lose its dynamism, to look inward, to concentrate more on the past than on the future, to be satisfied with form rather than content. In some places, notably Anatolia and Spain, the borders of the Muslim world had even receded.

Upon their arrival in the Middle East, the Seljuks by no means solved all the problems in that region. However, they did establish political unity in the area between Central Asia and the Egyptian border, rejuvinate Sunnism and greatly add to its strength, and lay the foundations for a new flowering of culture. In place of myriad, quarrelsome states, the Seljuks founded a single empire whose goal was world dominion. Under their rule, the bureaucracy, especially those branches concerned with taxation and land ownership, the judiciary, and the army were better organized and more efficient than ever before in Islam. In fact, with the Seljuks began the Turkish political or military domination of the Middle East that lasted until recent times.

As Sunnīs, the Seljuks came on the scene as liberators, rescuing the ʿAbbāsid caliph from his Shīʿī masters, and crushing heresy wherever they found it. Thanks to the Seljuks, Shīʿism would never capture the Muslim world. In the struggle against heresy, the Seljuks used both the sword and the pen. With respect to the latter, Islamic law schools, known as *madrasas,* were established under Seljuk auspices throughout the empire. After the mosque, the *madrasa* was the single most important Muslim institution ever created. It not only rejuvinated, strengthened, and promoted Sunnism, but also gave the ruling authorities certain opportunities to manipulate the religious class. The *madrasa* attracted the greatest minds of the age. A professor of one of these schools, the renowned philosopher al-Ghazzālī, is credited with reconciling the orthodoxy of the theologians with Ṣūfism, the widespread mysticism of the masses, thus assuring the triumph of orthodoxy over heresy. Indeed, while the Seljuks professed Sunnism, they also channeled much of their shamanistic past into different *ṣūfī* orders and consequently stimulated Islam on both levels.

Culturally, the Seljuk conquest of the Middle East brought major changes. The Turks, naturally, brought their own Central Asian traditions and customs with them. These included titles, ranks, symbols, music, dance, handicrafts, oral literature, and the like. Their contact with Central Asia, moreover, facilitated the spread of Chinese influence, especially in art, to the Islamic world. Perhaps most significantly, the Seljuk invasion marked the end of Arabic as the predominant language, or *lingua franca,* of the Muslim world and pushed the Arabs from center stage to stage left, for the center of Arabic language and culture then shifted from Baghdad to Cairo. With an empire based on the Iranian plateau and extending west into Anatolia, the Seljuks encouraged the development of first Persian and then Turkish as administrative and cultural languages. The Seljuks in fact stimulated a rebirth of Persian literature. Henceforth, the Middle East was divided between Arabic and Perso-Turkish linguistic and cultural zones. Finally, it should be mentioned that the Seljuks had a major influence on medieval Europe, indirectly via Byzantium, as they expanded the borders of Islam into Anatolia, and directly, as the primary antagonists of the Crusaders. As we know, it was Seljuk pressure on Byzantium and the fall of Jerusalem to Seljuk troops that led Pope Urban II to call for the First Crusade.

Despite the obvious importance of the Seljuks in Islamic history, there have been surprisingly few attempts in the West to write a systematic account of them. Between the appearance of Joseph de Guignes' *Histoire générale des Huns, des Turcs, des Mongols et des autres Tartares occidentaux* (books X–XI) in Paris between 1756 and 1758 and the first edition of the *Encyclopaedia of Islam* (abbreviated herein as *EI*) during the years 1913–42, no Western scholar showed any special interest in investigating their history, although there were certainly many references to them in such general works as Gustav Weil's *Geschichte der Chalifen* (Mannheim, 1846–51) and William Muir's *Caliphate, its Rise, Decline and Fall* (Oxford, 1891), and more particularly V. Barthold's classic *Turkestan Down to the Mongol Invasion* (Russian edition published in 1900, English ed. London, 1928).

Writing in the early forties, Jean Sauvaget, in his *Introduction to the History of the Muslim East* (recast by Claude Cahen, Berkeley: Univ. of Calif. Pr., 1965, p. 152), quite rightly attributed this neglect to the fact that Western Orientalists had "allowed themselves to be mesmerized by the so-called classical period of Muslim history," to which they directed most of their attention. He also noted (p. 151) that the "Eastern Question" in the nineteenth century "resulted in a strong and long-lasting prejudice in the West against Turkey and things Turkish." And this prejudice, of course, discouraged Western scholars from pursuing Turkish studies. There is certainly no doubt that in the nineteenth and early twentieth centuries Western Orientalists devoted most of their energy to studying Arabic and things Arab. They therefore tended to overemphasize the role of the Arabs in the development of Islam and Islamic civilization. However, given the occupation of Arab countries by European powers and the Orientalists' deep roots in Semitic studies, these scholars cannot really be blamed for their somewhat narrow approach to the field. It must also be admitted, without equivocation, that the study of the Turks in the Middle East before the

Ottomans is a very difficult task. Nomads do not write. It took time for the migrating tribes to settle, and many never did. "Urbanized" Turks were at first very few and tended to become acculturated by the indigenous inhabitants. Even where the Turks were in the majority, the Turkization of the local people went slowly. As a result, Turkish was not used as a language of administration or culture, apart from oral literature, until after the Turks had been in the Middle East in large numbers for several centuries. The early Turks, therefore, do not speak for themselves. Instead, one must rely on Arabic, Persian, Greek, Armenian, Syriac, Georgian, and even Latin and Old French sources. In short, one must approach them through intermediaries. In addition to these linguistic barriers, today's specialist in medieval Turkish history is also confronted with taking into account the important research now being carried out in English, French, German, Russian, *and* modern Turkish. In the event, the lack of Turkish sources and the multiplicity of non-Turkish sources thus presents a formidable obstacle. One may take some solace from the fact that most of the primary sources are in Arabic or Persian. The use of these sources, however, runs the risk, if only subliminaly, of forcing "Arabness" or "Persianess" on the Turks when completely unjustified, or, at the very least, of seeing them as a much less significant element than the Arabs and Persians in Islamic civilization. In a sense, because they did not write, or wrote very little in their own language, the Turks did not exist. Hence, during their first centuries in the Middle East, the Turks tend to become an invisible people. Consequently, great skill and perseverance are required in order to try to follow their progress in, and analyze their influence on, the Islamic world.

Perhaps the first systematic attempt in the West to describe the entire Seljuk period, albeit very briefly, is found in the article "Seldjuks" in the first edition of the *Encyclopaedia of Islam*. This article can be supplemented by the entries in the same work on the major Seljuk rulers and other leading personalities of the time. The article "Türks" should be included as well. A much better synthesis of the available material on the Seljuks was published by Claude Cahen in his chapter entitled "The Turkish Invasion: the Selchükids," in the first volume of *A History of the Crusades* edited by Kenneth Setton (1955–62; rpt. Madison, WI, 1969–). In the second volume of this work, he expanded on this subject in his chapter "The Turks in Iran and Anatolia before the Mongol Invasion." Given the very nature of this multivolume work, Cahen naturally gave particular attention to the Seljuks with respect to the Crusades. Be that as it may, Cahen's chapter in the first volume of *A History of the Crusades* remained the most up-to-date, indeed, the only, general account of the Seljuks of substance until the appearance of the fifth volume of the *Cambridge History of Iran,* edited by J. A. Boyle (Cambridge, 1968).

Of the many books and articles published in the West between 1955 and 1968 in the field of Islamic history, some discussed various aspects of the Seljuk period, but none examined it as a whole. I might mention, for example, C. E. Bosworth's *Ghaznavids: Their Empire in Afghanistan and Eastern Iran 994–1044* (Edinburgh, 1963) and George Makdisi's *Ibn ʿAqīl et la résurgence de l'Islam traditionaliste au XIe siècle* (Damascus, 1963). In 1963 there also appeared vol. 5 of *Handbuch der Orientalistik,* edited by B. Spuler (Leiden and Cologne, 1952–), entitled *Altaistik,* of which the first section was devoted to Turkology and the fifth (1966) to the history of Central Asia. In 1960 the second edition of the *Encyclopaedia of Islam* (Leiden and London) began to be published. It was a greatly expanded version of the first edition. Although as of 1987 it was only on the letter *M,* it nevertheless contained articles on such important figures as Alp-Arslan, Chaghrı Beg, and most of the sultans of Anatolia. These articles were frequently based on, or referred to, the more detailed information given under the same entries in the Turkish version of the first edition of this work, *İslâm Ansiklopedisi,* which began to appear in 1940 in Istanbul and was finally completed in 1987. More will be said shortly on this Turkish encyclopaedia.

The fifth volume of the *Cambridge History of Islam,* subtitled *The Saljuq and Mongol Periods,* contains a long chapter by C. E. Bosworth called "The Political and Dynastic History of the Iranian World (A.D. 1000–1217)." This is today the best survey in the West of the history of the Great Seljuks. In addition to Bosworth's contribution, this volume also contains substantial chapters on government administration, religion, science, art, and literature under the Seljuks. Altogether, it constitutes the best single book or collection of studies on the subject in a European language.

Since 1968, numerous works related to the Seljuks have of course continued to appear, but there have been no major general studies of note. However, one aspect of Seljuk history which deserves special reference is Anatolia. Perhaps because of their proximity and the leading role they played in the history of Byzantium and the Crusades, the Seljuks of Anatolia have attracted considerable attention in the West. This interest has been reflected primarily in articles, but it has also generated a number of books. The first comprehensive work in the West devoted to the Anatolian Seljuks was apparently the Russian study by V. Gordlevsky entitled *Gosudarstvo Seldzhukidov Maloy Azii.* Published in Moscow in 1941, it is now far out of date. Not only have various primary sources appeared since then, but this work also suffers from vagueness and a lack of scholarly criticism. Its attempt to apply a Marxist interpretation is too obviously forced. Twenty years passed before a comparable book appeared in English, namely, Tamara Talbot Rice's *Seljuks in Asia Minor* (New York, 1961). Although criticized for its superficial if not simplistic treatment of Seljuk history and culture, this work, like Gordlevsky's, was at least a beginning and contains many fine plates and drawings. Vastly superseding the books by these two writers is Claude Cahen's *Pre-Ottoman Turkey* (New York, 1968). A landmark study in the field, this work provides a highly competent and detailed account of the subject. It includes a good working bibliography and serves as the best available guide for students of the Seljuks of Anatolia. The author, however, has stated that this book represents a provisional synthesis and he has promised a more exhaustive study in French. Indeed, it must be admitted that the very nature of *Pre-Ottoman Turkey* makes it a somewhat frustrating text to read because of the many unanswered questions it raises. We are consequently rather fortunate to have Speros Vryonis' *Decline of Hellenism in Asia Minor and the Process of Islamization from the XIth to the XVth Century* (Berkeley, 1971), which does much to fill some of the gaps left by Cahen. Whereas Cahen deals strictly with the Seljuks and *beyliks,* Vryonis examines the decline of the Greek-speaking Christian population in Anatolia and its Islamization. He thus presents material on the Seljuks that would escape most Islamicists and is thus a welcome contribution.

Since the appearance of Vryonis' book, no major study has been published with regard to the Seljuks of Asia Minor. I might mention, though, several brief surveys that have been written on this topic in the past few decades: Cahen's chapter in the second volume of *A History of the Crusades,* cited above; F. Taeschner's chapter called "The Turks and the Byzantine Empire to the End of the Thirteenth Century" in *The Cambridge Medieval History,* vol. 4, *The Byzantine Empire,* part 1, edited by J. M. Hussey (Cambridge, 1966); and the somewhat more detailed chapter by Osman Turan entitled "Anatolia in the Period of the Seljuks and the *Beyliks*" in the *Cambridge History of Islam,* vol. 1, *The Central Islamic Lands,* edited by P. M. Holt et al. (Cambridge, 1970).

Finally, before very briefly describing Seljuk historiography in Turkey, I should state that there are four bibliographies that, together, give us an excellent, and fairly complete, picture of the work that has been done in this field. Sauvaget's book that I mentioned above gives the major primary sources as well as the most important contemporary books and articles that had been published in all languages up to 1965. In 1971, the General Directorate of the Turkish National Library in

Ankara issued a bibliography entitled *Selçuklu tarihi, Alp Arslan ve Malazgirt bibliyografyası* [A bibliography of Seljuk history, Alp-Arslan and Malazgird]. This 178-page bibliography lists primary sources, including manuscripts, in addition to modern works in the form of books, articles, and even newspaper stories. The emphasis is on works in Turkish, but many in Western and other languages are included. The length of this bibliography, however, belies somewhat the substance of the entries listed, for many do not directly concern the subject. Nevertheless, it is extremely useful and is the most serious attempt at compiling a comprehensive bibliography of works on the Seljuks. A few years later, Kosuke Shimizu published a *Bibliography on Seljuk Studies* (Tokyo, 1979). This work of 71 pages was based to a considerable extent on the aforesaid Turkish bibliography. It included books and articles in Western and Oriental languages, notably Persian. Lastly we have the well-known and indispensible *Index Islamicus,* compiled by J. D. Pearson, which has a section on the Seljuks and related topics. This work, which began publication in London in 1958, includes essentially all articles that have appeared in Western languages, and a few in Oriental languages, since 1906. Supplements are published periodically. In 1983, *Index Islamicus* issued its first supplement devoted to monographs (1976–80). So far no comprehensive bibliography of modern Arabic and Persian works has appeared. (For additional information on Seljuk historiography in the West, see Martin Strohmeier, *Seldschukische Geschichte und türkische Geschichtswissenschaft* [Berlin, 1984], pp. 22–28.)

2
Work in Turkey

With the rise of Turkish nationalism and, above all, the establishment of the Republic of Turkey, historical studies took a major step forward among the Turks themselves. Not surprisingly, contemporary Turkish scholars were immediately drawn to the Seljuks, and especially to the Seljuks of Anatolia, for their state was seen as the precursor of the modern Turkish republic. İbrahim Kafesoğlu, whose work forms the basis of this book, has sketched the development of Seljuk historiography in Turkey in an article called "Türkiye'de Selçuklu tarihçiliği" [Seljuk historiography in Turkey] published in *Cumhuriyetin 50. yılına armağan* [A commemorative volume on the fiftieth anniversary of the Republic {of Turkey}] (Istanbul, 1973). A translation by the present writer appeared in the *International Journal of Turkish Studies* 3(1985). According to Kafesoğlu, most modern Turkish historiography is now concerned with the Seljuk period and Turkish scholars are, on the whole, doing their best work in that field.

There is no doubt that the founder of contemporary Turkish historiography, on the Turks in general and the Seljuks in particular, was M. Fuad Köprülü who, in fact, was best known for his work on Turkish literary history. A man of extraordinary intellect and energy, he almost single-handedly created modern historiography in Turkey. In a sense, he was the "Atatürk" of Turkish scholarship. From 1916 until 1950, when he became the Turkish foreign minister, he produced a stream of publications that formed the basis of modern Turkish historical research. His books and articles are still used as the primary texts in history courses at Turkish universities. It was a tribute to his impact on Turkish historical studies that, although relatively little of his work appeared in English, he was made an honorary member of not only the American Oriental Society, but also the American Historical Association. With regard to the Seljuks, chiefly those in Anatolia, his seminal works included *Türk edebiyatında ilk mutasavvıflar* [Early mystics in Turkish literature] (Istanbul, 1918); "Anadolu'da islâmiyet" [Islam in Anatolia] (still in Ottoman), *Darülfünün Edebiyat Fakültesi Mecmuası* [The journal of the Faculty of Literature of Darülfünün {later Istanbul University}] 2(1922); "Bizans mütesseselerinin Osmanlı müessеselerine te'siri hakkında bâzı mülâhazalar" [Some observations on the influence of Byzantine institutions on Ottoman institutions], *THİT Mecmuası* 1(1931) [an English translation by the present writer is forthcoming as a monograph]; *Les origines de l'Empire ottoman* (Paris, 1935) [an English translation by the present writer is forthcoming]; and "Anadolu Selçukluları tarihinin yerli kaynakları" [Local sources for the history of the Seljuks of Anatolia], *Belleten* 7(1943) [an English translation by the present writer is forthcoming]. A bibliography of his most important writings can be found in the *Fuad Köprülü armağanı* [Fuad Köprülü Festschrift] (Istanbul, 1953). A contemporary of Köprülü was Mükrimin Halil Yınanç who attempted the first large-scale, comprehensive study of the Seljuks of Anatolia. However, only the first of his eight projected volumes appeared, *Türkiye tarihi, Selçuklular devri,* vol. 1, *Anadolunun fethi* [The history of Turkey, the Seljuk period, vol. 1, The conquest of Anatolia] (Istanbul, 1934). Yınanç was more a teacher than a writer, and he and Köprülü together trained a generation of Turkish historians.

This second generation was led by Faruk Sümer, Mehmet Köymen, İbrahim Kafesoğlu, and Osman Turan. Sümer has devoted most of his scholarly life to the study of the Oghuz clans. His outstanding work was the book *Oğuzlar (Türkmenler)* [The Oghuz Turks (Turkmen)] (Ankara, 1967). Köymen's chief interest has been in the Great Seljuks. In Ankara in 1954, he published the second of what were to be two volumes on this subject, namely, *Büyük Selçuklu imparatorluğu tarihi,* vol. 2, *İkinci imparatorluk devri* [The history of the Great Seljuk Empire, vol. 2, The second empire period]. This covered the period of Sultan Sanjar. The first volume on Toghrıl Beg, Alp-Arslan, and Malik-Shāh never appeared, for it became clear that these rulers would require more than one volume. This could be seen from the fact that three long articles (more than 250 pages) that he subsequently wrote called "Büyük Selçuklu imparatorluğunun kuruluşu" [The founding of the Great Seljuk Empire], parts 1–3, *DTCF Dergisi* 15(1957), 16(1958), only brought him up to Toghrıl Beg! He therefore had to abandon his original plan. Köymen then decided to begin work on a projected five-volume history of the Great Seljuks, of which the first volume would be an expanded version of his three articles in *DTCF Dergisi,* and the fifth volume would be an expanded version of his second volume mentioned above. The first volume was published as *Büyük Selçuklu imparatorluğu tarihi,* vol. 1, *Kuruluş devri* [The history of the Great Seljuk Empire, vol. 1, The foundation period] (Ankara, 1979). If completed, this will be a monumental work, the best on the Great Seljuks in any language. In the meantime, Köymen has written numerous other books and articles on various aspects of Seljuk history. Of Kafesoğlu and Turan, I shall have more to say later.

As might be expected, as the scholarly foundation was laid for this field and more sources were brought to light, the current generation of Turkish historians has begun to branch out and do more specialized work on the Seljuks. I can only mention here Nejat Kaymaz' *Pervâne Mu'înü'd-dîn Süleyman* [Parvāna Muʿīn al-Dīn Sulaimān] (Ankara, 1970); Erdoğan Merçil's *Kirman Selçukluları* [The Seljuks of Kirmān] (Istanbul, 1980); and Ali Sevim's *Suriye ve Filistin Selçukluları tarihi* [The history of the Seljuks of Syria and Palestine] (Ankara, 1983), a vastly expanded version of his *Suriye Selçukluları* [The Seljuks of Syria], vol. 1 (Ankara, 1965). By the third generation, Seljuk studies in Turkey had progressed to a level which easily justified the establishment of a special institute to promote, and serve as a focus for, research on this subject. Thus in 1966 the Selçuklu Tarih ve Medeniyeti Enstitüsü was founded in Ankara. From 1969 to 1972, it published an annual journal, *Selçuklu Araştırmaları Dergisi* [The journal of Seljuk research], which gives an excellent idea of current Turkish work on the Seljuks. In recent years the institute seems to have become less active, but books such as Köymen's appear from time to time under its auspices. For a list of current Turkish work on the Seljuks, one must consult the two periodicals *Türkiye Bibliyografyası* [The Turkey bibliography] for books that have appeared since 1928, that is, since Turkey adopted the Latin alphabet, and *Türkiye Makaleler Bibliyografyası* [The bibliography of articles on Turkey] for articles that have appeared since 1952.

Lastly, a few words are in order about the *İslâm Ansiklopedisi*. It is a revised and greatly expanded version of the first edition of the *Encyclopaedia of Islam*. In the *İA,* which is now finished, special emphasis is given to Turkish subjects. It therefore contains contributions, often important original works, by all the leading Turkish scholars who have specialized in the history of the Seljuks. The *İA* thus considerably supersedes the first edition of the *EI* and is still superior to the second edition of the same work on certain Turkish, and perhaps even non-Turkish, subjects. Indeed, as previously stated, entries in the second edition of the *EI* are sometimes based on, or refer to, corresponding articles in the *İA* that are generally much more detailed. For example, in the second edition of the *EI*, the article on the Anatolian Seljuk sultan Kai-Khusraw II is half a page in length, while in the *İA* it is nine pages. The real strength of the *İA*, in fact, lies in such contributions as those on the Seljuks. In many cases, these articles still represent the best work that has been done in any language on the subject in question. A translation of Kafesoğlu's specific article on the Seljuks consequently helps remind interested readers of the major scholarship to be found in the *İA*, and also gives them a chance to evaluate a significant contribution to that scholarship. (For further details on the *İA*, see A. Gabriel, "La Traduction turque de l'Encyclopédie de l'Islam [*Islam Ansiklopedisi*]," 236[1948]:115–22; for criticism, see B. Spuler, *Der Islam*, review section, 29[1949–50]:318–25, with a reply by Orhan F. Köprülü, "Bir tenkid hakkında bâzı mülâhazalar" [Some observations on a critique], *TM* 9[1951]:171–78; see also a review by A. F. Karamanlıoğlu in *Cultura Turcica* 3[1966]:127–30. Strohmeier discusses the leading Turkish Seljuk specialists, the development of Seljuk historiography in Turkey, and Turkish interpretations of Seljuk history in his *Seldschukische Geschichte*.)

İbrahim Kafesoğlu and His Work on the Seljuks

İbrahim Kafesoğlu was born Halil İbrahim in 1914 in the town of Tefenni in the province of Burdur in southwestern Turkey. Shortly thereafter, the First World War began and his father was killed on the Caucasus Front. He was then raised by his grandfather. He completed his elementary education in Tefenni in 1926, and upon showing great promise, he was sent to a secondary school in Izmir. After graduation in 1932, he worked as a teacher for almost three years in Afyon. In 1934, when the law of family names was issued in Turkey, he officially became İbrahim Kafesoğlu.

Because of his desire to pursue a higher education, he gave up teaching and won a scholarship to the Gazi Advanced Teachers' School in Ankara and later undertook training at the Dil ve Tarih-Coğrafya Fakültesi (Faculty of Language, History, and Geography) of Ankara University. There he became interested in Hungarology, medieval Turkish and Islamic history, and the Turkish language. After he finished his studies, he worked in the same faculty as a research assistant.

Between 1941 and 1943, Kafesoğlu did his military service and then was sent by the state to Budapest, at that time a thriving center of Turkology, to obtain a doctorate in Turkish history and culture. The

Second World War, however, greatly hampered his studies, and he was only able to complete two semesters of the 1943–44 academic year. But he studied with such well-known scholars as A. Alföldi, Gy. Nemeth, and D. Ligeti. The Russian occupation of Hungary, which he witnessed, put an end to his studies there and he was forced to return to Turkey. After a number of difficult months, he received an appointment as an assistant to the chair of medieval history at Istanbul University. He then began his professional, and sometimes stormy, academic life.

As an assistant, Kafesoğlu worked under Professor Mükrimin Halil Yınanç, who encouraged him to do research on Seljuk history. He subsequently earned his doctorate in 1949 with a monograph on Malik-Shāh. This was published as *Sultan Melikşah devrinde büyük Selçuklu imparatorluğu* [The Great Seljuk Empire during the reign of Malik-Shāh] (Istanbul, 1953). Four years later, he earned his assistant professorship (*doçentlik*) with a thesis on the history of the state of the Khwārazm-Shāhs. This was published as *Harezmşahlar devleti tarihi (485–618/1092–1220)* [The history of the state of the Khwārazm-Shāhs (485–618/1092–1220)] (Ankara, 1956). Although he became known primarily as a specialist on the Seljuks, he also had a great interest in various problems of Turkish history and culture in general. This eventually led him to devote most of his energy to investigating the pre-Islamic history of the Turks (Huns, Gök-Turks, Uighurs). He believed that it was essential to understand this period of Turkish history before one could properly grasp the Seljuk and Ottoman periods.

When Atatürk University was established in Erzurum in 1957, Kafesoğlu joined the faculty as a history teacher and, in fact, gave the opening lecture at that university. Two years later, he became a full professor and was appointed to the division of general Turkish history at Istanbul University. There he worked with Professor A. Zeki Velidi Togan. Upon Togan's death in 1970, Kafesoğlu was appointed to his chair and held that position until he retired in 1983. Shortly afterwards, on 17 August 1984, he died.

Kafesoğlu did research in France in 1958 and in England in 1968 and 1972, and frequently attended international conferences. He served on different committees in Turkey including the Ministry of Culture's commission for the publication of "1000 Basic Books," the editorial committee of the *İslâm Ansiklopedisi,* and the editorial committees of a number of journals. Altogether, he published 295 articles (including newspaper stories and reviews) and books. All his scholarly research came to fruition in 1977 with the publication of his greatest work, *Türk milli kültürü* [Turkish national culture], which had a far-ranging effect in Turkey. He received many awards for his contributions to

Turkish history and culture, including one in 1984 from the National Cultural Endowment of Turkey for service to Turkish national culture. Without a doubt, Kafesoğlu was a major figure in Turkish studies in this century in Turkey. Further details on his life and a list of his publications can be found in *Türk Kültürü Araştırmaları* [Research on Turkish Culture] 23(1985); see also Strohmeier, *Seldschukische Geschichte,* pp. 165–82.

As for Seljuk and related history, Kafesoğlu's most important works, none of which have heretofore been translated into a Western language, were his books on Malik-Shāh and the state of the Khwārazm-Shāhs, another book entitled *Selçuklu ailesinin menşei hakkında* [On the origin of the Seljuk family] (Istanbul, 1955), the monograph-length article on the Seljuks, as well as other entries, in the *İA,* and a number of serious shorter articles, such as "Doğu Anadolu'ya ilk Selçuklu akını (1015–1021) ve tarihi ehemmiyeti" [The first Seljuk incursion into eastern Anatolia (1015–1021) and its historical significance], in *Fuad Köprülü armağanı* (Istanbul, 1953), and "Selçuk'un oğulları ve torunları" [The sons and grandsons of Seljuk], *TM* 12(1955).

His last major publication on the Seljuks was the article in the *İA* that appeared between 1964 and 1965. (Later, in 1972, the Turkish Ministry of Culture in Ankara republished this encyclopaedia article in simplified form, without the references and in more "modern" Turkish, as a small book, *Selçuklu tarihi* [The history of the Seljuks].) Kafesoğlu's encyclopaedia article and volume 4 of the *Cambridge History of Iran* thus appeared about the same time. These two works therefore are the most recent surveys of the period. Afterwards, Kafesoğlu devoted most of his research, as mentioned, to the broader subjects of Turkish culture and nationalism. The encyclopaedia article, to a considerable degree, represented the epitome of his work, and that of other contemporary Turkish scholars, in this field of Turkish history. Furthermore, some of the themes presented in this article were later elaborated upon in Kafesoğlu's writings on Turkish culture. For example, he tries to show that certain elements of the steppe culture that was particular to the Turks were not lost upon the "Islamization" of the Seljuks. Indeed, in many respects the Seljuks "Turkized" Islam by making many contributions to Islamic civilization which greatly enriched it. Kafesoğlu later expanded on this theme as he developed his ideas about "cultural nationalism." He then put these ideas into final form in his book *Türk milli kültürü.* Thus in addition to giving us a general overview in English of the entire Seljuk period and a very good idea of what Turkish scholars have done in the field as of 1965, the translation that follows also presents an interpretation of this important chapter in world history by a leading, twentieth-century Turkish intellectual. This is an interpretation that is rarely seen in detail in the West and one that merits careful consideration, especially by those Islamists who are culture bound to other Muslim peoples.

Translator's Note

I have tried to render this translation into colloquial English. Many of the author's long and frequently complex sentences therefore had to be broken up and rearranged before they could be translated. However, some vestiges of the original Turkish syntax remain. At the risk of a certain tedium, Kafesoğlu's paragraphization has been retained in order to facilitate any comparison with the original work. Insignificant additions to the text and corrections of minor oversights or typographical errors have not been indicated in the translation. Major additions, primarily explanatory notes, have been placed in braces {} thusly. All Turkish titles have been translated when first given and placed in brackets. The author was not consistent in the manner in which he cited his references. They have therefore been recast according to contemporary Western practice. A full reference is given when a source is first cited, and an author/short-title reference is given if it is mentioned thereafter. Furthermore, in order to improve the readability of the work, all references have been extracted from the text and placed to the side as marginal notes. And all of Kafesoğlu's cross-references to other articles in the *İA* have been deleted. No attempt was made to confirm all of the author's statements or references. In a few instances where major discrepancies were found, they are so described in the marginal notes. The bibliography has also been recast according to Western practice and alphabetized. The full references to primary sources can be checked there. In some references to Persian works, the publication date is followed by the abbreviation *sh.* which indicates the solar year (*shamsī*) of the Muslim era. This solar year was adopted in Iran in 1925. I have replaced the author's single genealogical chart of the Seljuk dynasty with one for each major branch of the family. Moreover, these charts have been revised in light of the following works: Köymen, *Büyük Selçuklu imparatorluğu tarihi,* vol. 1, *Kuruluş devri;* Merçil, *Kirman Selçukluları;* and Sevim, *Suriye ve Filistin Selçukluları*. I have also added an appendix, a glossary, and two maps to the original text for further clarity. Finally, for the transliteration of Turkish, Arabic, and Persian words, the system employed in the *Cambridge History of Iran* has generally been used. This makes it easier to compare texts. Were it not for that work, the system found in the *Encyclopaedia of Islam* would have been preferable, although the second edition of this work may not reach the Seljuks for another generation. Some inconsistencies remain in this respect, but they should present no obstacles to readers. For those unfamiliar with Turkish, ç = ch, ş = sh, c = j, ö and ü are the same as the corresponding German vowels, ı = the o in *atom,* and ğ = gh as in *Edinburgh*.

Part Two

İbrahim Kafesoğlu's "Seljuks"

3
Political History

The name **Seljuk** was given to a Turkish collectivity which had an extensive and long-lasting influence on Turco-Islamic and world history by founding both a great empire in the Middle East in the eleventh century and successor states. This collectivity was composed of various Turkish groups, the great majority of whom were Oghuz. In the beginning, they were attached to Seljuk, one of the Oghuz commanders. Consequently, the dynasty which they founded was called by the same name. This dynasty lasted for more than 300 years in the states that it established in Iran, Iraq, Kirmān, Syria, and Anatolia.

The Appearance of the Seljuks on the Stage of History.

The pronunciation of the name *Seljuk,* the forefather of the dynasty, has been disputed. Marquart, who first pointed to the rule of vowel harmony in Turkish, proposed that the name should be pronounced "Salchuk" and gave as an example the work of the thirteenth-century Armenian historian Kirakos, where the name was recorded in this way.[1] Later, V. Barthold stated that the form "Selchük" was the most correct pronunciation, as determined by the famous eleventh-century Turkish scholar Maḥmūd Kāshgharī.[2] He also gave examples to confirm this from subsequent Turkish sources.[3] L. Rásonyi considered this problem somewhat later and insisted that the name should be "Selchük" (Seljük), using various kinds of evidence to support this claim.[4] He noted that this pronunciation was also clearly recorded by the twelfth-century

1. See J. Marquart, *Über das Volkstum der Komanen* (Berlin, 1914), p. 187.

2. See *Dīwān Lughāt al-Turk,* Turkish trans. Besim Atalay (Ankara: TDK, 1939–41), I, 478.

3. V. Barthold, *Orta Asya türk tarihi hakkında dersler* [Studies on the history of the Turks in Central Asia] (Istanbul, 1927), p. 91.

4. "Selçük adının menşe'ine dâir" [On the origin of the name *Seljuk*], *Belleten* 3(1939):377–84.

Arab author al-ʿAẓīmī[5] and by Qāḍī Burhān al-Dīn al-Anawī, the author of the Persian work *Anīs al-qulūb*.[6] Nevertheless, the pronunciation of the name as "Selchuk," which was written according to Arabic orthography as "Saljūq" by the great majority of Arab and Persian authors, has come down to us and been generally accepted in Turkish.

According to Rásonyi,[7] who proposed that *Selchük* originally meant "small torrent" {*küçük sel*}, the Oghuz commander Seljuk was born around Sel-Taġ, which was sometimes called Muz- (Buz-) Tağ by the Kirghiz, in Central Asia, and his name probably derived from this mountain. On the other hand, it has been mentioned that the word for "contender" {*mücâdeleci*} in Turkish can take the form *salçuġ*.[8]

As can clearly be seen from the historical sources, including coins and seals, the Seljuk family was related to the Qınıq subdivision of the Oghuz.[9] The father of the family had the name Duqaq or Tuqaq.[10] In some sources the mistaken form of Luqmān, corrupted from Duqaq, is found.[11] It should be mentioned that the byname {*laqab*} Temir-Yalıġ (*demir yaylı* {with iron bow}) was found among the Duqaq Oghuz. This esteemed and important byname indicated that its possessor occupied a high position.[12] According to our sources, the one who had this byname was recognized by all the Dasht-i Khazar Turkish tribes.[13] He was the chief of the Turks and their source of authority in all matters.[14] He was given such a name because he was powerful.[15] Apart from the fact that Duqaq had some kind of responsibility[16] in the Oghuz state around the Aral Sea,[17] we have no information about him.[18] Because he embodied the idea of attachment to a powerful dynasty among the Turks and was recognized by them as a powerful leader {*baş-buğ*} having the highest authority in the aforesaid region, he was apparently related to a family that had held the chief position for some time. In fact, even historical sources from the time of Toghrıl Beg agree on the noble descent of Duqaq. In a lost work, Ibn Ḥassūl, the head of Toghrıl Beg's chancery, linked the Seljuk family with the legendary Turkish ruler Afrāsiyāb.[19] In his work entitled *Tafḍīl al-atrāk*,[20] he made it clear that the family had an esteemed lineage. The famous Seljuk vizir Niẓām al-Mulk reported that members of the dynasty had been rulers from father to son.[21] Barhebraeus describes a letter that Toghrıl Beg sent to the caliph in 435/1043 and states that the sultan wrote in this letter that he was related to a family of royal descent.[22] This noble descent of his family is also mentioned in other sources.[23] Consequently, there is no need to discuss the groundless attempt to link the Seljuk dynasty, which clearly came from an old family of *khāns* {a title usually used for subordinate rulers} or *begs* {prince, chief, notable} to a tent-pole sharpener (*khargāh-tirāsh*) named

5. Ed. Cl. Cahen, "La Chronique abrégée d'al-ʿAẓīmī," *JA* 230(1938):360.

6. See M. Fuad Köprülü, "Anadolu Selçukluları tarihinin yerli kaynakları," *Belleten* 7(1943):474, text 501 f. {A translation of this article by Gary Leiser as "Local Sources for the History of the Seljuks of Anatolia," but minus the appendix on *Anīs al-qulūb*, is forthcoming.}

7. "Selçük adının," pp. 380 ff.

8. *Oeuvres Posthumes de P. Pelliot* (Paris, 1950), II, 176n. 2.

9. Ṣadr al-Dīn ʿAlī al-Ḥusainī, *Akhbār al-dawla al-saljūqiyya*, Turkish trans. N. Lugal (Ankara: TTK, 1943), p. 2; Kāshgharī, *Dīwān*, I, 55; al-ʿAinī, *ʿIqd al-jumān*, from *ʿUnwān al-siyar*, Turkish trans., Topkapı, Baghdad *köşk* MS 277, fol. 360b; Yazıcıoğlu, *Tawārīkh-i Āl-i Saljūq*, Topkapı, Revan *köşk* MS 1391, fol. 18a f.; Barhebraeus, *Abū 'l-Farac tarihi* [The history of Abū 'l-Faraj], Turkish trans. Ö. R. Doğrul (Ankara: TTK, 1945), I, 298; İbrahim Kafesoğlu, *Sultan Melikşah devrinde Büyük Selçuklu imparatorluğu* (Istanbul, 1953), p. 146.

10. See Ibn al-ʿAdīm, *Bughyat al-ṭalab fī taʾrīkh Ḥalab*, from the *Malik-Nāma*, Topkapı, Ahmet III MS 2925, III, fol. 268b; Ṣadr al-Dīn, *Akhbār*, pp. 1 f.; Ibn al-Athīr, *al-Kāmil fī 'l-taʾrīkh* (Cairo, 1357/1938–39), year 423 and the following. On the pronunciation of the name, see Ibn Khallikān, *Wafayāt al-aʿyān* (Cairo, 1299/1881–82), the biography of Toghrıl Beg.

11. E.g., Rāvandī, *Rāḥat al-ṣudūr*, ed. M. Iqbāl, *GMS*, N.S., vol. 2, (London, 1921), p. 88. Turkish trans. A. Ateş (Ankara: TTK, 1957), I, 86; Qāḍī Burhān al-Dīn, *Anīs al-qulūb*, pp. 475, 501; Yazıcıoğlu, *Tawārīkh*, fol. 18a; Ḥasan Yazdī, *Jāmiʿ al-tawārīkh-i Ḥasanī*, Fâtih Library MS 4507, fols. 171a f.

12. In ancient Turkish tradition, the bow was the symbol of sovereignty and represented supreme authority; see Osman Turan, "Eski Türklerde okun hukukî bir sembol olarak kullanılması" [The use of the arrow as a legal symbol among the ancient Turks], *Belleten* 9(1945):305–18.

13. Mīrkhwānd, *Rawḍat al-ṣafāʾ*, from the *Malik-Nāma* (Lucknow, 1308), IV, 85.

14. Ibn al-Athīr, *al-Kāmil*, year 423 and the following. Here the byname is translated by the author into Arabic as *al-qaws al-ḥadīd* {the iron bow}. In Ṣadr al-Dīn, *Akhbār*, where the name Duqaq is recorded as Yaqaq, the expression *demir yaylı* (p. 1) is believed to be a translation of Duqaq.

15. Barhebraeus, *Tarihi*, I, 292.

16. *Malik-Nāma*, which was cited in Ṣadr al-Dīn, *Akhbār;* Ibn al-Athīr, *al-Kāmil*, year 423; Barhebraeus, *Tarihi*, I, 292.

Kerakuji.[24] This was based on a sixteenth-century author[25] who passed on a baseless story in the *Jāmiʿ al-tawārīkh*.[26]

Because Duqaq and the groups that followed him lived north of the Aral Sea, there is still a dispute over whether or not they were subject to the Khazars or the state of the Oghuz *yabghu* {title of the Oghuz ruler}. Some researchers have pointed to the power of the Khazar state in the tenth century and proposed that Duqaq was bound to the Khazars. They based this on a report by the aforementioned Ibn Ḥassūl.[27] Nevertheless, this is certainly doubtful if one considers that, when Duqaq was probably alive, the Khazar state was very weak[28] and was forced to make an alliance with its Oghuz neighbors because of the pressure from the Pechenegs.[29] Indeed, it has been generally accepted, as stated by Cahen and Kurat, that Duqaq, who was the chief of the Oghuz in the Qıpchaq desert,[30] was not a commander subject to the Khazar king, but was probably an influential *baş-buğ* in the Oghuz state[31] or represented a *fédératif* force in it.[32] In fact, Duqaq was apparently the most important person in the Oghuz state after the yabghu because of his position of responsibility in the government. At one point he opposed a campaign that the yabghu wanted to carry out against a party of Turks and, as a result, a fight broke out in which he was wounded. However, he was able to strike the yabghu with a mace and knock him from his horse.[33] Some of the sources that discuss this dispute, in which Ibn Ḥassūl confused Duqaq with his son Seljuk, report that Duqaq prevented a campaign against the Muslim countries,[34] and wish to show this Oghuz *baş-buğ* as a defender of Islam. Although it is highly unlikely that Islam had spread among these Oghuz by the time this event took place, probably between 875 and 885,[35] the religious status of the Qınıq tribe, the Duqaq family, and other Oghuz at that period is not clear. Because the names Isrāʾīl and Mikhāʾīl were found at that time among the Seljuk family, it has been proposed that they were Christians[36] or Jews.[37] As there is no other evidence to support either contention, there is no firm basis for these claims. The Oghuz only began to adopt Islam in the second half of the tenth century,[38] and although Seljuk was depicted as the first Muslim from the family of Duqaq,[39] this does not mean that there was no possibility that Duqaq himself might have had contact with Islam.[40] It would not be a mistake, however, to conclude that the Seljuk family still believed in *kamlık* (shamanism) at that time.

Seljuk was born around the beginning of the tenth century and was seventeen or eighteen years old when his father, Duqaq, died.[41] He grew up under the tutelage of the yabghu, later occupied his father's high position in the state, and became the *sü-başı* ("army commander")

17. Cf. O. Pritsak, "Der Untergang des Reiches des Oġuzischen Yabġu," in *Fuad Köprülü armağanı* (Istanbul, 1953), pp. 397– 410; Mehmet Köymen, "Büyük Selçuklu imparatorluğu'nun kuruluşu I," *DTCF Dergisi* 15(1957):97 ff.

18. Ibn Ḥassūl, *Tafḍīl al-atrāk*, ed. and Turkish trans. Şerefeddin Yaltkaya, *Belleten* 4(1940):265, where it is said that he was at the side of the king of the Khazars.

19. Alp Er-Tunga, see Ḥamd Allāh Mustawfī Qazvīnī, *Taʾrīkh-i Guzīda, GMS*, vol. 14 (London, 1911), I, 434.

20. Ibn Ḥassūl, p. 265.

21. *Siyāsat-Nāma*, ed. Ch. Schefer (Paris, 1891), p. 7, ed. ʿA. Khalkhālī (Tehran, 1310 *sh.*), p. 6.

22. *Tarihi*, p. 299.

23. E.g., Muntajab al-Dīn Badīʿ al-Kātib Juvainī, *ʿAtabat al-kataba*, ed. ʿAbbās Iqbāl (Tehran, 1329 *sh.*), p. 33; Rāvandī, *Rāḥat*, p. 91, Turkish trans., pp. 90 f.

24. Z. V. Togan, *Umûmî türk tarihine giriş* [A general introduction to Turkish history] (Istanbul, 1946), pp. 175 ff.

25. Seyyid Loqmān, see F. Babinger, *Die Geschichtsschrieber der Osmanen und ihre Werke* (Leipzig, 1927), pp. 164 f.

26. By Rashīd al-Dīn. See Topkapı, Hazîne MS 1653, fol. 302b.

27. Pritsak, "Der Untergang," p. 400; D. M. Dunlop, *The History of the Jewish Khazars* (Princeton, 1954), pp. 258 f.

28. On the defeats of the Khazars in 965 and 969, see Akdes N. Kurat, *Peçenek tarihi* [The history of the Pechenegs] (Istanbul, 1937), pp. 90 f.

29. Cf. Cahen, "Le Malik-Nameh et l'histoire des origins Seljukides," *Oriens* 2(1949):42.

30. *Malik-Nāma*, in Ṣadr al-Dīn, *Akhbār*.

31. Köymen, "Büyük Selçuklu," p. 103.

32. Kafesoğlu, *Selçuklu âilesinin menşe'i hakkında* (Istanbul, 1955), pp. 21–25; Faruk Sümer, "X. yüzyılda Oğuzlar" [The Oghuz in the tenth century], *DTCF Dergisi* 16(1958):149 f.

33. Mīrkhwānd, *Rawḍat*, from the *Malik-Nāma*, IV, 85.

34. Ṣadr al-Dīn, *Akhbār*, p. 1; Ibn al-Athīr, *al-Kāmil*, year 432.

35. Köymen, "Büyük Selçuklu," p. 102.

36. Barthold, "Orta Asya'da Moğol fütûhâtına kadar hıristiyanlık" [Christianity in Central Asia until the Mongol conquests], *TM* 1(1925):78.

37. Dunlop, *Jewish Khazars*, p. 261.

38. Sümer, "Oğuzlar," p. 145.

39. Ṣadr al-Dīn, *Akhbār*, p. 2; Ibn al-Athīr, *al-Kāmil*, year 432.

40. Cf. Cahen, "Le Malik-Nameh," p. 42.

41. Köymen, "Büyük Selçuklu," p. 102.

for the Oghuz yabghu. Because the Turks had felt attracted to old and noble dynasties throughout history and had an ancient tradition based on the belief that the ruler's family was of divine origin,[42] Seljuk was, like his father, certainly at the head of large Oghuz groups and at that time controlled the military power of the state with the title *sü-başı* ("governor," "commander"). Although it appears that Seljuk had a falling out with the yabghu and played a role in the secret struggle for power, the story that his wife (the wife of the yabghu) incited her husband against Seljuk[43] and the allegation that Seljuk therefore fled the country with one hundred horsemen[44] seem to be without sound foundation. There must have been a more serious reason for the great Oghuz migration that began with the movement toward the south by Seljuk—whose position in the state and country we have described—and which Barthold tried to explain by the pressure on the Oghuz from the Qıpchaqs to the north.[45] Indeed, there is sufficient information in our sources to clarify this. As with most of the great Turkish migrations in history, here too the primary impetus seems to have been a lack of land and pasturage. Sharaf al-Zamān Marvazī[46] states that the migrations from Central Asia toward the west and the Near East generally resulted from a lack of land for the tribes in the area. Indeed, some of the sources that specifically mention the Seljuk migration explain that the tribes under the leadership of Seljuk descended toward Transoxiana because their numbers were large and their lands were no longer sufficient.[47] It is known that the Seljuks were very numerous when they were in Transoxiana and Khurāsān. This is corroborated by the fact that when Seljuk, together with other Oghuz groups subordinate to the Qınıq tribe, left Yengi-Kent—the winter capital of the Oghuz state located between the Caspian and Aral seas[48]—they brought a great many horses, camels, sheep, and cattle with them.[49]

Seljuk came to Jand, which was also an Oghuz city, on the left bank of the Jaxartes (Syr Darya, Ṣayhūn) probably after 960. It was not far from Yengi-Kent and, as Barthold states, was a border city between the Turks and the Islamic countries where Muslim emigrants from Transoxiana lived.[50] The coming of Seljuk to Jand marked a watershed in history. It was during this period that a large number of Turkish groups began to adopt Islam en masse. Indeed, the Islamic milieu was not unfamiliar to the religious views of many of them and others were already at home in it.[51] Seljuk believed in the necessity of adopting Islam not only because of the need to live in this Muslim environment, but also for political reasons. With great skill and statesmanship, he grasped the political and social conditions of this new milieu, and after deciding with his associates to carry out this conversion, requested religious officials from neighboring Islamic lands like Bukhārā and

42. See Kafesoğlu, *Melikşah*, pp. 141 f.

43. Ṣadr al-Dīn, *Akhbār*, p. 2; Ibn al-Athīr, *al-Kāmil*, year 432; Barhebraeus, *Tarihi*, I, 292; Mīrkhwānd, *Rawḍat*, IV, 85.

44. Köymen, "Büyük Selçuklu," pp. 106, 110.

45. See *Dersler*, p. 102.

46. *Ṭabā'i' al-ḥayavān*, ed. and trans. V. Minorsky, as *On China, the Turks and India* (London, 1942), pp. 29 ff., 95; text p. 18.

47. Rāvandī, *Rāḥat*, p. 86, Turkish trans., p. 85; Jamāl al-Dīn Qarshī, *Mulḥaqāt al-ṣurāḥ*, ed. Barthold, *Turkestan*, I, 135. {This refers to one of the texts that Barthold included in the original Russian edition of his *Turkestan Down to the Mongol Invasion* (St. Petersburg, 1900) but which were not included in the English translation (London, 1928 and 1968). Cf. the latter, pp. 51–52, 257; *Encyclopaedia of Islam*, 2d ed., *Supplement*, "Djamāl Ḳarshī."} Qazvīnī, *Guzīda*, I, 434.

48. Today called Jan-Kent, the ruins of which can still be seen, see Barthold, *Dersler*, p. 53.

49. Barhebraeus from the *Malik-Nāma*, *Tarihi*, I, 292.

50. See *Dersler*, p. 53.

51. See Kāshgharī, *Dīwān*, III, 149.

Khwārazm. He and the Oghuz loyal to him then became Muslims.[52] This Turkish mass, to which our sources refer on the one hand as the Seljuks (*saljūqiyyān, salājiqa*) and on the other as the Turkmen—which was not the name of a particular Turkish group but was apparently used as a political term, first among the Qarluqs and then among the Oghuz even before the adoption of Islam—then acquired a new political and social identity.[53] Seljuk, saying that he would not give *kharāj* {tax} to nonbelievers, namely, the officials of the Oghuz yabghu who came to Jand to collect the annual taxes, forced them to leave and undertook a struggle against the Oghuz state as a *ghāzī* {warrior for the faith} ready to embark upon a *jihād* {holy war against non-Muslims} for Islam.[54] From the fighting that constantly broke out, and as a result of which Seljuk was later called "al-Malik al-Ghāzī,"[55] he gained two important advantages: first, he obtained the help of some Muslims and the allegiance of those Turks who wanted to participate in the battles; and second, he was successful in overcoming the authority of the yabghu in Jand and its surrounding area and in establishing an independent government. Seljuk gradually increased his power and obtained a position of great importance in the international arena when the neighboring states (e.g., the Sāmānids in Transoxiana) acknowledged being subject to this independent entity. His position was confirmed when the Sāmānid state requested his help against the Qarakhānids, and he defeated them with forces he sent under the command of his son Arslan (Isrā'īl). As a result, the Seljuks were given new lands (*yurt,* homeland) around the town of Nūr facing the Qarakhānids on the border between Bukhārā and Samarqand. Ḥamd Allāh Mustawfī Qazvīnī gives the year 378/985–86 for this event and describes it as the time when the Seljuks came to Transoxiana.[56] But because the Qarakhānid ruler, Hārūn Bughra Khān, appears to have been subject to attacks from surrounding Oghuz forces while returning from Samarqand in 382/992,[57] this event must have taken place no later than 992–93. The Seljuks who came to the Nūr area were Turkmen under the command of Arslan. With political skill and courage, the Seljuks successfully faced up to the new reality of being between two large organized states like those of the Qarakhānids and Sāmānids, one Turkish and the other Iranian, that were struggling for Transoxiana. In 992, the Qarakhānid Hārūn Bughra Khān captured the Sāmānid capital of Bukhārā but withdrew because of illness and pressure from the Turkmen. Later, after the death of Nūḥ II b. {i.e., *ibn,* son of} Manṣūr (997), the Sāmānid ruler who had again governed Transoxiana thanks to Oghuz support, continuous internal disorders in the Sāmānid state (the struggles of Fā'iq, Abū ʿAlī Sīmjūrī, and Bektüz) and such events as the murder of Nūḥ II's son Manṣūr II and his replacement

52. Barhebraeus, *Tarihi,* I, 293; Mīrkhwānd, *Rawḍat,* IV, 85.

53. See Kafesoğlu, "Türkmen adı, mânası ve mâhiyeti" [The meaning and nature of the name *Turkmen*] in *Jean Deny armağanı* [Jean Deny Festschrift] (Ankara: TDK, 1958), pp. 121–33, Fr. trans. as "À propos du nom Turkmen," *Oriens* 11(1958):146–50.

54. Ibn al-Athīr, *al-Kāmil,* year 432; Mīrkhwānd, *Rawḍat,* IV, 72.

55. Ibn Funduq, *Ta'rīkh-i Baihaq,* ed. Aḥmad Bahmanyār (Tehran, 1317/1938), p. 71.

56. *Guzīda,* I, 434.

57. Al-'Utbī, *al-Ta'rīkh al-Yamīnī,* with commentary by Manīnī (Cairo, 1286/1869), I, 176; Barthold, *Turkestan,* p. 260.

by his brother ʿAbd al-Malik II—not to mention the interference of the Ghaznavids, who had created a new and powerful state to the south, in the affairs of Khurāsān against the Sāmānids—all increased the interest of the Seljuks in Transoxiana. In November 999, the Qarakhānid Naṣr II İlig-Khān recaptured Bukhārā and sent ʿAbd al-Malik II and other members of the dynasty to his own capital of Öz-Kent. Although the Sāmānid state had therefore essentially collapsed, Abū Ibrāhīm al-Muntaṣir, a relative of ʿAbd al-Malik II, succeeded in escaping and tried to regain power. But when the struggle in Khurāsān proved fruitless, he sought refuge and assistance with the Oghuz. In alliance with al-Muntaṣir, the Seljuks defeated the Qarakhānid commander, the *sü-başı* Tegin, and in a night raid in the vicinity of Samarqand, defeated Naṣr II İlig-Khān (August 1003). Afterwards, at Ushrūsana in June 1004, they routed the Qarakhānid forces for a third time, as well as al-Muntaṣir who had broken with them somewhat earlier.[58] It was again Turkmen loyal to Arslan who played a role in all of these events that resulted in the failure and death of this last Sāmānid representative who had become estranged from the Seljuks. The fact that each member of the dynasty here had his own forces and tribes seems to be an example of an old Turkish custom. Indeed, in addition to this practice, which we know later continued in the Seljuk family, titles like *yabghu, yınal, ınanch, beg,* and so forth, which members of the family held, show that the organization of the old Oghuz state was also applied to the new government established under Seljuk's authority. Seljuk, who is described in the sources as living to an old age, thus laid the foundation of the empire named after him and its successor states, all of which would have a lasting influence on world history. After he had organized this empire and made it secure in battle, he died around 1009, near the age of one hundred in Jand,[59] the place where the great Turco-Islamic state was established and whose political and historical importance as a border city was always appreciated.[60]

It was said that Seljuk had married the daughter of one of the Turkmen rulers.[61] He had four sons: Mikhāʾīl, Arslan (Isrāʾīl), Yūsuf, and Mūsā. The oldest, Mikhāʾīl, died in battle while Seljuk was still alive (after 995). His two sons, Chaghrı and Toghrıl, were therefore raised by their grandfather Seljuk.[62] Arslan, who held the title of "Yabghu," succeeded Seljuk as head of the government in conformity with the organization of the state. Yūsuf, who probably died young (after 995) and had the title of "Inal," and Mūsā, who lived to an old age (d. after 1064) and probably had the title "Inanch," and was later the yabghu, held positions as Arslan's assistants. As for the brothers Chaghrı and Toghrıl, who at that time must have been fourteen or fifteen years old

58. Al-ʿUtbī, *Ta'rīkh,* Manīnī's commentary, I, 176; Ibn al-Athīr, *al-Kāmil,* year 432; Gardīzī, *Zain al-akhbār,* ed. Muḥammad Mīrzā Qazwīnī (Tehran, 1315 *sh.*), pp. 49 ff.; Barthold, *Turkestan,* pp. 259–76; Köymen, "Büyük Selçuklu," pp. 126–40.

59. Ṣadr al-Dīn, *Akhbār,* p. 2; Ibn al-Athīr, *al-Kāmil,* year 432; Cahen, "Le Malik-Nameh," pp. 44 f.

60. See Kafesoğlu, *Harezmşahlar devleti tarihi* (Ankara: TTK, 1956), pp. 91 f.

61. Ibn Aybak al-Dawādārī, *Kanz al-durar,* Topkapı, Ahmet III MS 2932, I, fol. 99b, cited in Köymen, "Büyük Selçuklu," p. 118n. 3.

62. *Malik-Nāma,* cited in Mīrkhwānd, *Rawḍat,* IV, 72.

at the most, they took their places in the administration as *begs*.[63] Although Arslan held the high authority of the yabghu, the members of the Seljuk family, as mentioned above, adhered to the old state system. Thus when they descended upon Transoxiana, each did so at the head of the Turkmen groups loyal to him. Meanwhile, their "ally," the Sāmānid state, had ceased to exist and, moreover, because the Bukhārā-Samarqand region had passed into the hands of the Qarakhānids, who had come to an understanding with the Ghaznavids, the Seljuks found themselves in direct opposition to the Qarakhānids. But the Qarakhānid Naṣr II İlig-Khān was apprehensive about the Seljuks and wanted to reach an agreement with them, if possible, by which he could benefit from their forces. However, because of the feeling of mutual distrust, a struggle broke out between them. In the course of it, Chaghrı Beg and Toghrıl Beg decided to have recourse to the other Qarakhānid ruler Bughra Khān. Although they went to the area around Talas according to his wishes, he detained Toghrıl there and relations between them soured. Chaghrı Beg then defeated the forces of Bughra Khān in a ferocious surprise attack and took some of his commanders prisoner. Toghrıl Beg was thus rescued and rejoined the other Seljuks.[64] This incident reveals the difficult position in which the groups bound to the sons of Mikhā'īl found themselves. As for their return to Transoxiana, they came to Bukhārā upon the death of Naṣr II İlig-Khān in 403/1012–13 and encountered the opposition of the Qarakhānid ʿAlī-Tegin, whose family had established an independent state there. According to Fakhr al-Dīn al-Rāzī,[65] ʿAlī-Tegin wrote a letter to the "kings and sultans of Turkistan" asking help to drive away the Seljuks who were in the plains of Kish (*yeşil şehir*) and Nakhshab.[66] The subsequent political pressure and shortage of land were the reasons for the famous incursion of the Seljuks, under Chaghrı Beg, into eastern Anatolia (1016–21).

The Coming of the Seljuks to Khurāsān and the First Seljuk State

ʿAlī-Tegin became an ally of Arslan Yabghu. At one time, Arslan Khān, one of the Qarakhānid rulers, captured him but he later escaped from prison. When he came to Transoxiana, he and Arslan Yabghu seized Bukhārā (411/1020–21). ʿAlī-Tegin settled there and, with Arslan's assistance, built up his strength and worked to gain a more commanding position compared to the other branches of the Qarakhānids.[67] Thus one of the natural results of the *fédératif* organization among the Seljuks at that time was an alliance between some of them and the Qarakhānids. As will be seen later, this was because the

63. On the question of Seljuk's sons, which is very confused, see the most recent study by Kafesoğlu, "Selçuk'un oğulları ve torunları," *TM* 13(1958):117–30.

64. Mīrkhwānd, *Rawḍat,* IV, 72.

65. *Jāmiʿ al-ʿulūm,* Nuruosmaniye Library MS 3760, fol. 75a.

66. Yazdī, who cites Abarqūhī, *Jāmiʿ,* Fâtih Library MS 4507, fol. 171b.

67. Ibn al-Athīr, *al-Kāmil,* year 432; Sibṭ b. al-Jawzī, *Mirʾāt al-zamān,* Topkapı, Ahmet III MS 2907, XII, fol. 91b; Mīrkhwānd, *Rawḍat,* IV, 72.

members of the dynasty were free to act in their own interests. The power and influence of Arslan Yabghu, ʿAlī-Tegin's supporter, increased and he attracted the attention of the Qarakhānids on the one hand and the Ghaznavids on the other. Transoxiana was a country that tempted the expansionist ambitions of these two great states. Therefore, while the Qarakhānid ruler, Yūsuf Qadır Khān (d. 1032), wanted his brother ʿAlī-Tegin to be ejected from there, Sultan Maḥmūd of Ghazna (d. 1030) wanted to extend his own rule toward Transoxiana, after having already taken possession of the territory of Khwārazm to the north in 407/1016–17. In 1024, the Qarakhānid ruler Manṣūr, "the Great Qaghan," had abdicated his position and Yūsuf Qadır Khān took his place. While ʿAlī-Tegin was taking sides against Yūsuf because he did not recognize him as "the Great Qaghan," Sultan Maḥmūd was receiving letters from the people of Transoxiana complaining of ʿAlī-Tegin. Although both of these rulers wanted to recover the Bukhārā area from their troublesome neighbor, Arslan Yabghu and his Turkmen gave them second thoughts. It was for this reason that a historic meeting was held in Transoxiana between Yūsuf Qadır Khān and Sultan Maḥmūd (1025). In this remarkable meeting, described in detail by Gardīzī,[68] all "Iranian and Turanian" problems were discussed.[69] Yūsuf Qadır Khān characterized the Seljuks as a numerous and warlike people who could not be controlled and asked the sultan to have them rounded up and removed from Turkistan and Transoxiana before they became a dangerous problem for even the Ghaznavid state. As can be seen in the famous anecdote about sending his arrows {a signal for his kinsmen to mobilize}, Arslan had tens of thousands of horsemen in Turkistan and the Balkhān mountains.[70] Moreover, he was described as "the son of Seljuk feared by all rulers of Turkistan and the Afrāsiyābids for his valor, warlikeness, and the way he fell upon his prey like lightening."[71] Sultan Maḥmūd, therefore, used shrewdness and cunning to have him brought to Samarqand, where he was arrested and then banished to the fortress of Kālinjār in India. The arrest of Arslan Yabghu, who eventually died in the fortress after seven years of captivity (1032), had important consequences. First, the Seljuk authority in the aforesaid places ended. The leaderless Turkmen were scattered here and there without land. To this was added the pressure from the sons of Mikhā'īl who wanted to subordinate them to their own authority.[72] Their *begs* finally petitioned Sultan Maḥmūd and, as a result, about 4,000 families were moved to Khurāsān, despite the vehement opposition of the Ghaznavid governor of Ṭūs, Arslan Jādhib, who sensed a future threat. They settled around Nasā, Bāvard, and Farāva (these were to be known as the Turkmen of Iraq). Second, the brothers Chaghrı and Toghrıl and the sons of Arslan, that is, the branch that established the Anatolian

68. *Zain al-akhbār,* pp. 65–67.
69. Jūzjānī, *Ṭabaqāt-i Nāṣirī,* ed. ʿAbd al-Ḥayy Ḥabībī Qandahārī (Kabul, 1342–43/1963–64), I, 209.

70. See Rāvandī, *Rāḥat,* p. 89, Turkish trans., I, 88, cited here from other sources.

71. Jūzjānī, *Ṭabaqāt,* I, 209.

72. Gardīzī, *Zain,* p. 67.

Seljuk state, did not take kindly to Arslan's arrest and did not forget this unjust action. This would appear to be the basis of the Seljuks' desire for revenge against the Ghaznavids. Third, upon the arrest of Arslan, the imperial line was transferred to the descendants of Mikhā'īl via Chaghrı and Toghrıl, who moved to the forefront of Seljuk history.[73]

As we have seen, Chaghrı and Toghrıl were in a difficult position in Transoxiana. And so, they decided to carry out a reconnaissance operation to find more suitable areas for themselves. While Toghrıl Beg withdrew into the plains, which were safe from attack, his brother moved to the west, toward Anatolia, at the head of 3,000 horsemen. The Byzantine frontier had been known to them for some time. Already in 964 and 966, throngs of volunteers had come to the region of Armenia to fight as *ghāzī*s.[74] Apparently there had been Turks among them, for Chaghrı Beg encountered them around Āzarbāījān. He passed through Khurāsān and that region in 1018, with "long-haired Turkmen armed with bow and lance on horses which flew like the wind," and appeared in the Armenian kingdom of Vāspūrakān around Lake Van.[75] Chaghrı Beg routed the Armenian forces that went out against him, took control of the western section of the country, and then headed north toward the lands of the Shaddādids. Because the Georgian forces around Nakhchivān did not dare engage him in battle and withdrew, he went on to carry out various military operations. Further north he used steppe-warfare tactics to defeat the large army organized by Vasak Pahlavu, the commander of the fortress of Bıjnı in the Armenian kingdom of Ani, who tried to stop him. Vasak was killed in the fighting.[76] Because of the heavy Turkish pressure resulting from this raid, the Armenians under the authority of Senacherim, the king of Vāspūrakān, left their homeland and went to central Anatolia. After staying for a while in all the Armenian and Georgian countries, Chaghrı Beg returned to Toghrıl Beg in Transoxiana. The Ghaznavid forces were not able to prevent this movement back and forth from Transoxiana. As clearly reported by Barhebraeus,[77] Chaghrı Beg described the results of this great campaign to his brother saying that the Seljuks could go to the region of Armenia that he had reconnoitered because there were no forces there that could oppose them.[78]

After Chaghrı Beg's campaign in eastern Anatolia, which ended successfully with respect both to showing his military power and to acquiring booty, the influence and fame of the two brothers increased in Transoxiana. Moreover, the number of their followers multiplied, especially after the arrest of their uncle Arslan. They thus obtained a powerful position. Although they were the effective chiefs of the Turkmen, they selected another of their uncles, Mūsā (Inanch), as yabghu according to tribal protocol. At the time that Sultan Maḥmūd of Ghazna

73. Köymen, "Büyük Selçuklu," pp. 145–64.

74. Ibn al-Athīr, *al-Kāmil,* years 353 and 355; Ibn Funduq, *Ta'rīkh,* p. 124.

75. Aristaces, cited in J. Laurent, *Byzance et les Turcs Seldjoucides dans l'Asie occidentale jusqu'en 1018* (Paris, 1914), p. 16n. 6; E. Dulaurier, *Chronique de Matthieu d'Edesse* (Paris, 1858), p. 41, Turkish trans. H. D. Andreasyan, *Urfalı Mateos vekayi-nâmesi* (Ankara: TTK, 1962), pp. 48 ff.

76. Vartan, *History,* Turkish trans. H. D. Andreasyan as "Türk fütûhât tarihi, 889–1269" [The history of the Turkish conquests, 889–1269], in *Istanbul Üniversitesi Edebiyat Fakültesi Tarih Semineri Dergisi* [The journal of the history seminar of the Istanbul University Faculty of Literature], 1(1937):166; Chamichian, *Ermeni tarihi* [The Armenian history] {in Armenian} (Venice, 1875), II, 901, 904; for an inscription dating from 1029 concerning Vasak's death in battle, see L. Alishan, *Chirag* (Venice, 1881), p. 148.

77. *Tarihi,* I, 293.

78. See Kafesoğlu, "Doğu Anadolu'ya ilk Selçuklu akını (1015–21) ve tarihî ehemmiyeti," *Fuad Köprülü armağanı,* pp. 259–74; idem, "Réponse à la critique par Cl. Cahen de l'article 'Dogu Anadolu'ya ilk Selçuklu akını (1015–21) ve tarihî ehemmiyeti,'" {under "Comptes Rendus"} *JA* 244(1956):129–34; idem, "Selçuklu tarihinin mes'eleleri" [Problems of Seljuk history], *Belleten* 19(1955):480–85.

had come to the famous meeting in Transoxiana, ʿAlī-Tegin had fled from Bukhārā but returned after the sultan departed, and maintained his rule. Believing that he could keep conditions as they had been in the time of Arslan, he sent ambassadors to Chaghrı Beg and Toghrıl Beg and proposed that they join the Qarakhānid state, as Arslan had previously done.[79] However, the offer was rejected by the Seljuk chiefs, who felt that it was a trick, just as Maḥmūd's earlier proposal that they come to Khurāsān had been rejected. ʿAlī-Tegin was anxious about this and therefore sought an opportunity to undermine the solidarity among the Seljuks and turn them against each other. He successfully made contact with Yūsuf (the son of Mūsā Yabghu) and, in return for generous *iqṭāʿs* {land grants}, wanted to appoint him the yabghu of the Turks ("Inanch Yabghu") and send him against Chaghrı Beg and Toghrıl Beg. When Yūsuf would not be party to this, he was killed in a raid against the Seljuks carried out by Alp-Qara, a Qarakhānid commander under the orders of ʿAlī-Tegin. But before long Mūsā Yabghu together with the brothers Chaghrı Beg and Toghrıl Beg, defeated the Qarakhānid army in revenge for this grave attack and killed Alp-Qara (Muḥarram 420/January 1029). This event is important for revealing the inner solidarity among the leading Seljuk families under the direction of Chaghrı Beg and Toghrıl Beg.[80] However, as a result of rather severe losses inflicted by the combined forces of ʿAlī-Tegin, which attacked from all sides, the Seljuks were compelled to withdraw toward Khwārazm. There they stayed in an area set aside for them by the Khwārazm-Shāh Altun-Tash, the Ghaznavid governor. Around that time Sultan Maḥmūd died (421/1030) and his son Masʿūd succeeded him on the throne. A change then occurred in Ghaznavid policy, namely, Masʿūd ordered Altun-Tash to go on campaign against ʿAlī-Tegin at Bukhārā. When Altun-Tash subsequently died, his son Hārūn, who had been given control of Khwārazm in his place by the sultan, launched a war of independence in 425 (spring of 1034). All this was to be to the advantage of the Seljuks, for just as ʿAlī-Tegin, who had threatened the capital, was compelled to draw near the Seljuks, so too Hārūn, a friend of the Turkmen with whom he had reached an agreement against the Ghaznavids, felt it necessary to show great respect to the Seljuks from whom he expected major support. Consequently, a tripartite alliance was created against the Ghaznavids, which meant that Chaghrı Beg and Toghrıl Beg were united with the Turkmen of the yabghu and the Turkmen loyal to Yınal (Ibrāhīm Yınal, who was the son of Yūsuf Yınal and half-brother {on his mother's side} of Toghrıl Beg) and that the Seljuks who lived in the region between Bukhārā and Khwārazm would again play a role in international relations.[81] But by that time two events had occurred in rapid succession which placed

79. Mīrkhwānd, *Rawḍat,* IV, 73.

80. Ibn al-Athīr, *al-Kāmil,* year 432; Mīrkhwānd, *Rawḍat,* IV, 73; Barthold, *Turkestan,* pp. 297 f.; Kafesoğlu, "Selçuk'un oğulları," p. 124.

the Seljuks once more in difficult straits. One was the terrible attack that befell them at the hands of the son of ʿAlī, the yabghu of Yengi-Kent, and Abū 'l-Fawāris Shāh-Malik[82] who were from the Baranlı (Koyunlu) tribe of the Oghuz,[83] which had been the primary enemy of the Seljuks since ancient times. Between the two a bitter and bloody hostility had prevailed.[84] Shāh-Malik had followed the Seljuks step by step. He secretly crossed the desert road and caught the Turkmen by surprise, killing 7,000–8,000 of them (the last day of Kurban Bayram 425/November 1034). He also captured a great many horses and slaves. Although the Seljuks were thrown into disarray and were forced to leave their homeland in Khwārazm and cross the Oxus, they later returned upon the request and assurances of Hārūn who was afraid to lose their support. The Seljuks urged him to oppose Shāh-Malik, who therefore hesitated to pursue them and face the 30,000-man force of Hārūn. The second event was the death of ʿAlī-Tegin at the beginning of 1035. According to the statements of the Ghaznavid vizir Aḥmad b. ʿAbd al-Ṣamad, it appears that it was not considered to be particularly difficult to deal with the matter of the rebellious Hārūn, who was without allies. From the Ghaznavid point of view, the main problem was that the Seljuks were in a difficult situation and could only cross into Khurāsān because of the pressure from the sons of ʿAlī-Tegin, not to mention the undiminished hostility of Shāh-Malik.[85] The position of the "Turkmen of Iraq" in Khurāsān was clear.[86] As we have seen, these Turkmen, who were called "Nawbakī" {or Nāvakiyya} (*yabghulu?*), were moved to the area around Nasā, Bāvard, and Farāva after the arrest of Arslan Yabghu. They were led by chiefs named Qızıl, Bogha (Buka), Yaghmur, and Gök-Tash.[87] After living there a short time, their numbers increased when they were joined by new groups coming from Turkistan and the Turkmen scattered about Iran.[88] They then began to carry out undisciplined actions that broke down public order. Although Sultan Maḥmūd ordered the governor of Ṭūs, Arslan Jādhib, to pursue them when the people of the area complained of their behavior, the Turkmen would not submit. It was impossible for the Ghaznavid forces to be completely successful against them because they would sometimes withdraw to the Dihistān and Balkhān mountains whence they could make repeated counterstrikes. It was for these reasons that Sultan Maḥmūd himself had to go on campaign (418/1028), after accusing Arslan Jādhib of a lack of effort. And he inflicted a resounding defeat on them at Ribāṭ-i Farāva. Among the Turkmen who were consequently scattered were the Qızılı and Yaghmurlu (i.e., those under the command of Qızıl and Yaghmur) who withdrew to the Dihistān and Balkhān areas. Some even went to Kirmān.[89] Although Maḥmūd expelled the Turkmen from Khurāsān, he was not able to

81. Ibn al-Athīr, *al-Kāmil,* year 432; Abū 'l-Faḍl Baihaqī, *Ta'rīkh-i Baihaq,* eds. Q. Ghanī and 'A. Fayyāḍ (Tehran, 1324/1945), pp. 445, 471, 680 ff.; Barthold, *Turkestan,* pp. 296 f.

82. See Pritsak, "Der Untergang," p. 407.

83. Ibn Funduq, *Ta'rīkh,* 51.

84. Baihaqī, *Ta'rīkh,* p. 682.

85. Ibid., p. 445.

86. Ibn al-Athīr, *al-Kāmil,* year 432.

87. Baihaqī, *Ta'rīkh,* pp. 68, 266, 445; Jūzjānī, *Ṭabaqāt,* I, 291.

88. Kasrawī Tabrīzī, *Shāhriyārān-i gumnām* (Tehran, 1928–30), II, 57.

make them completely obedient. Because he even tried to pursue them beyond the borders of his own state, it is clear that he considered them to be a constant danger. Those who went to Kirmān passed through Iṣfahān upon the death of the Būyid ruler of that province in 1028 and took refuge with ʿAlā' al-Dawla Kākūya. However, as a result of Maḥmūd's political pressure, arrangements were made to annihilate them. They escaped with difficulty and together with the Turkmen masses in their company moved toward the west. Their leaders were Bogha, Gök-Tash, and two others. Meantime, Maḥmūd had died and his son Masʿūd, who was then the governor of Rayy, wanted to succeed him. But he needed support. So he turned to the Oghuz and invited Bogha and Gök-Tash, who had gone toward Āzarbāījān, and Yaghmur, who, as we mentioned, had withdrawn to the Balkhān area, back to Khurāsān. In November 1030, some of these Turkmen, who were in the Ghaznavid army, showed their courage in the capture of Makrān. They also provided important services in Iraq, India, and Lahor.[90] But Sultan Masʿūd still did not trust the Oghuz and, over the well-founded objections of his vizir, tried to subordinate the Turkmen to the control of Ḥājib Khumār-Tash, one of the Ghaznavid commanders, and in this respect ordered Tash Farrāsh, the commander-in-chief of Iraq, to begin to put pressure on them. Finally, some fifty chiefs of the Oghuz (who were separate from the Turkmen), who had been sent to Iraq under the leadership of Yaghmur, were put to death by Tash Farrāsh (424/spring 1033).[91] All this caused the Turkmen masses, whose number had increased by the continuous arrival of newcomers from Transoxiana, to revolt and seek revenge. Thus, primarily under the leadership of Yaghmur's son, war broke out with the Ghaznavids in the Marv, Tirmidh, Ṭūs, Sarakhs, Nasā, Bādghīs, Bāvard, and Dihistān areas of western Khurāsān. Masʿūd was forced to take various measures to seal off Khurāsān from the influence of the tripartite alliance that faced him across the Oxus. Although he dispatched his vizir and top commanders on different roads into this region and even took the field himself, he could not stop the Turkmen who wreaked havoc in the environs of Rayy and Dāmghān, routed the elephant-equipped Ghaznavid army, and killed Tash Farrāsh and other important commanders. After overcoming other Ghaznavid resistance (1034), they headed for Āzarbāījān and joined their kinsmen who had already gone there.[92]

It was not difficult to eliminate the Khwārazm-Shāh Hārūn, who had prepared to seize Khurāsān with the help of the Seljuks, as mentioned above, by assassination (Jumāda II 426/April 1035). Indeed, it became clear that the greatest problem facing the Ghaznavid state, at home or abroad, was that of the Seljuk-Turkmen, and that the opinion

89. Gardīzī, *Zain,* pp. 70 f.; Ibn al-Athīr, *al-Kāmil,* year 432; Baihaqī, *Ta'rīkh,* pp. 88, 521, and see Köymen, "Büyük Selçuklu imparatorluğu'nun kuruluşu II," *DTCF Dergisi* 15(1957):29 ff.

90. Baihaqī, *Ta'rīkh,* pp. 68, 404; Ibn al-Athīr, *al-Kāmil,* year 432.

91. See ibid.; Baybars al-Manṣūrī, *Zubdat al-fikra,* Fayzullah Efendi Library MS 1459, fol. 57a.

92. Jūzjānī, *Ṭabaqāt,* I, 292 f.; see also Köymen, "Büyük Selçuklu II," pp. 34, 36–40.

of the Ghaznavid vizir about them was correct once again. With the death of Hārūn, the Seljuks were deprived of support and at the same time were pressed by Shāh-Malik on the one hand and the sons of ʿAlī-Tegin on the other. They were also weakened by their most recent attack. The Seljuks had no choice but to head for Khurāsān without the permission of the Ghaznavids.[93] In May 1035, Chaghrı Beg and Toghrıl Beg, together with Mūsā Yabghu and his forces, and the followers of Yınal and their forces, crossed the Oxus and entered Ghaznavid territory. Their numbers were small, but increased as they advanced toward Marv and Nasā.[94] The leaderless Turkmen, as well as the Khwārazmians who had been in Khurāsān, did not hesitate to join these two renowned members of the old Seljuk princely family. The passage of the Seljuks to Khurāsān thus constituted one of the major events in history, for the brothers Chaghrı and Toghrıl, one of whom became famous for his courage and bravery and the other for his high statesmanship and political acumen, laid the foundations in Khurāsān for the Seljuk Empire, the first of the two greatest Turco-Islamic political entities.

When the Seljuk chiefs arrived in Nasā, they wrote a letter to the Ghaznavid vizir of Khurāsān describing their difficult position resulting from their lack of land, and asked him to intercede with the Sultan so that they could be given a homeland there.[95] The high officials of the Ghaznavid state were seized by alarm at this news. They immediately held a conference in which it appears that they wanted Sultan Masʿūd to march quickly on the Seljuks while the vizir, who had more correctly analyzed the problem of the Seljuks—who were known to have an army at that time of 10,000 horsemen—and had carefully observed their actions and taken precautions from the beginning, recommended dealing cautiously with them. Because the vizir's view prevailed, the sultan did not go to Nasā to oppose the Seljuks but for the time being went to Nīshāpūr. There he set about putting his own plans into operation and prepared an army "capable of capturing all Turkistan."[96] However, this army, which set out under the command of Ḥājib Begtoghdi and was reinforced with elephants, suffered a terrible defeat at the hands of the Seljuks on the plains of Nasā (Shaʿbān 426/last week of June 1035).[97] This was the first victory that the Seljuks won against the Ghaznavids and was a sign to them that, not only could they rely to a very great extent on themselves, but they also had an opportunity to found a state here. In fact, after the victory the two sides exchanged "ambassadors" and a kind of autonomy was granted the Seljuks by the Ghaznavids. The provinces of Nasā, Farāva, and Dihistān were given to the three Seljuk chiefs. In addition, robes of honor, patents of office,

93. Baihaqī, *Ta'rīkh*, pp. 687 f.; Jūzjānī, *Ṭabaqāt*, I, 292.

94. Baihaqī, *Ta'rīkh*, pp. 687, 470.

95. Ibid., pp. 470 f.

96. Ibid., pp. 482, 488.

97. Ibid., p. 483; Gardīzī, *Zain*, pp. 80 f.; Ṣadr al-Dīn, *Akhbār*, pp. 3 f.

and banners were sent to them (August 1035).[98] But the Seljuks were not satisfied. This is clear from their disrespect for the treaty, the raids they launched as far as Balkh and Sīstān, the political relations they established with the Khwārazm-Shāh Ismāʿīl, and their desire for more than three provinces of Khurāsān. Consequently, Sultan Masʿūd again assembled a great army, this time to drive the Turkmen completely out of Khurāsān. But as has been described to this point, Masʿūd, who was a man of little political insight and, furthermore, addicted to amusement and pleasure, simply left the prosecution of the war against this formidable danger, which swirled about the head of the Ghaznavid state, to his commanders and himself set out to conquer India. The great Ḥājib Sü-Bashı, the commander of the Ghaznavid army which was at Nīshāpūr, moved against the Seljuks on the direct order of the sultan in India. In the battle that took place near Sarakhs (third week of May 1038), he suffered a major defeat, thanks above all to the great efforts of Chaghrı Beg.[99] This second Seljuk victory was in reality a battle in a war for independence. It brought the region of Khurāsān directly under Seljuk sovereignty. In accordance with an old Turkish tradition, the Seljuk chiefs divided their country among themselves: Chaghrı Beg acquired Marv, Mūsā Yabghu took Sarakhs, and "the just ruler" Toghrıl Beg received Nīshāpūr, the leading city of Khurāsān.[100] Ibrāhīm Yınal came to Nīshāpūr, which had been abandoned by the Ghaznavid forces, and held talks with the people in his capacity as the vanguard and representative of the Seljuks. From these talks it was clear that the goal of the Seljuk chiefs was to establish the state that they had heretofore so intently wanted to bring to reality, and make Toghrıl Beg the head of that state. While the *khuṭba* {Friday sermon} was read in the name of Chaghrı Beg in Marv with the title "Malik al-Mulūk" {King of Kings},[101] in June 1038, with brilliant pagentry, Toghrıl Beg entered Nīshāpūr where Ibrāhīm Yınal had begun to have his name read in the *khuṭba* in May with the title "al-Sulṭān al-Muʿaẓẓam" {the Great Sultan}. With Toghrıl Beg were 3,000 horsemen and he carried a bow in his hand as a symbol of Turkish rule. Qāḍī Ṣāʿid, the most respected man in the city when Sultan Masʿūd had ascended the throne there, addressed Toghrıl Beg as *efendimiz* {our master}.[102] The new Seljuk state was immediately organized, officials were appointed to its various regions, and, in accordance with another old Turkish tradition, the territories to be conquered were conferred upon other Seljuk chiefs by Toghrıl Beg. When the ʿAbbāsid Caliph al-Qā'im bi-Amr Allāh sent an ambassador to Nīshāpūr, the Seljuks were justifiably pleased, for this meant that the caliph recognized Toghrıl Beg as the ruler of Khurāsān and leader of all the Turkmen.[103]

98. Baihaqī, *Ta'rīkh,* p. 492; Jūzjānī, *Ṭabaqāt,* I, 294.

99. Baihaqī, *Ta'rīkh,* pp. 536–45; Köymen, "Büyük Selçuklu II," pp. 67–88.

100. Baihaqī, *Ta'rīkh,* p. 552.

101. Ibn al-Athīr, *al-Kāmil,* year 432.

102. Baihaqī, *Ta'rīkh,* p. 553.

The Seljuk War of Independence and Subsequent Conquests

When Sultan Masʿūd learned of the events in Khurāsān, he hastely set out with his forces. Meanwhile Chaghrı Beg was struggling to capture the area around Ṭāliqān and Fāryāb and some of his cavalry even appeared at the gates of Balkh. The sultan, at the head of an army composed of 50,000 horsemen and foot soldiers and equipped with 300 war elephants, came to Balkh and quickly headed in the direction of Sarakhs. Under the command of Masʿūd, this army was so large and well-equipped that nothing in all Turkistan could resist it.[104] And it was continuously augmented by new forces that joined it from various regions. Chaghrı Beg was in Sarakhs. Toghrıl Beg mobilized and marched there from Nīshāpūr. With the arrival of Mūsā Yabghu, who joined them with 20,000 cavalry from Marv, the Seljuk chiefs all met at the same point. Chaghrı Beg in particular was among those in favor of going to war. In the fighting, which began in Ramaḍān 430/May 1039 and lasted for a long time, the Seljuks could not continuously face all the sultan's forces. And so they spread out and withdrew to the desert, where it was impossible for the Ghaznavid army to follow them, and fought a war of attrition. Meanwhile Masʿūd entered Nīshāpūr (Ṣafar 431/November 1039). Harassed by ceaseless hit-and-run attacks, the Ghaznavid army occupied itself with training for desert warfare. When spring arrived, the Seljuks decided, again at the insistance of Chaghrı Beg, to go out and confront the sultan. The Ghaznavid army, under the command of the sultan, was gradually drawn away from Sarakhs, to the desert north of that city. In this trackless wasteland the Seljuks had destroyed all the wells. Left without water and subject to a series of uninterrupted attacks and raids from behind, the morale of this army of some 100,000 men was consequently shaken. Finally, near Marv before the fortress of Dandānqān the Seljuks gave battle and inflicted a terrible defeat on the Ghaznavid army, which had fought nonstop with all its strength for three days, and destroyed a large section of it (7–9 Ramaḍān 431/22–24 May 1040).[105] The Seljuks seized their treasure and an untold amount of weapons and supplies. Although Masʿūd was able to escape with about 100 followers and headed for India, he was later killed on the way by his own men.[106] This was the battle for Seljuk independence. Now, after the long hard struggle, which had begun from the time they had come to Jand, they obtained their wish: they succeeded in founding an independent state in Khurāsān. On the last day of the fighting, in the meeting they held after the Friday prayer, they proclaimed Toghrıl Beg the sultan of the Seljuk state. According to the custom of the period, *fetḥnāme*s {victory

103. ʿImād al-Dīn al-Iṣfahānī, *Zubdat al-nuṣra*, Turkish trans. Kıvâmüddin Burslan, as *Irak ve Horasan Selçukluları tarihi* [The history of the Seljuks of Khurāsān and Iraq] (Istanbul: TTK, 1943), pp. 4 f.; Barhebraeus, *Tarihi*, I, 296; Baihaqī, *Ta'rīkh*, pp. 550–54; Köymen, "Büyük Selçuklu II," p. 100.

104. Baihaqī, *Ta'rīkh*, pp. 554, 569.

105. Yāqūt, *Mu'jam al-buldān*, 2d ed. F. Wüstenfeld (Leipzig, 1924), II, 477.

106. Baihaqī, *Ta'rīkh*, pp. 571 ff., 616–26; Gardīzī, *Zain*, pp. 85 f.; Ṣadr al-Dīn, *Akhbār*, pp. 8 f.; ʿImād al-Dīn, *Zubdat*, p. 5; Ibn al-Athīr, *al-Kāmil*, year 432; Jūzjānī, *Ṭabaqāt*, I, 296 f.; Rāvandī, *Rāḥat*, pp. 100 f.; for details, see Köymen, "Büyük Selçuklu imparatorluğu'nun kuruluşu III," *DTCF Dergisi* 16(1958):1–53.

announcements} were sent to neighboring rulers. Later in the same month, important decisions were made in a great assembly convened in Marv and opened with a speech by the new sultan. A letter based on these decisions and bearing the signature of Toghrıl Beg was sent to Baghdad with the Seljuk ambassador Abū Isḥāq al-Fuqqāʿī. This letter was addressed to the caliph and described the current situation. It stated that justice had been established in Khurāsān, there would be no deviation from the path of God, and that the Seljuks would be loyal to the Commander of the Faithful.[107] Among the decisions that were put into effect was one based on the Turkish concept of conquests, which was related to the conquest of the world. In accordance with the old Turkish tradition of state, the country that had been conquered and those to be conquered in the future were divided among the three chiefs of the Seljuk dynasty: the area between the Oxus and Ghazna, the center of which was Marv, but also including the cities of Sarakhs and Balkh, was given to Malik al-Mulūk Chaghrı Beg; the Bust and Sīstān regions, the center of which was Herāt, were given to Mūsā Yabghu; Toghrıl Beg, who remained in the capital of Nīshāpūr as sultan, was given Iraq and the area to the west. Among the members of the dynasty who were of secondary rank, Ibrāhīm Yınal was assigned to Kūhistān; Qutalmısh (Arslan Yabghu's son) was assigned to Gurgān and Dāmghān; and Qāvurt, Chaghrı Beg's son, was assigned to the districts of Kirmān. All of them were at the command of the sultan.[108] The Seljuk conquests continued on this basis. Mūsā, also called Yabghu Kalan,[109] captured Herāt with 5,000 cavalry. In the meantime, Er-Tash, i.e., the son of Yūsuf Yınal and the brother of Ibrāhīm Yınal, went to Sīstān at the end of 1040. In November, he established his authority there and had the Yabghu's name read in the *khuṭba*. With his help and that of Abū 'l-Faḍl, the ruler of Sīstān who had offered his allegiance to the Seljuks, Mūsā Yabghu then took complete control of that region and the area around Bust. Er-Tash died in 440/1048–49. In 1051 Zarang, the principal city of Sīstān, passed into the hands of the Ghaznavid grand chamberlain Toghrıl. Although Mūsā, who usually lived at Herāt, and his son Qara-Arslan Böri came to retake it, they were attacked by surprise and forced to retreat. After Toghrıl Beg left, Sīstān again reverted to Mūsā's control. In Rajab 446/October 1054, Chaghrı Beg's son, Yāqūtī, came to Sīstān and brought the region of Makrān on the coast of the Indian Ocean under Seljuk sovereignty. Toghrıl Beg, however, intervened to prevent his attempt to have the *khuṭba* read in his father's name in that region.[110] Later, in 1064, Mūsā Yabghu, who also had the bynames "Muʿizz al-Dawla" {the Fortifier of the State} and "Fakhr al-Mulk," {the Glory of the Realm} was arrested in the fortress of Herāt, where he had taken refuge after claiming the

107. Baihaqī, *Ta'rīkh,* p. 628; 'Imād al-Dīn, *Zubdat,* p. 5; Barhebraeus, *Tarihi,* I, 299; Rāvandī, *Rāḥat,* pp. 103 f., Turkish trans., p. 102.

108. 'Imād al-Dīn, *Zubdat,* p. 7; Rāvandī, *Rāḥat,* pp. 102, 104, Turkish trans., pp. 101 f.; Köymen, "Büyük Selçuklu III," pp. 57 ff.

109. "The Great Yabghu," see Rāvandī, *Rāḥat,* p. 104.

110. Anonymous, *Ta'rīkh-i Sīstān,* ed. Malik al-Shuʿarā' Bahār (Tehran, 1314/1935), pp. 371–75, 381 f.

sultanate from Alp-Arslan, and was brought before the sultan. Alp-Arslan forgave his great uncle and was satisfied simply to detain him close at hand.[111] He later granted him Māzandarān as an *iqṭā'*.[112] Böri, who represented his father in Sīstān, protected that region with Abū 'l-Faḍl. The last word we have on this concerns the fact that in August 1056 he came to Zarang where he was greeted with honor.[113] Er-Tash meanwhile had returned to Khurāsān because of a falling out with Mūsā Yabghu. But when Mawdūd, the son of the Ghaznavid Sultan Mas'ūd, tried to recover Sīstān from the Seljuks with an army led by his commander Qaimaz, Abū 'l-Faḍl sent word to him and he suddenly appeared in Sīstān in July 1042, defeated the Ghaznavid forces, and drove them from the region. In the same year while Toghrıl Beg was on campaign in Khwārazm, Er-Tash captured the well-known Seljuk enemy Shāh-Malik, the amīr of Jand (who had fled to Kirmān), and sent him to Chaghrı Beg.[114] Er-Tash, who had made a great contribution to the establishment of Seljuk rule in Sīstān, was assassinated in Ṭabas in 440/1048–49.[115]

As mentioned, Chaghrı Beg's son Qara-Arslan Qāvurt[116] was sent to Kirmān. He went into action there against the Būyids in 1041. Although the Turkmen forces under his command met stiff resistance, he entered Sardsīr, the northern part of Kirmān, at the head of 5,000–6,000 cavalry in Sha'bān 442/beginning of 1051. He finally captured the major city of the area from the *nā'ib* {representative} of the Būyid Abū Kālījār, who had been blockaded there. Moreover, by carrying out a raid in which he put the chiefs of the Qufṣ and Qufa tribes to the sword, he also rescued Garmsīr, the mountainous region of southern Kirmān, from their banditry.[117] He thus brought all of Kirmān under Seljuk control. Qāvurt then went to the Arabian peninsula via the amirate of Hormuz, which had offered allegiance on its own, and created for himself a large country by adding Oman to the Seljuk domain. When his younger brother Alp-Arslan ascended the throne, Qāvurt claimed the sultanate and rebelled. But because Alp-Arslan quickly appeared in Kirmān, interrupting his Caucasus campaign, Qāvurt asked for and received forgiveness. Nevertheless, in 459/1067 he rebelled again because he did not want to have the name of Alp-Arslan's son, Malik-Shāh, read in the *khuṭba* as the heir apparent. When the imperial forces arrived in Kirmān, he asked for mercy and was again forgiven. While on his deathbed, Alp-Arslan advised, among other things, that Qāvurt, who had also become ruler of Fārs after 460/1068 by defeating Faḍlūya Shabānkāra,[118] and the countries in his possession, be kept under tight control.[119] When Malik-Shāh ascended the throne, Qāvurt declared himself sultan, went on the

111. Ibn al-Athīr, *al-Kāmil,* year 456.
112. Kafesoğlu, "Selçuk'un oğulları," pp. 119 f.
113. Anonymous, *Sīstān,* p. 382.
114. Ibn al-Athīr, *al-Kāmil,* year 437.
115. Anonymous, *Sīstān,* pp. 367–69; Kafesoğlu, "Selçuk'un oğulları," pp. 128 f.
116. In Barhebraeus, *Tarihi,* I, 326, Kawrath, Karut, probably another pronunciation for the Turkish word *kurt* {wolf}; see M. T. Houtsma's introduction to the *Ta'rīkh-i Saljūqiyyān-i Kirmān* by Muḥammad b. Ibrāhīm in the work he edited entitled *Recueil des textes relatifs à l'histoire des Seldjoucides* (Leiden, 1886), I, xiin. 1, and cf. G. Moravcsik, *Byzantinoturcica* (Budapest, 1943), II, 144.
117. Afḍal al-Dīn Kirmānī, *Badā'i' al-azmān fī ta'rīkh Kirmān,* ed. Mahdī Bayānī (Tehran, 1326/1927), pp. 5–8, cited by Muḥammad b. Ibrāhīm, *Ta'rīkh-i Saljūqiyyān-i Kirmān,* ed. Houtsma, in *Recueil,* I, 5 ff.
118. Qazvīnī, *Guzīda,* I, 433, 442.
119. Barhebraeus, *Tarihi,* I, 325 f.

march, and took Rayy. But in a battle near Hamadān, he was defeated and captured by forces sent by Malik-Shāh and his vizir, Niẓām al-Mulk (4 Shaʿbān 465/16 May 1073). In order to make sure that he would not cause further trouble, he was secretly strangled with his own bowstring.[120] Qāvurt was the founder of the Seljuk dynasty in Kirmān (see below). As for Chaghrı Beg, he also went on to conquer the countries left to him at the east of the Seljuk state.[121] In the fall of 1040, he besieged and captured the important city of Balkh and defeated the Ghaznavid army. He subsequently became the ruler of Gūzgān, Bādghīs, Khuttalān and other cities of Tukhāristān. In 434/1043, he made a joint campaign with Toghrıl Beg in Khwārazm. The Khwārazm-Shāh Ismāʿīl Khandān, who had previously cooperated with the Seljuks, had been defeated by Shāh-Malik (Jumādā I 432/February 1041), who had been given sovereignty over Khwārazm by Sultan Masʿūd. As ruler of Khwārazm, Shāh-Malik became the most important ally of the Ghaznavids. Chaghrı Beg and Toghrıl Beg surrounded Gurgānj (Jurgāniyya), the capital of Khwārazm, and routed Shāh-Malik. While Khwārazm was thus being absorbed by the Seljuks, Shāh-Malik fled to take refuge with the Ghaznavids but, as stated above, was captured by Er-Tash and handed over to Chaghrı Beg. He died in prison.[122] When Chaghrı Beg became ill in 435/1043–44, his son Alp-Arslan looked after his territory. Alp-Arslan's first victory occurred when he defeated and drove off the new Ghaznavid forces. Chaghrı Beg went on to conquer Tirmidh and its environs and subsequently entrusted Alp-Arslan with all these territories under his control.[123] When the Qarakhānid Arslan Khān appeared and tried to take over the countries that he governed, Alp-Arslan drove him back. The Qarakhānid ruler then reached an agreement with Chaghrı Beg whereby he recognized Seljuk sovereignty over these lands. Chaghrı Beg made a fruitless attempt to seize Ghazna, but in the long struggle Alp-Arslan in particular revealed his great abilities. In the spring of 1050, he took the province of Fārs and drove out the Būyids.[124] Finally, Chaghrı Beg concluded a peace treaty with the new Ghaznavid sultan, Ibrāhīm, when he ascended the throne in 1059.[125] This treaty, which made the Hindu Kush mountain range the border between the two states, lasted about a half century.

After these last events, Chaghrı Beg became ill and passed away in the city of Sarakhs at the age of seventy (Ṣafar 452/March 1060). His body was later transferred to the *türbe* {tomb} built by Alp-Arslan in Marv. With astonishing courage and great ability to command, Chaghrı Beg had played the primary role in the foun-

120. Afḍal al-Dīn, *Badā'iʿ*, p. 13; ʿImād al-Dīn, *Zubdat*, p. 49; Ibn al-Athīr, *al-Kāmil*, year 465; Ibn Khallikān, *Wafayāt*, II, 587.

121. ʿImād al-Dīn, *Zubdat*, pp. 3 ff., called Chakır.

122. Baihaqī, *Ta'rīkh*, pp. 686–90; Ibn al-Athīr, *al-Kāmil*, year 434.

123. Ṣadr al-Dīn, *Akhbār*, p. 19.

124. Ibn al-Athīr, *al-Kāmil*, year 442.

125. Jūzjānī, *Ṭabaqāt*, I, 282.

dation of the Seljuk state from the beginning. But his modesty was such that he consented to his younger brother Toghrıl Beg, whose intelligence and superior political acumen he respected, becoming chief of state. Chaghrı Beg was the ancestor of all the Seljuk dynasties except for the Anatolian Seljuk family, and one of his daughters married the Caliph al-Qā'im. Meanwhile as the sovereignty of the Seljuk state thus spread east, north, and south, conquests were also made on a large scale in the west under the direction of Toghrıl Beg.

While Toghrıl Beg was adding the area around Gurgānj and Ṭabaristān, where he went in person, to the state and receiving the allegiance of the Ziyārid (Vashimgīrī) and Bāvandid dynasties there (433/1041–42),[126] Ibrāhīm Yınal captured Rayy, one of the most important cities of Iran. He made it his base of operations and took Burūjird and beyond it Hamadān, the city of the Jibāl region, from the Kākūyids. In 437/1045–46, Hamadān was transferred to the Seljuks once and for all. Toghrıl Beg left Nīshāpūr and made Rayy the capital, for it was closer to the fields of conquest. When he entered that city in 434/1042, he was met with great pomp by Ibrāhīm Yınal. The sultan also ordered various construction projects to be undertaken in the city.[127] He subsequently added Ṭabarak, Qazvīn, Iṣfahān, Dihistān and their environs to the Seljuk state by accepting the allegiance of some of the local rulers and removing others. The armies dispatched under the direction of Ibrāhīm Yınal and Qutalmısh captured Dīnawar, Karmisīn {Kirmanshah} and Ḥulwān (433–39/1042–48). In these regions, which were taken from Būyid possession, the *khuṭba* was read in the names of Toghrıl Beg and Ibrāhīm Yınal.[128] After Ibrāhīm Yınal took Kinkiver, the fortress of Sarmāj, and then Shāhrazūr, he went to Āzarbāījān on Toghrıl Beg's orders. Meanwhile, in order to stop the destruction caused by the Turkmen, who had recently arrived in those areas from Turkistan before Toghrıl Beg, the Caliph al-Qā'im sent the well-known Muslim legal scholar and chief *qāḍī* {judge} al-Māwardī,[129] the author of the famous *al-Aḥkām al-sulṭāniyya,* to the sultan. Toghrıl Beg met the ambassador with honor at a distance of four parasangs from Rayy and told him that the Seljuks had a vast number of "troops" and that their current lands were not sufficient.[130]

Some of the Oghuz who were described above as the "Turkmen of Iraq" and were led by such commanders as Qızıl (d. 1041), Bogha, Gök-Tash, Manṣūr, and Nasoghlu[131] entered the Van region (Vāspūrakān) and wandered as far as Erzurum on horses that were "swift as eagles."[132] As for the other Oghuz masses, they advanced

126. See Ibn al-Athīr, *al-Kāmil,* year 433; Ibn Isfandiyār, *Ta'rīkh-i Ṭabaristān,* ed. 'Abbās Iqbāl (Tehran, 1320 *sh.*), II, 26.

127. Ibn al-Athīr, *al-Kāmil,* year 434.

128. See Kafesoğlu, "Selçuk'un oğulları," pp. 125 f.

129. See Ibn Khallikān, *Wafayāt,* I, 586, II, 440.

130. Ibn al-Athīr, *al-Kāmil,* year 435; Barhebraeus, *Tarihi,* I, 302.

131. Matthew of Edessa, *Chronique,* p. 82, Anazugli.

in the direction of Diyārbakr to the lands of the Marwānids, to the Mayyāfāriqīn (Silvan) and Mārdīn areas and to Jazīrat Ibn ʿUmar. Some of them entered the environs of Sinjār, Naṣībīn, and Ḥulwān. But these Oghuz were stopped by the Marwānids and the ʿUqailids who ruled Mosul. Because of the heavy losses they suffered, they headed for Āzarbāījān. There a clash occurred between the Aras {Araxes} and Murad rivers. Another group of Turkmen also advanced toward the Caucasus via Ṭabaristān. It entered the Arrān region and together with the Shaddādids made raids on Armenian territory and fought the Georgians.[133] In the reign of Emperor Basil II (d. 1025), known as Bulgaroctonus and a famous figure in Byzantine history, the Byzantine Empire had begun to follow a policy of annexation in the East and this policy had continued up to the period in question.[134] In order to put pressure on the Armenians and Georgians and, at the same time, march against the Turks to stop their raids, Emperor Constantine IX Monomachus (1042–55) dispatched the army to Ani on one hand, and to Dvin, the capital of the Shaddādids, on the other. When the Byzantines began to exert their power in this manner, Toghrıl Beg sent Qutalmısh, who was then conquering ʿIrāq al-ʿAjam with Ibrāhīm Yınal, to Āzarbāījān at the head of a great army. Mūsā Yabghu's son, Ḥasan, also participated in this operation. The Seljuk forces inflicted a defeat on the Byzantine army before Ganja (438/1046). Ḥasan subsequently set about conquering Pasinler {east of Erzurum}, but when he moved south from there he was ambushed in Vāspūrakān by a combined Byzantine, Armenian, and Georgian force under the command of the Georgian prince Liparit and was killed (1047).[135] Meanwhile Qutalmısh, who had been left alone, made no progress in his siege of Ganja. And so, the sultan sent Ibrāhīm Yınal, whom we mentioned above in the Shāhrazūr area, as the governor of Āzarbāījān against the Byzantines, and Qutalmısh set out to join him. The Seljuk princes advanced as far as the plain of Erzurum and first captured the large and rich city of Erzen (Kara-Erzen, today's Karaz), which was near Erzurum. At that moment, on the orders of the emperor, a 50,000-man Byzantine army under the command of Katakalon, and reinforced with all the Georgian and Abkhazian forces led by Liparit, appeared on the plain of Pasin {Phasiane, Basean, Basian, Hasan-Kale}. The two armies met before Hasan-Kale. The savage battle ended in the defeat of the Byzantine army. Tens of thousands of prisoners were taken, and among the large number of captured commanders was the Georgian Liparit (18 September 1048).[136] Thousands of wagons full of booty were also taken.[137] And Erzurum was occupied as

132. Aristaces, Fr. trans. Ev. Prud'homme, *Histoire d'Arménie, comprenant la fin du Royaume d'Ani et le commencement des invasions des Seldjoucides* (Paris, 1864), p. 72.

133. Ibn al-Athīr, *al-Kāmil,* years 432, 434, 437–40; Barhebraeus, *Tarihi,* I, 303; Matthew of Edessa, *Chronique,* pp. 82 f.; Mükrimin Yınanç, *Türkiye tarihi I, Anadolunun fethi* (Istanbul, 1944), pp. 38–44; Cahen, "La Première Pénétration turque en Asie-Mineure [seconde moitié du XIe siècle]," *Byzantion* 18(1948):52 ff..

134. See Kafesoğlu, "Doğu Anadolu'ya," pp. 264 ff.

135. Joannes Zonaras, Fr. trans. M. de S. Amour, *Chronique ou annales de Jean Zonare* (Lyon, 1560), p. 97a; Aristaces, *Histoire,* pp. 72 f.; Yınanç, *Türkiye,* p. 46.

136. See Minorsky, *Studies in Caucasian History* (London, 1953), p. 61n. 2.

well. While Ibrāhīm Yınal took the prisoners, the most prominent of whom was Liparit, and the booty to Toghrıl Beg at Rayy, the Turks spread out in the area from the environs of Lake Van to Trebizond.[138] Because of this great victory at Pasinler {*sic*}, the first that the Seljuks won against the Byzantines, Emperor Constantine IX Monomachus was forced to come to terms with the sultan. The Byzantine ambassador, who sent expensive gifts to Toghrıl Beg by way of the Marwānid Naṣr al-Dawla, tried to rescue Liparit in return for ransom. The sultan freed Liparit without a ransom and sent him with his own ambassador, Sharīf Nāṣir al-Dīn b. Ismāʿīl,[139] to the Byzantine capital to conduct peace talks (441/1049–50). According to the agreement that was reached, the emperor would repair the mosque in Constantinople, which had fallen into ruin; would have lamps hung within it; would permit the *imām* {prayer leader} sent by the caliph to perform the prayers five times a day; and would have Toghrıl Beg's name read in the *khuṭba* there. The emperor, however, did not agree to pay an annual tribute and, because he was apprehensive about the Seljuks, began to strengthen his fortresses and the walls of his cities in the east.[140]

Ibrāhīm Yınal, whose important role in the foundation and development of the Seljuk state we have noted earlier, had become the most powerful figure in ʿIrāq al-ʿAjam, al-Jazīra, and Āzarbāījān, especially after the victory over Byzantium, and was ready to rebel. He asked Toghrıl Beg to relinquish the Jibāl area to him but was refused. Unable to hold out against the sultan, he took refuge in the fortress of Sarmāj where he was forced to surrender. He was not only forgiven but also placed in charge of Jibāl and Āzarbāījān.[141] Toghrıl Beg then went to Iṣfahān and after a year-long siege took it from Farāmurz, the son of Ibn Kākūya, who had been inclined toward the Būyids in Baghdad. Some of his forces also began to occupy Khūzistān. Except for Baghdad, which was controlled by al-Malik al-Raḥīm Khusraw Fīrūz, Būyid Shīʿī rule was being overthrown everywhere. Thus, after ʿIrāq al-ʿAjam, the Seljuks absorbed Fārs, Ahvāz, Khūzistān and al-Jazīra. Toward the end of 1054, the *khuṭba* was read in the name of Toghrıl Beg in Karmisīn, which had been in the hands of the ʿUqailid rulers of Mosul.[142] At the same time, the sultan made plans for another campaign in eastern Anatolia via Āzarbāījān. The emperor, who, as we know, refused to pay an annual tribute to the Seljuk state, had sent a Byzantine army supported by the Georgian king Baghrat to Ganja. Qutalmısh had besieged it there and then had to withdraw toward Tabrīz.[143] Later, in 446/1054, while Qutalmısh was besieging Kars, Toghrıl Beg came to Āzarbāījān, received the allegiance

137. Aristaces, *Histoire*, p. 106; Zonaras, *Chronique*, p. 97b; Matthew of Edessa, *Chronique*, pp. 86 f.; Vartan, *History*, p. 75; Ibn al-Athīr, *al-Kāmil*, year 440; Barhebraeus, *Tarihi*, I, 306; Laurent, *Byzance*, p. 22; Yınanç, *Türkiye*, pp. 46 f.

138. Aristaces, *Histoire*, pp. 73 f.; Ibn al-Athīr, *al-Kāmil*, year 440.

139. See Ibn Khallikān, *Wafayāt*, II, 441.

140. Aristaces, *Histoire*, p. 103; Zonaras, *Chronique*, p. 97b; Ibn al-Athīr, *al-Kāmil*, year 441; Barhebraeus, *Tarihi*, I, 304 f.; Minorsky, *Studies*, p. 68.

141. ʿImād al-Dīn, *Zubdat*, p. 6; Ibn al-Athīr, *al-Kāmil*, year 441.

142. Ibid., years 442–46.

143. M. Brosset, *Histoire de la Géorgie* (St. Petersburg, 1849), I, 323.

of the Rawwādids Manṣūr and Vahsūdān and the Shaddādid Abū 'l-Aswār by having the *khuṭba* read in his name in Tabrīz and Ganja, and captured Barkiri. He then came to Arjīsh "like a black cloud spurting fire,"[144] took the city and laid siege to the redoubtable fortress of Malazgird, which was defended by Vasil {not further identified}. While he was there the Marwānids of Diyārbakr, who had declared their allegiance to him, joined him with their forces and together they advanced as far as Erzurum. As the Turkish forces took possession of the Choruh and Kelkit valleys, he returned to Malazgird, where other troops had been left to continue the siege. But their strong attacks were fruitless. After the Greeks burned the Seljuk catapults and it began to snow, Toghrıl Beg returned to Rayy.[145] He ordered Yāqūtī, the son of Chaghrı Beg, to advance against Anatolia in the company of large forces and sent him to Āzarbāījān. Yāqūtī and the Turkmen under his command carried out continuous raids {in Anatolia} even though the emperor had assigned the renowned general Nicephorus Bryennius to that region.[146]

Because of the increasing oppression of the Shīʿī Būyids, Khusraw Fīrūz' proclamation of an ʿAlawī *khuṭba* in Shīrāz, and the persecution of Seljuk supporters in the capital of the caliphate by the Būyid commander-in-chief, Arslan al-Basāsīrī, who received continuous support from the Fāṭimids in Egypt, Toghrıl Beg headed for Baghdad on the invitation of the Caliph al-Qā'im. In a letter that the caliph sent with his ambassador Hibat Allāh b. Muḥammad al-Ma'mūn, the sultan was asked to come quickly to the capital.[147] As the sultan and his vizir, ʿAmīd al-Mulk al-Kundurī, approached Baghdad with an army equipped with elephants, al-Basāsīrī's anxiety increased. He finally informed Egypt of the situation and retreated from Baghdad to the north. The Būyid ruler al-Malik al-Raḥīm proclaimed his obedience to Toghrıl Beg. Al-Qā'im ordered the *khuṭba* to be read in the name of the Seljuk sultan in Baghdad and the entire Sunnī world, and prepared to greet him with brilliant pagentry. After the caliph received a courtesy letter from Toghrıl Beg requesting permission to enter the seat of the caliphate, the sultan entered Baghdad on 25 Ramaḍān 447/17 January 1055. The next day, however, there was great tumult in the city. The Shīʿīs living in the Karkh quarter were involved in it, and when the situation became serious the instigators were punished. When Toghrıl Beg subsequently arrested and imprisoned al-Malik al-Raḥīm and his men, the Shīʿī Būyid state, which had ruled for more than 120 years, came to an end. The sultan appointed the commander Ai-Tegin as the *shiḥna* {chief of security} of Baghdad, coined money,

144. Matthew of Edessa, *Chronique*, p. 100.

145. Aristaces, *Histoire*, pp. 90–101; Matthew of Edessa, *Chronique*, pp. 100 ff.; Ibn al-Athīr, *al-Kāmil*, year 446; Barhebraeus, *Tarihi*, I, 306; Samuel of Ani, *Tables*, Fr. trans. Brosset, *Collection d'historiens arméniens* (St. Petersburg, 1874–76), II, 449.

146. Yınanç, *Türkiye*, p. 51.

147. ʿImād al-Dīn, *Zubdat*, p. 7; Rāvandī, *Rāḥat*, p. 105; Ibn al-Jawzī, *al-Muntaẓam* (Hyderabad, 1357–59/1938–41), VIII, 163.

and seized the treasury. He also set aside 50,000 dinars and 500 "*kor*" of wheat to add to the caliph's annual allowance. Later, in the palace that he had built for himself in Baghdad, Toghrıl ascended a gold throne adorned with precious stones that the caliph had given to him as a gift. Thus he added the territories of Baghdad and ʿIrāq al-ʿArab, over which the Seljuk Oghuz had spread, to his own state. At the same time, by acting as the protector of the ʿAbbāsid caliph, he took on the defense of the Sunnī Muslim world. And thanks to the marriage of Chaghrı Beg's daughter, Khadīja Arslan Khātūn, to al-Qā'im, a strong relationship was established that strengthened the tie between the Seljuk dynasty and the family of the caliph.[148]

148. ʿImād al-Dīn, *Zubdat*, pp. 8 f.; Ṣadr al-Dīn, *Akhbār*, p. 13; Ibn al-Athīr, *al-Kāmil*, years 447–48; Rāvandī, *Rāḥat*, p. 105; Barhebraeus, *Tarihi*, I, 307 f.

The Great Seljuk Empire

With the help of the Fāṭimids, Arslan al-Basāsīrī collected his forces at Raḥba and defeated Qutalmısh, who had been sent against him (end of Shawwāl 448/January 1057). Toghrıl Beg was therefore forced to take the field. When the sultan headed for Mosul with Ibrāhīm Yınal and Yāqūtī, who set out in the same month, al-Basāsīrī fled to Syria. Sinjār and Jazīrat Ibn ʿUmar were attacked and taken. The Marwānid ruler and the ruler of Ḥilla again declared their obedience. The sultan entrusted Ibrāhīm Yınal with the area around Mosul and Sinjār and then returned to Baghdad where he was greeted with great pagentry by the caliph's vizir. He was invited by al-Qā'im to the caliphal palace, and there a ceremony was held legitimizing Toghrıl Beg's assumption of the defense of the Muslim world. In this ceremony, which was attended by all the leading men of the Seljuk state and the caliphal officials, al-Qā'im thanked the sultan for the services he had rendered and had him sit on a specially prepared throne next to his own. The sultan in turn paid his respects to the caliph. Afterwards, al-Qā'im placed a crown on the head of Toghrıl Beg, to whom he had also given banners and robes of honor. Girding him with a gold sword, he declared him to be the "ruler of the East and West" (26 Dhū 'l-Qaʿda 449/25 January 1058). In addition, he gave him the *kunya* {patronymic/surname} "Abū Ṭālib" {the Father of Ṭālib}, the *laqab* {byname} "Rukn al-Dunyā wa 'l-Dīn" {Pillar of Worldly Affairs and the Faith}, and the title "Yamīn Amīr al-Mu'minīn" {Right Hand of the Commander of the Faithful, namely, the caliph}.[149] Toghrıl Beg's sovereignty over the Muslim world was thus confirmed. At the same time, it was proclaimed that he was the ruler of the world. All of this was completely in line with his previously held desire

149. ʿImād al-Dīn, *Zubdat*, pp. 10 ff.; Ṣadr al-Dīn, *Akhbār*, pp. 12 f.; Ibn al-Athīr, *al-Kāmil*, year 449; Barhebraeus, *Tarihi*, I, 311 f.; Rāvandī, *Rāḥat*, p. 105; anonymous, *Mujmal al-tawārīkh wa 'l-qiṣaṣ*, ed. Malik al-Shuʿarā' Bahār (Tehran, 1318/1939), p. 429; Ibn al-Jawzī, *al-Muntaẓam*, VIII, 181 ff.

and policy to eliminate Shīʿism on the one hand, and continue the conquests to the west on the other. However, he soon had to crush a revolt by Qutalmısh's brother, Rasūl-Tegin, in Khūzistān. Afterwards Ibrāhīm Yınal left Mosul without orders and went to his former territory, Hamadān. This prompted al-Basāsīrī to invade the Mosul region. Toghrıl Beg consequently set out on a second campaign. When he had advanced as far as Naṣībīn, he learned that Ibrāhīm Yınal, who was not to be punished for leaving his post without permission (thanks to the intervention of the caliph), had openly rebelled with the encouragement of the Fāṭimids and al-Basāsīrī. The sultan quickly returned to Baghdad where he left his wife, part of his army and his vizir, ʿAmīd al-Mulk, and personally began the pursuit of the rebellious prince. However, Ibrāhīm Yınal was not only in an area that he controlled but was also greatly strengthened by the troops of Muḥammad and Aḥmad, the sons of his brother Er-Tash. When Toghrıl Beg could make no progress against him, he requested help from Baghdad. Toghrıl Beg also called the sons of Chaghrı Beg to join him immediately: Alp-Arslan from Khurāsān, Qāvurt from Kirmān, and Yāqūtī from the Anatolian frontier. Near Rayy, Toghrıl Beg defeated the rebel army in a fierce battle on 9 Jumādā II 451/22 July 1059. Muḥammad and Aḥmad were taken prisoner and executed. Ibrāhīm Yınal was strangled with his own bowstring.[150] While the sultan was thus occupied, al-Basāsīrī went on the march again and reached Baghdad. He removed the caliph from the city, had the *khuṭba* recited in the name of the Fāṭimids, had the call to prayer made in the Shīʿī manner, and attempted to capture Baṣra and its environs. But when he learned that Toghrıl Beg was victoriously on his way to Baghdad, he fled. After the sultan reached Baghdad, he greeted the caliph, who had returned from captivity, and personally took complete control by taking him to his palace and placing him on the throne. Then, at the head of a vast army that included such important commanders as Sav-Tegin, Khumar-Tegin, Gümüsh-Tegin, and Erdem, he immediately set out after al-Basāsīrī. He caught up with his forces at Ḥilla. They were defeated and al-Basāsīrī was killed (Dhū 'l-Ḥijja 451/January 1060). This event caused great pleasure in Baghdad and the entire Sunnī world.[151] Meantime Toghrıl Beg's beloved wife, who had been influential in state affairs, passed away and the sultan wanted to marry the daughter of al-Qā'im.[152] Although the caliph was not very enthusiastic about giving his daughter to someone outside the caliphal family, he eventually agreed to it. The marriage ceremony was performed in Shaʿbān 454/August 1062. But Toghrıl Beg, who

150. See Kafesoğlu, "Selçuk'un oğulları," pp. 127 f.

151. ʿImād al-Dīn, *Zubdat,* pp. 12–17; Ṣadr al-Dīn, *Akhbār,* p. 15; Ibn al-Jawzī, *al-Muntaẓam,* VIII, 202 ff., 194 ff. {sic}; Ibn al-Athīr, *al-Kāmil,* year 450; Barhebraeus, *Tarihi,* I, 313 ff.

152. Ibid., I, 315.

was now rather old, could not devote much attention to the matter of this marriage because he had to fight Qutalmısh, who had rebelled. As we have seen, Qutalmısh had cooperated with Ibrāhīm Yınal. After the latter's defeat, he maintained his own claim to the sultanate and withdrew to the fortress of Gird-kūh with his brother Rasūl-Tegin. Although he drove off the forces that had immediately been sent against him, he was later besieged by Vizir ʿAmīd al-Mulk. Meanwhile the sultan had come to Baghdad, where his wedding was held with great rejoicing. After returning to Rayy with his wife, he became ill and could not rise. Finally, on 8 Ramaḍān 455/4 September 1063, at the age of seventy, he died and was buried in his *türbe* at Rayy.[153] All the sources testify to his justice and piety. Moreover, he was distinguished among the members of the Seljuk family by his quick mind and the insightfulness of his political views. It was for these reasons that he became the first sultan of the Seljuk state. Toghrıl Beg laid the foundation for the Great Seljuk Empire during the twenty-five years of his sultanate. As one who eliminated the religious differences in the Near East and established public order, he provided for the development of the empire on a firm political structure. For this reason, Toghrıl Beg occupies an important position in Turkish and Islamic history.

Toghrıl Beg had no children. He therefore made his nephew, Chaghrı Beg's son, Sulaimān, the heir apparent. Upon the sultan's death, Vizir ʿAmīd al-Mulk broke off the siege of Qutalmısh and quickly returned to the capital. He abided with the succession of Sulaimān and proclaimed him as sultan, but Alp-Arslan, while unable speedily to reach Rayy from Marv, tried to take command of the situation with the help of Er-Sıghun, the son of Yūsuf Yınal and brother of Ibrāhīm Yınal,[154] and Erdem, who had the *khuṭba* read in his name in Qazvīn. Meanwhile, Qutalmısh proclaimed himself sultan and came to the capital at the head of a large army. He met Alp-Arslan near Damghān and was defeated. As he fled he fell from his horse and was killed. He was buried next to Toghrıl Beg. Furthermore, his brother Rasūl-Tegin was taken prisoner. On 7 Jumādā I 456/27 April 1064, Alp-Arslan ascended the throne at Rayy. He was thirty-six years old.[155] The new sultan dismissed ʿAmīd al-Mulk and replaced him with Niẓām al-Mulk, who had been his vizir in Marv. He also made changes among the other high state officials. After putting down the revolt of Mūsā Yabghu in Herāt by bringing this aged uncle of his over to his side and pardoning his brother Qāvurt for claiming the sultanate in Kirmān, Alp-Arslan continued the Seljuk conquests. Indeed, he had come

153. ʿImād al-Dīn, *Zubdat,* pp. 24 f.; Ṣadr al-Dīn, *Akhbār,* p. 16; Ibn al-Athīr, *al-Kāmil,* years 454 and 455; Rāvandī, *Rāḥat,* pp. 111 f.; Barhebraeus, *Tarihi,* I, 316; Ibn Khallikān, *Wafayāt,* II, 438–42.

154. See Kafesoğlu, "Selçuk oğulları," pp. 129 f.

155. Ibn al-Athīr, *al-Kāmil,* years 420 and 455; ʿImād al-Dīn, *Zubdat,* pp. 26 f.; Cahen, "Qutlumush et ses fils avant l'Asie Mineure," *Der Islam* 39(1964):14–27.

to Kirmān from the Caucasus. The Turkish masses there were constantly on the move against Byzantium. Moreover, even after Toghrıl Beg had sent an ambassador to the Byzantine capital and received a great many gifts and money from the Empress Theodora, columns of Turkmen had penetrated as far as Erzurum, Akhlāṭ, Mūsh, and Malatya.[156] They took possession of this last city and eastern Kara-Hiṣār {Colonea} and besieged Edessa. Furthermore, they also advanced toward the Qızıl Irmak {Halys River} region and captured Sivas {Sebastea} in 1060. In the following year, they defeated the Byzantine forces sent by Emperor Constantine X Ducas.[157] All these forces, whose operations were under the direction of Dinar, Karpar, Jemjem, Tugh-Tegin, Sālār-i Khurāsān and other chieftains, were under the command of Yāqūtī and returned to Āzarbāījān each winter.[158]

In the spring of 1064, Alp-Arslan set out for Āzarbāījān. After receiving the allegiance of the little Armenian kingdom of Lori in Arrān, he entered Georgia. His son Malik-Shāh and Niẓām al-Mulk were with him and they captured Sürmari (Sürmeli-Çukuru) on the Aras River as well as the famed redoubtable fortresses and surrounding area of Maryam-Nishīn, which were noted for their churches.[159] Alp-Arslan was very pleased with his son's success. When Malik-Shāh and Niẓām al-Mulk rejoined him, he took Sipez-Shāhr by storm. He subsequently marched on Ani, which was the capital of the Bagratid dynasty but a dependency of Byzantium defended by the Greeks. After fierce attacks against the city's renowned walls, the sultan finally captured it on 16 August 1064.[160] He then entered Kars with Prince Gagik, who had come to the sultan and offered his allegiance.[161] The conquest of Ani caused great rejoicing in the Islamic world. *Fetḥnāmes* were sent everywhere. The caliph himself issued a declaration describing Alp-Arslan's successes and thanking him and his fighters for the faith. He also gave the sultan the title "Abū 'l-Fatḥ" {the Conqueror}. This campaign, "the conquest of 24 provinces,"[162] which resulted in the capture of an enormous booty and thousands of prisoners, forced the Byzantine Emperor to reach an accommodation with Alp-Arslan.[163]

The sultan returned to Rayy, settled the affair of Qāvurt, and then went to Marv. In the latter city he married his son Malik-Shāh to a Qarakhānid princess—later famous as Terken Khātūn (Jalāliyya)—who was to have great influence over the future sultan.[164] Afterwards, he appointed his other sons and relatives as *maliks* {king, ruler} to various places in the country. Thus his old uncle Mūsā Yabghu was sent to Māzandarān; his brothers Sulaimān

156. Barhebraeus, *Tarihi,* I, 312.

157. Matthew of Edessa, *Chronique,* pp. 107 ff.

158. Laurent. *Byzance,* p. 24; Yınanç, *Türkiye,* pp. 53 ff.

159. Ṣadr al-Dīn, *Akhbār,* pp. 24 ff.; Ibn al-Athīr, *al-Kāmil,* year 456.

160. See Samuel of Ani, *Tables,* II, 449 f.

161. Matthew of Edessa, *Chronique,* pp. 119–22; Ṣadr al-Dīn, *Akhbār,* pp. 26 ff.; Ibn al-Athīr, *al-Kāmil,* year 456; Barhebraeus, *Tarihi,* I, 316 f.; Yınanç, *Türkiye,* pp. 58 f.

162. Vartan, *History,* p. 177.

163. Sibṭ, *Mir'āt,* Topkapı, Ahmet III MS 2907, XII, 222a.

164. Ibn al-Athīr, *al-Kāmil,* year 456.

to Balkh, Arslan-Arghun to Khwārazm, Ilyās to Tukhāristān and Saghāniyān; his sons Arslan-Shāh to Marv, and Toghan-Shāh to Herāt. Er-Tash's two sons Mas'ūd and Mawdūd were appointed to Baghshūr and Isfizār respectively. As for the sultan's other sons, Ayaz later replaced Sulaimān in Balkh; Tutush went to Syria; Böri-Bars to Herāt; and Arslan-Arghun to Hamadān and Sāveh.[165] Alp-Arslan also went on campaign in the East again. In 457/1065, he crossed the Oxus and entered Turkistan. In Manqıshlaq on the shores of the Caspian Sea, he fought the chief of the Qıpchaqs and forced him to submit. He then headed for Jand in order to visit the tomb of his great-grandfather Seljuk. The ruler of Jand offered his allegiance and greeted the sultan with gifts. After this visit, Alp-Arslan returned to Marv via Gurganj, the capital of Khwārazm (Jumādā II 458/May 1066). By this first Turkistan campaign, he added to the Seljuk state all the regions of the country of his ancestors that bordered on Transoxiana. Near Nīshāpūr, the sultan came to Rādkān, "an example of the highest heaven,"[166] and performed the ceremony making Malik-Shāh the heir apparent. In the middle of Ramaḍān/July in the same year (458/1066), he went to Nīshāpūr. He subsequently crushed the last revolt of Qāvurt, the *malik* of Kirmān (459/1067), and, by marching from Kirmān toward Shīrāz, brought the fortress of Iṣṭakhr under control.[167] He then concentrated all his attention on the western frontier, that is, Anatolia, which the Turkmen forces continued to raid incessantly and which had become necessary to conquer because the Turks had streamed into that region in great masses from Central Asia. In compliance with the orders received from the sultan, Gümüsh-Tegin, Afshin, Aḥmad-Shāh, and Sālār-i Khurāsān appeared in the districts of Malatya, Ergani, Akhlāṭ, Siverek {Sevaverak, Severak}, Āmid {Diyārbakr}, Mayyāfāriqīn, Edessa, Adıyaman, Ḥarrān, Naṣībīn, Sarūj, Dulūk {Teloukh}, Ra'bān, and Antioch (1065–66). They seized fortresses here and there, entered cities, fought and won victories, and withdrew. They carried out their duties in a regular manner. Afshin was particularly distinguished among these chieftains for routing a Byzantine army near Malatya, invading the area, and capturing Kayseri {Caesarea} (1067). From there he fell upon Cilicia. At this time the Turkish masses swarmed over places in central and eastern Anatolia, and the raiding intensified.[168] Upon the death of Emperor Constantine X Ducas in 1067, the empress sought to place a powerful general at the head of the empire in order to stop the Turks and, if possible, remove them from Anatolia. She therefore married Romanus Diogenes, who had been successful against the Pecheneg Turks in the Balkans. After he was proclaimed

165. Ibid., year 458; Kafesoğlu, *Melikşah*, p. 14n. 16.

166. Mīrkhwānd, *Rawḍat*, IV, 83.

167. Ṣadr al-Dīn, *Akhbār*, pp. 28 ff.

168. Matthew of Edessa, *Chronique*, pp. 123 ff., 133 ff,; Barhebraeus, *Tarihi*, I, 317 f.; Laurent, *Byzance*, p. 24; Yınanç, *Türkiye*, pp. 61 f.

emperor as Romanus IV Diogenes at the beginning of 1068, he set out to expel the Turks from Anatolia. Despite his advance with a large army to Kayseri and then as far as Aleppo, and the efforts of newly appointed Byzantine commanders like Philaretus in Malatya and Manuel Comnenus in Sivas, neither the destruction of Niksar {Neocaesarea} by the Turks nor the capture and destruction of the famous city of Amorium (Amorion, ʿAmmūriyya) by Afshin, who had set out from his base at Akhlāṭ and penetrated as far as the environs of Eskishehir {Dorylaeum}, could be prevented.[169] During Romanus' second operation in central Anatolia in 1069, the Turks seized and pillaged Konya {Iconium}.[170] Meanwhile Ibrāhīm Yınal's brother Er-Sıghun had claimed the sultanate, rebelled, and headed for Anatolia with Qāvurt. While being pursued by Afshin under the orders of Alp-Arslan, this Seljuk prince had defeated Manuel Comnenus, the commander of the Byzantine forces, at Sivas but then joined him and went to Constantinople. While following his trail, Afshin entered western Anatolia, captured and plundered the city of Khunas {Chonae} near Denizli {Laodicea}, and from there reached the shores of the Sea of Marmara.[171] It was finally decided to drive the Turks from Anatolia once and for all and, if necessary, march on the capital of the Seljuk Empire. After long preparations, Romanus set out from Constantinople at the head of an enormous army on 13 March 1071. He billeted his troops on the banks of the Sakarya {Sangarius} and in Erzurum and then came to Malazgird. For forty years Turkish forces had been forcing open the Byzantine door. In accordance with the intentions and plans of the Seljuk rulers, in eastern and central Anatolia they continuously struck at the border guards and military concentrations and destroyed the cities and towns. After the defensive network had broken down, the Seljuk Empire realized that Anatolia was ready for conquest, and Malazgird would be the place where the Seljuks would finally settle their account with the Byzantines. Meantime, for the purpose of ending the disturbances in Shīrvān and pursuing Er-Sıghun, who had fled before him, Alp-Arslan had made arrangements for a second Caucasus campaign. In 1068, with Niẓām al-Mulk at his side and the great commander Sav-Tegin leading the vanguard, he advanced to that region, took the Sheki {Shakki} area, and entered Tiflis.[172] When word reached him that the Qarakhānid ruler had died, he turned back. The following year he appointed Sav-Tegin to be the head of the Caucasian forces and himself set out (July 1070) via Āzarbāījān to achieve a primary goal of Seljuk state policy, the overthrow of the Fāṭimid caliphate in Egypt. The time seemed right, for while Syria was

169. Zonaras, *Chronique,* p. 104b; Ibn al-Athīr, *al-Kāmil,* year 499; Barhebraeus, *Tarihi,* I, 319.

170. Zonaras, *Chronique,* p. 105a.

171. Attaliates, cited in Laurent, *Byzance,* p. 58.

172. Ṣadr al-Dīn, *Akhbār,* pp. 30 ff.; Yınanç, *Türkiye,* pp. 63 ff.; Minorsky, *Studies,* p. 65.

being occupied by Turkmen under the command of Atsız, Egypt was exhausted after the struggle between her pro-Seljuk vizir and the commander-in-chief of her army, Badr al-Jamālī. The sultan captured Malazgird, laid siege to Edessa for a time and then arrived before Aleppo. But when he learned there that the Byzantine army had advanced to eastern Anatolia, he quickly turned back (3 Rajab 463/7 April 1071). By a forced march he reached Malazgird where he completely destroyed the Byzantine army (26 August 1071) and captured Romanus IV Diogenes. With the destruction on the Malazgird plain of the last and most powerful Byzantine army to be sent against the Turks, the Byzantine defenses collapsed. As a result of this incomparable victory, which was to have great repercussions in the Islamic and Western worlds, Alp-Arslan sealed the fate of Anatolia, which would become a Turkish homeland.[173]

173. Kafesoğlu, "Selçuklu tarihinin," pp. 475–80.

After this victory, the sultan prepared for a campaign in Transoxiana because of a war between {his brother} Malik Ilyās, who was then in Khwārazm, and the Qarakhānid ruler Shams al-Mulk Naṣr Khān. During this campaign, he was stabbed by the commander of a local fortress, who had been taken prisoner, and consequently died on 10 Rabīʿ I 466/25 November 1072. Famous for his courage, this great sultan was one of the most distinguished figures in Turkish and Islamic history. He was forty-five years old at his death and held the *kunya* "Abū Shujāʿ" {the Courageous}, the *laqab* "ʿAḍūd al-Dawla" {the Strength of the State}, and the title "Burhān Amīr al-Mu'minīn" {the Proof of the Commander of the Faithful}.

Malik-Shāh, who headed a force of 15,000 experienced cavalry and had served on the Caucasus front as well as in Khwārazm, Khūzistān, Shīrāz, and Iṣfahān, was declared sultan on 25 November 1072.[174] Alp-Arslan had frequently reconfirmed him as the heir apparent in order to prevent fratricidal quarrels, which were highly likely to occur because of the well-known Turkish view of sovereignty. When Malik-Shāh ascended the throne, Niẓām al-Mulk, who was of major influence, was retained as vizir. In the first two years of his reign, Malik-Shāh had to defend the borders and contend with the domestic struggles that his father had anticipated. In the winter of 1072–73, when the Qarakhānids and Ghaznavids attacked the borders, Malik-Shāh's uncle, Qāvurt, the *malik* of Kirmān, would not recognize him as sultan and rebelled. On the advice of Niẓām al-Mulk, the sultan first defeated and captured Qāvurt (4 Shaʿbān 465/10 May 1073). This success strengthened Malik-Shāh's position within the country and the caliph confirmed his sultanate. The forces of Malik-Shāh under the command of

174. ʿImād al-Dīn, *Zubdat,* p. 47; Ṣadr al-Dīn, *Akhbār,* p. 38; Ibn al-Athīr, *al-Kāmil,* year 465; Rāvandī, *Rāḥat,* p. 123.

Sav-Tegin then went on the march in the East and expelled the Qarakhānids from the country. They advanced as far as Samarqand and at that point forgave the Qarakhānid ruler Shams al-Mulk Naṣr Khān.[175] Moreover, an army sent under the command of Anūsh-Tegin, who was the predecessor of the Khwārazm-Shāhs, and Gümüsh-Tegin Bilge forced the Ghaznavid ruler Ẓahīr al-Dawla Ibrāhīm to make peace.[176] The two dynasties then became related by marriage.

When these difficulties were overcome, Malik-Shāh, who had transferred the capital of the empire to Iṣfahān, began large-scale conquests. After the battle of Malazgird, Romanus IV Diogenes had been sent back to his country under the protection of a Turkish detachment. Upon his death, after his eyes had been gouged out by the new Emperor Michael VII Ducas, the order that Alp-Arslan had given to conquer Anatolia was put into effect.[177] The sons of Qutalmısh, namely, Sulaimān-Shāh, Manṣūr, Alp-İlig, and Dolat, with the forces at their disposal, and the Turkmen subject to such chiefs as Artuq Beg and Tutak, marched toward the interior of Anatolia. The Byzantine armies, supported by Frankish mercenaries, were under the command of Isaac Comnenus. He had been in charge of the eastern armies which included special detachments called the "Immortals" that Emperor Michael VII had organized against the Turks.[178] The Byzantine armies were defeated in various places and routed near Sabanja. A short distance to the west they also clashed with Turkish forces around Izmit {Nicomedia}.[179] At the same time, Sulaimān-Shāh, who had made Birejik his headquarters, carried out raids on Antioch, took the governor prisoner, and then laid siege to Aleppo, forcing it to recognize Seljuk sovereignty (1074). Meanwhile, other Turks who had seized Ala-Shehir {Philadelphia} penetrated as far as Miletus on the Aegean.[180] On 3 April 1078, when General Nicephorus Boteniates donned the emperor's crown after having rebelled with Turkish help, Izmit and all of Koja-eli {the peninsula between the Black Sea and Sea of Marmara opposite Constantinople} passed under Turkish control and Byzantine resistance in Anatolia ended.[181] Except for the coastal region, the entire country was invaded by the Turks. After Sulaimān-Shāh eliminated his brother Manṣūr, with whom he had broken for claiming the sultanate, with an army dispatched by Malik-Shāh under the command of Bursuq, he received from the caliph a robe of honor and a *manshūr* {patent} confirming his sovereignty over Anatolia. He assumed command of all military forces in Anatolia and, in his capacity as a supporter of General Nicephorus Melissenus, who had rebelled against the emperor, took over a great

175. Ṣadr al-Dīn, *Akhbār,* pp. 42 f.; Ibn al-Athīr, *al-Kāmil,* year 466.

176. Ṣadr al-Dīn, *Akhbār,* p. 73.

177. Aristaces, *Histoire,* p. 147; Matthew of Edessa, *Chronique,* p. 144; Zonaras, *Chronique,* p. 108a.

178. Anna Comnena, *Alexiad,* Fr. trans. B. Leib (Paris, 1937), I, 18.

179. Nicephorus Bryennius, *Histoira,* Fr. trans. Cousin in *Histoire de Constantinople* (Paris, 1685), III, 531 f.

180. Laurent, *Byzance,* p. 93.

181. Ibid., cited from Attaliates.

many fortresses and cities in western Anatolia. He entered Iznik {Nicaea} in 1078 and made this historic city his capital. This made it possible for him to advance to Üsküdar {Chrysopolis} and control the Bosphorus.[182] It was this event that caused the Byzantine emperor to send a delegation to China in 1081 in order to try to bring pressure on the Seljuks from the East, for their domain extended as far as Turkistan.[183] By 1085, the country of the Marwānids, which included above all Āmid and Mayyāfāriqīn plus Mārdīn, Ḥiṣn Kaifā {Castrum Cepha}, Jazīrat Ibn ʿUmar, and some thirty fortresses, was incorporated into the Seljuk Empire during the conquest of Anatolia. This was done through the efforts of the Turkmen forces, the armies brought from the *shiḥnalık* {security forces} of Baghdad to the governor general of ʿIrāq al-ʿAjam under the direction of Saʿd al-Dawla Gawhar-Āʾīn, Artuq Beg, Chubuk Beg, Monjuk-Böri, Chökermish, and Ḥājib Altuntaq, and with the help of the Marwānid vizir Fakhr al-Dawla Muḥammad b. Jahīr. In the same year, Qasīm al-Dawla Aq-Sonqur and other Turkmen chiefs entered Mosul and annexed the surrounding lands of the ʿUqailids to the Seljuk Empire.[184] The "always victorious" great Turkmen *beg* Artuq Beg forced the submission of al-Aḥsāʾ and the islands of Bahrain, which were inhabited by Shīʿī Qarmathians.[185] Furthermore, because the struggle against Shīʿism was one of the main political policies of the Seljuk Empire, the elimination of the Fāṭimid state in Egypt was a major goal of the Seljuk sultans, for it was the primary source of this creed that had caused a schism and fearful enmity in the Muslim world. Ai-Tegin, the *shiḥna* of Baghdad, had been ordered to capture Damascus during Alp-Arslan's last years (May 1071). As we have seen, the Turkmen *beg* Atsız was also sent to Syria. He went on to take Palestine which had previously been occupied by the Nāvakiyya Turkmen (the Oghuz of Iraq) who had come there under their *baş-buğ*.[186] He also captured Jerusalem, fought Badr al-Jamālī at the fortress of Acre (1072), seized Damascus after three sieges (10 June 1076), ended the Shīʿī call to prayer, and had the names of the ʿAbbāsid caliph and Malik-Shāh recited in the *khuṭba*. However, Atsız' Egyptian campaign in 469/1077 met with failure before Cairo.[187] Malik-Shāh then appointed his own brother Tāj al-Dawla Tutush the *malik* of Syria. After forcing the Egyptian army, which had laid siege to Damascus, to retreat, Tutush eliminated Atsiz and became the unrivaled master of the area (Rabīʿ I 471/September 1078).[188]

Because of quarrels in the country of the Shaddādids and the disobedience of the Georgian king Giorgi II, Malik-Shāh made a campaign in that region and returned after placing Sav-Tegin in

182. Bryennius, *Historia*, p. 593; C. Lebeau, *Histoire du Bas-Empire* (Paris, 1824–36), XV, 81.

183. See W. Eberhard, *Oriens* 1(1948):146 {refers in *Oriens* to the contents of vol. 2 of *Philobiblon*, Sept. 1947, a quarterly review of Chinese publications}.

184. See Kafesoğlu, *Melikşah*, pp. 40–56; Ibn Wāṣil, *Mufarrij al-kurūb*, ed. Jamāl al-Dīn al-Shayyāl (Cairo, 1953), I, 11 ff.

185. Sibṭ, *Mirʾāt*, al-Yunīnī's text, Türk-İslam Eserleri Müzesi MS T. 2135, XII, 32.

186. Ibid., fols. 4a–5a {sic}.

187. Ibn al-Qalānisī, *Dhail Taʾrīkh Dimashq*, ed. H. F. Amedroz (Leiden, 1908), p. 108; Ibn Muyassar, *Annales d'Égypte*, ed. H. Massé (Cairo, 1919), p. 25; Ibn al-Athīr, *al-Kāmil*, year 469.

188. See Kafesoğlu, *Melikşah*, pp. 31–38.

charge of the Caucasus (1076). However, the Georgian king rebelled again and Gagik, the former King of Ani, also tried to regain his crown. So the sultan had to march to the Caucasus a second time.[189] Malik-Shāh went to Georgia via the Aras. Even though he strengthened the position of Sav-Tegin (471/1078–79), he was compelled to send Turkmen forces there under the command of Aḥmad, Abū Yaʿqūb, and ʿĪsā Böri in 1080. They recovered Kars, Oltu {Ukht'ik'}, and Erzurum from the Byzantines and completely occupied the region of Ajaralar as far as Kutayis, the Choruh valley and everything up to the Black Sea coast.[190] Trebizond was also taken in the process.[191] In 1084 the Kingdom of Kakhetia submitted, and by 1087 all of Armenia was added to the empire.[192] Malik-Shāh gave the subject areas of the Caucasus and Arrān to the son of his uncle Yāqūtī, Quṭb al-Dīn Ismāʿīl, the governor general of Āzarbāījān. The conqueror of Anatolia, Abū 'l-Fawāris Sulaimān-Shāh, who had signed a treaty with Emperor Alexius I Comnenus in 1082 making the border the Dragos {Dracon} River on the Anatolian side of the Bosphorus near Constantinople, came to Antioch and captured this fortified city, the key to Syria and al-Jazīra, from General Philaretus (12 January 1085). This caused a breach between him and Tutush, the *malik* of Syria. Sulaimān-Shāh's siege of Aleppo in April 1086 put the two Seljuk princes in conflict. In the ensuing battle that took place at ʿAin Salm, Sulaimān-Shāh's army was shattered and he killed himself (18 Ṣafar 479/5 June 1086). The sultan, who was greatly distressed by this, marched from Iṣfahān with a large army. With him were Bursuq, Mujāhid al-Dawla Bozan, Qasīm al-Dawla Aq-Sonqur, and others who were among the commanders of his special guard. He advanced by way of Mosul and Ḥarrān and left Bozan to besiege Edessa. After taking the castles of Jaʿbar and Manbij, he came to Aleppo (Ramaḍān 479/December 1086). He appointed Yaghı-Sıyan the governor of Antioch, and Aq-Sonqur the governor of the Aleppo region. He continued as far as Suwaidiyya {St. Simeon}, where, facing the waves of the Mediterranean, he gave thanks to God for the great conquests that had been granted him.[193] Meanwhile Lādhiqiyya {Laodicea}, Shaizar {Larissa}, and other fortresses surrendered. On 28 February 1087 Bozan captured Edessa and was made its governor. When the disorder in this region was settled, the entire land of Syria up to the Sinai Desert took shape as a kingdom governed by Tutush in Damascus. Artuq Beg, who had joined Tutush in the war against Sulaimān-Shāh and had provided important assistance, was given possession of Jerusalem and its environs.

189. Chamichian, *Ermeni tarihi,* II, 996.

190. Brosset, *Géorgie,* I, 359.

191. Anna Comnena, *Alexiad,* Fr. trans. Cousin, IV, 247 f.

192. Matthew of Edessa, *Chronique,* p. 171.

193. Ibn al-Qalānisī, *Dhail,* p. 119; Ibn Wāṣil, *Mufarrij,* I, 19; Rāvandī, *Rāḥat,* p. 129, Turkish trans., pp. 126 f.; Matthew of Edessa, *Chronique* p. 172; Barhebraeus, *Tarihi,* I, 334.

Leaving Aleppo, Malik-Shāh went to Baghdad and was greeted by the caliphal officials amidst an enthusiastic popular demonstration. In a great ceremony arranged in the Dār al-Khilāfa, Caliph al-Muqtadī bi-Amr Allāh, girded the sultan with two swords while again describing him as "the ruler of the East and West" (17 Muḥarram 480/25 April 1088). It was then that Malik-Shāh's daughter, Mehmelek, who had meantime come to Baghdad from Iṣfahān with Terken Khātūn in the company of leading commanders, was married to the caliph. The magnificent wedding, for which Mehmelek brought an amazingly rich trousseau, and the public rejoicing that lasted for days in Baghdad are noteworthy indications of the grandeur and might of the Seljuk Empire.[194]

194. For details, see Kafesoğlu, *Melikşah,* pp. 86–98.

When Sulaimān-Shāh went to Antioch, he left Abū 'l-Qāsim in his place in Iznik. While building a Turkish fleet in the Gulf of Gemlik {an inlet on the Sea of Marmara}, he was won over by Emperor Alexius I Comnenus. He was taken to Constantinople where he took sides against the sultan. He was eliminated, however, by Bursuq, who was dispatched by Malik-Shāh, and the forces under the command of Bozan that followed.[195] Abū 'l-Qāsim was replaced by his brother Abū 'l-Ghāzī, who kept Iznik until the appearance of Sulaimān-Shāh's son Qılıch-Arslan I in 1092.

195. Anna Comnena, *Alexiad,* Fr. trans. Cousin, pp. 184, 189; Lebeau, *Histoire,* XV, 192–97.

The *beg* of Izmir {Smyrna}, Chakan {or Chaka}, created another powerful Turkish force which presented a serious threat to the Byzantines because of its strong fleet. Chakan Beg captured the islands off Anatolia and defeated the Byzantine fleet numerous times. He even contemplated seizing Constantinople and becoming the emperor. For this purpose, he sought to bring about the collapse of the Byzantine Empire by making an alliance with the Pecheneg Turks, who had descended from the Balkans as far as eastern Thrace, and with the Seljuks, who were on the coast of the Sea of Marmara, and thus squeezing the empire from three sides: Üsküdar, Edirne {Adrianople}, and Chanakkale. However, Alexius I Comnenus, one of the most outstanding Byzantine emperors, was able to save the empire from this critical position thanks to the terrible battle of Levunium (29 April 1091), which took place on the banks of the Maritsa between the Pechenegs and Cuman Turks.[196]

196. See Kafesoğlu, *Melikşah,* pp. 107–12.

Because of popular complaints against Aḥmad Khān, the ruler of Samarqand, Malik-Shāh organized a campaign to Transoxiana (May 1087). On the way he took the castles and fortified positions one by one and then seized Bukhārā. Afterwards he besieged Samarqand and took Aḥmad Khān prisoner, thus bringing the western branch of the Qarakhānids into the Seljuk Empire. He then received the allegiance of the governor of Taraz.[197] The governors of Balāsāghūn and Isfījāb agreed to pay taxes. When the sultan arrived in Öz-Kent, Hārūn Bughra Khān, the ruler of Kāshghar, came to him and offered his allegiance.[198] Consequently, the Seljuks also incorporated the eastern branch of the Qarakhānids. At that point (482/1090) the frontier of the Great Seljuk Empire stretched as far as the Great Wall of China. In 1091, Malik-Shāh made a second campaign in Turkistan to end disturbances there. In the fall of the same year, in his second visit to Baghdad, he convened a war council (Ramaḍān 484/November 1091) in which he ordered Sa'd al-Dawla Gawhar-Ā'īn, Qasīm al-Dawla Aq-Sonqur and Bozan, accompanied by Tāj al-Dawla Tutush, to capture the coastal areas of Syria; resolve the matters of the *khuṭba* in Mecca and the sovereignty over Medina, which had been points of political conflict and rivalry with the Fāṭimids; and conquer Yemen and the province of Aden. The Seljuk army, under the direction of such commanders as Tirsek, Chabaq, and Yarın-Kush, subsequently added the entire region of the Ḥijāz to the empire and then annexed Yemen and the province of Aden to the Turkish dominion.[199]

One of the problems that Malik-Shāh had to face in the Sunnī-Shī'ī quarrel was the *bāṭinī* {Shī'ī-Ismā'īlī} activity within the empire that centered about Ḥasan al-Ṣabbāh.[200] Although the sultan dispatched such commanders as Yorun-Tash, Qızıl-Sarıgh, and Qol-Tash to destroy his nest of *rāfiḍīs* {heretics}, who became particularly significant after they seized Alamūt in September 1090, the operation could not continue, for in the meantime the sultan had died in Baghdad.[201] The ambitious Terken Khātūn had wanted to make her own son Maḥmūd the heir apparent instead of prince Berk-Yaruq. She had conspired with Caliph al-Muqtadī, who had been offended by Malik-Shāh, and poisoned the sultan (16 Shawwāl 485/20 November 1092).[202] Malik-Shāh was thirty-eight years old when he died. He had succeeded in creating one of the largest empires in the world, extending from Kāshghar to the Bosphorus and the Mediterranean; and from the Caucasus and the Aral Sea to Yemen and the Indian Ocean. He had hoped to expand the borders of the Seljuk state even further: to capture Egypt and the Maghrib, and establish world dominion. Malik-Shāh was the greatest Seljuk ruler and one of the greatest Turkish emperors in history. Because he was the sovereign of a great many sultans and *malik*s, he was called "al-Sulṭān al-A'ẓam" {the Greatest Sultan}, "Sulṭān al-'Ālam" {Sultan of the World}, and also bore the title "al-Sulṭān al-'Ādil" {the Just Sultan} and the title "Abū 'l-Fatḥ." In addition he was given the bynames "Jalāl al-Dunyā wa 'l-Dīn" {the Glory of the World and the Faith} and the title "Qasīm Amīr al-Mu'minīn"

197. Talas, 'Imād al-Dīn, *Zubdat*, p.89; Ṣadr al-Dīn, *Akhbār*, p. 50.

198. Ibid. p. 50; Ibn al-Athīr, *al-Kāmil*, year 480.

199. 'Imād al-Dīn, *Zubdat*, p. 69; Ibn al-Athīr, *al-Kāmil*, year 485.

200. See 'Alā' al-Dīn 'Aṭā' Malik Juvainī, *Ta'rīkh-i Jahān-Gushā*, ed. Mīrzā Muḥammad Qazvīnī, *GMS* (London, 1912–37), III, 146 f.

201. Anonymous, *Sīstān*, p. 386; Ibn al-Athīr, *al-Kāmil*, year 485; Juvainī, *Ta'rīkh*, I, 19, III, 202 f.

202. 'Imād al-Dīn, *Zubdat*, pp. 85, 235; Ṣadr al-Dīn, *Akhbār*, p. 49; Ibn al-Athīr, *al-Kāmil*, year 485; Ibn al-Jawzī, *al-Muntaẓam*, IX, 64; anonymous, *Mujmal*, p. 408; Ibn Funduq, *Ta'rīkh*, p. 76; Vartan, *History*, p. 184; Kirakos of Gantzag, *History* (Venice, 1863), p. 60; Matthew of Edessa, *Chronique*, pp. 178, 226; Barhebraeus, *Tarihi*, I, 334.

(the Partner of the Caliph). Because of his justice and compassion and the deep respect and affection that he aroused in the empire, his death was mourned by Christians, including Armenians and Assyrians, and members of other religions as much as by Turks and the Muslim world in general, and funeral marches were held everywhere.[203]

203. For details, see Kafesoğlu, *Melikşah,* pp. 211 ff.

4
The Dissolution of the Great Seljuk Empire

About one month before the death of the sultan, the renowned Niẓām al-Mulk, who had been the Seljuk vizir for some thirty years, was murdered by the *bāṭinīs*. Consequently, when Malik-Shāh passed from the scene, the empire fell into a state of confusion resulting from the unavoidable struggles for the throne and was divided into four sections: (1) the Seljuk state of Iraq and Khurāsān (the continuation of the Great Seljuks), until 1194; (2) the Seljuk state of Kirmān, 1092–1187; (3) the Seljuk state of Syria, 1092–1117; and (4) the Seljuk state of Anatolia, 1092–1308. During the reigns of the four sons who were the successive rulers after Malik-Shāh, indeed in the reign of the very first son, Anatolia separated from the empire. It remained formally bound to the center of power until 1116, when the Seljuk family in Syria passed from the scene. After Sanjar (d. 1157), the last "Great Sultan," the three remaining Seljuk states went their separate ways.

The Seljuks of Iraq and Khurāsān

With the exception of Sultan Sanjar, the general history of the Seljuk state of Iraq and Khurāsān is a chronicle of brave but inept rulers devoid of political sense and unworthy of their ancestors, ambitious and devious state officials, and *bāṭinī* crimes. By spending large sums to win the support of the commanders, Terken Khātūn declared her son Maḥmūd the new sultan, although he was only five years old. While the *khuṭba* was being read in his name, Berk-Yaruq, who was supported as heir apparent by the followers of Niẓām al-Mulk, was declared sultan in Rayy. When her forces met defeat in battle at Burūjird, Terken Khātūn married the *malik* of Āzarbāījān, Quṭb al-Dīn Ismāʿīl, and tried to bring him to power. But he was also defeated. Meanwhile Tāj al-Dawla Tutush, who had himself declared sultan in Damascus and had his name recited in the *khuṭba* in Syria, inflicted a defeat on Qasīm al-Dawla Aq-Sonqur, an ally of Berk-Yaruq and governor of Aleppo, which resulted in his death. Tutush also killed Bozan, the governor of Edessa, for the same reason.[1] He then advanced toward al-Jazīra and Diyārbakr at the head of their combined armies. During the struggle that she had undertaken on behalf of her son, Terken Khātūn was finally removed from the scene by assassination. Tutush came to Rayy via Āzarbāījān and in the ensuing battle with Berk-Yaruq was defeated and killed (7 Ṣafar 488/26 February 1095). But his sons in Syria, Fakhr al-Mulūk Riḍwān and Shams al-Mulūk Duqaq, with the encouragement of the *atabeg* {majordomo} Tugh-Tegin, did not recognize Berk-Yaruq and had the *khuṭba* read in their own names. Tutush's uncle, Tekish, who had twice previously rebelled against Malik-Shāh, had cooperated with Tutush and rebelled again to set himself up in Balkh. Berk-Yaruq, therefore, seized him in 1094 and had him strangled. At this critical time, the sons of Qāvurt in Kirmān also broke away from the center of power, and Sulaimān-Shāh's son Qılıch-Arslan I, who had been in Khurāsān, went to Iznik at the head of the great Oghuz Yıva tribe (1092) and took over the government from Abū 'l-Ghāzī as the second Seljuk sultan of Anatolia. Berk-Yaruq had not been able to prevent this. Indeed, although he succeeded in securing part of the Seljuk domain thanks to the illness and death of Maḥmūd, he was forced to fight his uncle Arslan-Arghun, who had declared his independence in Khurāsān, in order to retain the territories in the East. The sultan sent his younger brother Sanjar, along with the *atabeg* Kamach, against him in Khurāsān. He also marched there himself. Arslan-Arghun was assassinated in 1097. Berk-Yaruq made Sanjar the *malik* of Khurāsān and entrusted him with the province of Balkh up to the Ghaznavid border. In the same year (1097), Kochkar-oghlu Ekinji, a Qıpchaq Turk who was governor of Khwārazm, was killed by the supporters of Arslan-Arghun. "Tashtār" {*tast-dār*} Muḥammad b. Anūsh-Tegin was appointed the Khwārazm-Shāh in his place.[2] In 1099, Berk-Yaruq's other brother, Muḥammad Tapar, the *malik* of Āzarbāījān, rebelled. With the help of Malik Sanjar, Īl-Ghāzī b. Artuq, Kür-Bugha, Gawhar-Ā'īn, and other leaders, commanders, and *beg*s, he succeeded in capturing Iṣfahān, the capital of the empire. Although he defeated Berk-Yaruq in 1100, he was later beaten by him near Hamadān. When the two armies came face to face for the third time in November 1101,

1. Ibn Wāṣil, *Mufarrij,* I, 22–27.

2. See Kafesoğlu, *Harezmşahlar,* pp. 37 f.

the two brothers agreed to divide the state through the mediation of the caliph. Thus Muḥammad Tapar received Āzarbāījān, al-Jazīra, and Diyārbakr as *malik*. Sanjar kept his position, and Berk-Yaruq was accepted as sultan. However, this was simply for appearances. In fact Muḥammad declared himself sultan again but without success. Although he assembled new forces in Āzarbāījān, where he had withdrawn, and then set out against Berk-Yaruq, he was defeated once more before Khoy. Nevertheless, by cooperating with such eastern Anatolian Turkish *beg*s as ʿImād al-Dīn ʿAlī in Erzurum and Sukmān in Akhlāṭ, he forced Berk-Yaruq to divide the state officially: with the Safīd Rūd in Āzarbāījān as the border, the Caucasus and the entire country as far as Syria was given to Muḥammad and the *khuṭba* was recited in the name of the new sultan in this area (1104).[3] Rukn al-Dīn Abū 'l-Muẓaffar Berk-Yaruq, who had been forced to fight ever since he was an adolescent, became ill from various hardships and died while only twenty-six or twenty-seven years old (December 1104). He was succeeded by his son Malik-Shāh II, but Muḥammad Tapar quickly deposed him and became sultan (1105).

During those critical days in which Berk-Yaruq was making every effort to hold together the dissolving Great Seljuk Empire, the underground *bāṭinī* movement, on the one hand, spread throughout the country[4] and zealots from the medieval Christian world, on the other, swept into Muslim Turkish territory like a torrent. However much Pope Urban II may have called the Western world to arms (27 November 1095) in order to save the Christians in the East who were allegedly suffering from Muslim oppression, the main reason for launching the Crusades by inciting the religious feelings of Europeans was to save the country of the Byzantine Emperor Alexius I Comnenus, who, after the loss of Antioch, believed his capital was in danger. Furthermore, when we realize that Christian parties under the leadership of ascetics and nobility had been able to come from Europe to Jerusalem and perform the pilgrimage[5] at a time when Turkish forces under such *başbuğ*s as Han-oghlu (Ibn Khān al-Turkī) and Qarali (or Qurlu) were present in the area stretching from Aleppo to Tiberias and some Turkmen had begun to settle in Palestine and around Tripoli,[6] it is clear that the importance of Jerusalem was secondary. This would also be borne out by later events. After a rather large undisciplined company of Crusaders led by two hermits was conveyed to the coast of Anatolia by the Byzantines and subsequently was destroyed while still on the Koja-eli peninsula (fall of 1096), the first genuine Crusader army organized and controlled by counts and dukes took Iznik from the Seljuks of Anatolia (June 1097). Bohemond, the commander of the vanguard, headed for Syria and laid siege to Antioch, the gateway to

3. Ibn al-Jawzī, *al-Muntaẓam,* IX, 104 f.; ʿImād al-Dīn, *Zubdat,* pp. 83–88; Ṣadr al-Dīn, *Akhbār,* pp. 52–55; Ibn al-Qalānisī, *Dhail,* p. 137; Rāvandī, *Rāḥat,* pp. 139–51; Ibn al-Athīr, *al-Kāmil,* years 485–94; Barhebraeus, *Tarihi,* I, 334 f. II, 340–43.

4. See M. G. S. Hodgson, *The Order of Assassins* (The Hague, 1955), pp. 72–98.

5. Cf. M. Michaud, *Histoire des Croisades* (Tours, 1853), p. 16.

6. Ibn al-ʿAdīm, *Zubdat al-ḥalab fī ta'rīkh Ḥalab,* ed. Sāmī al-Dahhān (Damascus, 1951), I, 294–96; Ibn al-Qalānisī, *Dhail,* p. 92.

Jerusalem. While the governor of Antioch, Yaghı-Sıyan, was defending this fortified city, Berk-Yaruq sent Kür-Bugha, the ruler of Mosul, to help him. However, because of the delay caused by attempting to recover Edessa—which had meanwhile been captured and made the {center of} a county by the Crusaders—and the assistance that the Crusaders besieging Antioch received by sea, Kür-Bugha was not able to succeed against them even though he was reinforced by the troops of Duqaq, the *malik* of Damascus, and his *atabeg* Tugh-Tegin; the Artuqid Sukman, who possessed Jerusalem and al-Jazīra; and others; and he had surrounded them and forced them to the point where they were almost ready to surrender (5 June 1098). The Crusaders seized Antioch and the road to mastering Syria was open to them.[7] While the Turks were busy at Antioch, the Fāṭimids had seized the opportunity to occupy Jerusalem, but it later fell to the Crusaders on 15 July 1099. As a result of this success, the Crusaders were able to found, in addition to the County of Edessa (1098–1144), the Frankish states called the Principality of Antioch (1098–1268), the Kingdom of Jerusalem (1100–87 in Jerusalem, 1187–1291 in Acre), and the County of Tripoli (1109–1289) within the Turco-Islamic nation. In order to destroy these states and save the Muslim lands, the Turks had to fight and shed blood for centuries.

7. *Histoire anonyme de la Première Croisade*, ed. and Fr. trans. L. Bréhier (Paris, 1924), pp. 97 f., 110 f.; Matthew of Edessa, *Chronique*, pp. 192–98; Barhebraeus, *Tarihi*, II, 339 f.; Rāvandī, *Rāḥat*, p. 140; R. Grousset, *Histoire des Croisades* (Paris, 1948), I, 71 f., 88–108.

After arresting his cousin Mengü-Bars, who had rebelled in Nihāvand, and imprisoning the sons of his uncle Tekish, who had joined him, Sultan Muḥammad Tapar had to deal with Chavlı, Chökermish, Aq-Sonqur al-Bursuqī, the Arab amīr of Ḥilla, namely, Saif al-Dawla Ṣadaqa, and the Anatolian Seljuk sultan Qılıch-Arslan I concerning claims of sovereignty over Mosul (1105–08). Furthermore, he had to wage a fierce struggle against those *bāṭinīs* who were notorious for assassinating leading statesmen and commanders, beginning with Niẓām al-Mulk. He defeated Aḥmad b. ʿAbd al-Malik al-ʿAṭṭāsh, one of the most famous Ismāʿīlī *dāʿīs* {propagandist}, seized the castle in which he had taken refuge and wiped out all the *bāṭinīs* found there (1107). In 1108, with Vizir Ḍiyā' al-Mulk and Chavlı, Muḥammad marched on Alamūt and inflicted heavy losses. At the same time he also sent forces that drove off the Georgians who had attacked Ganja (1108). Some of the attacking Georgian forces were Qıpchaq (Cuman) Turks who had lived on the plains north of the Caucasus, were converted to Christianity through the efforts of the Georgian king David II (d. 1125), and then were attracted to the Caucasus. David married his son to the daughter of Atrak, son of Karahan, their *baş-buğ,* thus establishing a relationship by marriage. It was also these Qıpchaqs who had played a role in earlier Georgian attacks in the Caucasus.[8]

8. Brosset, *Géorgie*, I, 362 f.

Muḥammad Tapar went to Baghdad to be present at the wedding of his sister who married Caliph al-Mustaẓhir bi-Allāh. While the country enjoyed a relatively peaceful period, he entered the struggle against the Crusaders. In 1111 he sent an army under the command of Mawdūd, the nephew of Kür-Bugha, the *atabeg* of Mosul, that besieged Edessa, the capital of the Frankish county. He was accompanied by Sukmān al-Quṭbī, who was the *shāh* {king} of Akhlāṭ, and the two sons of Bursuq. These forces went on to Aleppo where Tugh-Tegin {the *atabeg* of Damascus} joined them. In 1113 Muḥammad sent a second army under the command of Mawdūd, which was strengthened by Artuqid forces from Mārdīn, that advanced as far as Hama. There Mawdūd was again joined by Tugh-Tegin, and they {went on to} lay siege to Tiberias. But the leaders of these Turkish armies did not have full confidence in each other. In the first campaign {for example}, Riḍwān closed Aleppo to Mawdūd. In the second, Mawdūd was murdered by *bāṭinīs* in the cathedral mosque of Damascus (October 1113). A third army that the sultan dispatched under the command of Aq-Sonqur al-Bursuqī also suffered from dissention—even though supported by İl-Ghāzī, the Artuqid ruler of Mārdīn; Lu'lu', the *nā'ib* of Aleppo; and Tugh-Tegin—and could make no progress against the Franks (1115). Just as this lack of success allowed the Crusaders to become fully entrenched along the Syrian coast, new forces sent against Alamūt under the command of Anūsh-Tegin Shīrgīr left in the middle of the siege, which was succeeding, because of the death of Ghiyāth al-Dīn Abū Shujā' Muḥammad Tapar (April 1118).[9] The sultan, who died at the age of thirty-six, was succeeded by his son and heir apparent Mughīth al-Dīn Maḥmūd. While Maḥmūd was fighting his rebellious brother Toghrıl, Sanjar, the *malik* of Khurāsān, declared himself sultan and marched on his nephew. In the fierce battle of Sāveh (2 Jumādā I 513/11 August 1119), he defeated and captured Maḥmūd. According to the agreement that was reached, the western parts of the empire, except for Rayy, which would belong to Sanjar, were given to Maḥmūd along with the title of sultan on condition that he be subject to Sanjar. Thus the Seljuk state of Iraq, the capital of which was first Iṣfahān and then Hamadān, came into being. In the struggles for the throne that began after the death of Malik-Shāh, Sanjar invaded and took control of the states that had broken away from Seljuk rule (in 1113, while *malik*, he made a campaign to Samarqand against the Qarakhānids and in 1114 entered Ghazna, the capital of the Ghaznavid state). He later added the Ghūrid territories and established his control over Iraq, Āzarbāījān, Ṭabaristān, Iran, Sīstān, Kirmān, and Khwārazm as well. When combined with the area of the Ghaznavid sultanate, Afghanistan, Kāshghar, and Transoxiana, his domain approximated that of his father

9. 'Imād al-Dīn, *Zubdat*, pp. 90–115; Ṣadr al-Dīn, *Akhbār*, pp. 55 ff.; Ibn al-Athīr, *al-Kāmil*, years 499–511; Matthew of Edessa, *Chronique*, pp. 221 ff., 227 f., 231 f., 236 f., 241 ff., 246–54; Vartan, *History*, p. 191; Barhebraeus, *Tarihi*, II, 345–55; Grousset, *Histoire*, pp. 265–80.

and he took the title "al-Sulṭān al-Aʿẓam."[10] Sanjar's former seat of power, Marv, became the capital of the empire.

Maḥmūd was only a youth of fourteen when he came into conflict with his younger brothers Toghrıl and Masʿūd, or more correctly, their *atabegs*. Georgian forces took advantage of the continuing disorders to occupy Tiflis in 1121.[11] Because relations were not good between the sultan and the caliph, al-Mustarshid bi-Allāh, bloody clashes occurred in Baghdad between the Seljuk forces and the Arabs. The sultan was incapable of facing up to these events and devoted himself to hunting and other amusements. He died on 10 September 1131 at the age of thirty-one. Sanjar arrived to place Maḥmūd's brother al-Malik Rukn al-Dīn Toghrıl on the throne and succeeded in doing so in March 1131 in Hamadān after defeating {his other brother} al-Malik Masʿūd, who had opposed this, and his allied forces.[12] Toghrıl brought his brothers Masʿūd and Dā'ūd, whom Maḥmūd had designated the heir apparent,[13] to terms, but had no sooner secured the sultanate than he suddenly died (October 1134). Giyāth al-Dīn {i.e., al-Malik} Masʿūd, in whose name the *khuṭba* had been previously read in Baghdad, became the Seljuk ruler of Iraq after reaching an understanding with Sanjar (1134–52). It should also be noted here that the caliphs, who had been restricted to concerning themselves with religious matters and had been isolated from worldly affairs since the time of Toghrıl Beg, slowly began to get involved in affairs of state. The first to become active was the aforesaid al-Mustarshid (1118–35). This caliph did not approve of the Hamadān government and provoked fratricidal conflict over the Seljuk throne. In return for receiving direct personal control of ʿIrāq al-ʿArab as a caliphal state (agreement of 1132), he supported Masʿūd against Toghrıl and even attempted to send a robe of honor to Atsız, the Khwārazm-Shāh, to get his support.[14]

Masʿūd, who had been sent to Mosul as *malik* by his father, Muḥammad Tapar, was joined in the struggle for the sultanate by Mawdūd and Ai-Aba. Mawdūd, who, as we have seen, was dispatched from Mosul against the Crusaders, had previously been appointed Masʿūd's *atabeg*. Ai-Aba (also known as Chavush Beg) was later appointed to the same position. When Masʿūd became preoccupied with Qızıl, Sonqur, Chavlı and other commanders who had rebelled, the caliph took advantage of this to strengthen his power materially by besieging Mosul (July 1133). Although Masʿūd forced al-Mustarshid to leave Baghdad (1135), the caliph was able to gather sufficient forces to attack Masʿūd (24 June 1135). But "Turks being inclined to Turks," he was taken prisoner by Masʿūd when the Turkish soldiers in his army deserted to the sultan.[15] Although an agreement was reached between them at

10. Ibn al-Athīr, *al-Kāmil,* year 513; Ṣadr al-Dīn, *Akhbār,* pp. 61–64; ʿImād al-Dīn, *Zubdat,* pp. 117, 121–24; Ibn al-Jawzī, *al-Muntaẓam,* IX, 141, 144, 205, 216; Rāvandī, *Rāḥat,* pp. 167–71.

11. Brosset, *Géorgie,* I, 365 f.

12. ʿImād al-Dīn, *Zubdat,* pp. 148 ff.; Ṣadr al-Dīn, *Akhbār,* p. 71; Ibn al-Jawzī, *al-Muntaẓam,* X, 25 f.; Ibn Wāṣil, *Mufarrij,* I, 49 f.

13. Ṣadr al-Dīn, *Akhbār,* pp. 71–74.

14. Ibn al-ʿAmīd, *al-Majmūʿ al-mubārak,* Laleli Library, MS 2002, fol. 181a.

15. ʿImād al-Dīn, *Zubdat,* p. 164.

Marāgheh, the caliph was murdered by the *bāṭinīs*. Baghdad and its environs reverted to Seljuk rule. Because al-Rāshid bi-Amr Allāh, who succeeded al-Mustarshid as caliph, had cooperated with ʿImād al-Dīn Zangī and went to Mosul while the sultan laid siege to Baghdad, he was dethroned by Masʿūd and al-Muqtafī li-Amr Allāh (1136–60) was made caliph in his place.[16] While struggling with Dā'ūd, who claimed the sultanate, the sultan succumbed to certain suggestions to try to eliminate Qara-Sonqur, who had been of great service—the sultan had previously sent him against Dā'ūd, and at the same time he had defended Arrān and Āzarbāījān against Georgian attacks. The attempt failed (1139) and the sultan thus fell more under the oppression {of the Turkish amīrs}. In 1143 Dā'ūd was murdered by the *bāṭinīs*. After Qara-Sonqur died in 1141, the commander Boz-Aba revolted. The sultan met him in battle near Hamadān (1147) and defeated him,[17] thus escaping from oppression. This time he entrusted the administration of the state to Beg-Arslan (Khāṣṣ-Beg). Masʿūd was invited to Rayy by Sanjar and there received the favors of the great sultan. He then went to Baghdad (April 1150). At that time he ruled an area extending from Rayy to Aleppo and Erzurum. However, he soon became ill and died (1 Rajab 547/2 October 1152) {in Hamadān} where he was buried. With the death of Masʿūd, the prosperity of the Seljuk dynasty of Iraq can be said to have come to an end. İl-Ghāzī b. Artuq and the eastern Anatolian *beg*s joined in battle against the Georgians and Qıpchaqs (1121–24); the *atabeg* of Damascus, Tugh-Tegin, received a *manshūr* from Muḥammad to rule Syria; and Tāj al-Dīn Böri pleaded with Maḥmūd for help against the Crusaders in 1128.[18] But even though there was a need for a common front against foreign enemies, signs of loyalty to the Iraqi government simply disappeared. The power in the state had shifted to the *atabeg*s of Mosul (Zangids), Āzarbāījān (Eldigüzids), and Fārs (Salghurids).

We have seen that Sanjar closely followed events in the Seljuk state of Iraq and that he came to Rayy several times at the head of an army to settle disputes among members of the dynasty or to set aright the actions of the ʿAbbāsid caliphs against their rulers. By subduing the Ghūrids (1121), who had revolted in the east of the empire; continuing the fierce struggle that Maḥmūd had previously opened against the *bāṭinīs;* overcoming the troubles in Samarqand caused in particular by the Qarluqs (1130); settling Maḥmūd Khān, his sister's son, in Transoxiana; and securing the empire against the dangers to come from the steppes in the form of the Khwārazm-Shāh Quṭb al-Dīn Muḥammad (1097–1128) and his son Atsız, the sultan brought peace and order to a great part of the eastern Islamic world and showed himself to be the sole great ruler whose name was recited in the *khuṭba* everywhere, as

16. Ibn al-Azraq, *Ta'rīkh Mayyāfāriqīn,* British Museum Or. MS 5803, fol. 165a.

17. ʿImād al-Dīn, *Zubdat,* p. 200.

18. Ibn al-Qalānisī, *Dhail,* pp. 193, 219.

all the sources testify. In Ramaḍān 527/July 1133, Sanjar sent a *ferman* {edict} that clearly confirms this state of affairs to the vizir of Caliph al-Mustarshid. Although it was addressed to the caliph, it was sent in answer to a letter from the vizir and is a document that is as important for its historical content as it is with respect to diplomatics.[19] According to this document, Sanjar, who is given the byname "Muʿizz al-Dunyā wa 'l-Dīn," the titles "Burhān Amīr al-Mu'minīn," and "Abū 'l-Ḥārith" {Lion}, "received the submission of all kings and sultans, all Turkistan and other provinces as far as the borders of the land of China, the Wall of Gog and Magog, Qandahār and Sumnat." In addition, "the lands and tribes of Baghdad, Mecca, Medina, Rum, and India, the Arabs and Yemen further increased his power daily." Thanks to the favor of almighty God, he rose to become "the sovereign {*pâdişâh*} of the world," and was characterized as the "world conqueror," a designation that he inherited from his father (Malik-Shāh). He always looked after the best interests of his subjects, eliminated oppression, and was sensitive to the great men of religion.[20] However, the appearance of the Qara-Khitai in Central Asia changed everything. As Islam advanced toward inner Asia via Turkish rule, the Qara-Khitai state, which was of Mongol origin, formed the first barrier to it and for the first time subjected a Muslim political entity to non-Islamic rule.[21] This state held dominion over Transoxiana for some eighty years and was of great importance in Turco-Islamic history with regard to later facilitating the flow of the Naimans and, right after them, the Mongols into the Turco-Islamic world. In 1128, in the vicinity of Kāshghar, the Qara-Khitai suffered a defeat at the hands of the Qarakhānid ruler Aḥmad Khān and were driven off. However, in 1137, in cooperation with the Qarluqs in Transoxiana, they defeated the Khān of Samarqand. On 5 Ṣafar 536/9 September 1141, Sanjar lost the battle against them at Qaṭvān and his army was annihilated.[22] All of Transoxiana thus slipped from his hands. Earlier, in 1138, in his first Khwārazm campaign, Sanjar had defeated the Khwārazm-Shāh Atsız (1128–56), who had rebelled in the hope of establishing an independent state, and forced him to submit. Later, in 1140, Atsız seized Bukhārā. And after the defeat at Qaṭvān, the sultan could not prevent the Khwārazm-Shāh from invading Khurāsān and taking Sarakhs and Nīshāpūr (1141–42), even though he had previously compelled him to make an oath of fidelity. In his second Khwārazm campaign, however, the sultan was able to drive Atsız from Khurāsān and penetrate as far as Gurgānj. Despite this victory, Sanjar had to make a third campaign in Khwārazm (1147) and defeat Atsız once more. Each time the sultan defeated the rebellious Khwārazm-Shāh he forgave him and sent him back to his country. This was because of his desire to maintain security by having

19. *Majalla-i Yādgar,* no. 9–10, pp. 134–55, partial ed. Barthold, *Turkestan,* I, 35; see Köymen, "Selçuklu devri kaynaklarına dâir arastırmalar I" [Research on the sources for the Seljuk period, I], *DTCF Dergisi* 8(1951):577.

20. For details, see Köymen, *Büyük Selçuklu imparatorluğu tarihi II: Ikinci imparatorluk devri* (Ankara: TTK, 1954), pp. 219–36.

21. See Barthold, *La Découverte de l'Asie,* Fr. trans. B. Nikitin (Paris, 1947), p. 87.

22. See Yāqūt, *Mu'jam al-buldān,* IV, 139.

a courageous Khwārazm-Shāh guard the northern border of the Seljuk Empire at such places as Jand and Manqıshlaq. Indeed, the serious consequences of the continuously increasing pressure on the Turco-Islamic nation from the steppes were not long in coming. Following the defeat of the Ghūrid Saif al-Dīn Sūrī by the Ghaznavid Sultan Bahrām-Shāh and Sanjar's return to Rayy for the third time to make the sultan of Iraq, Masʿūd, confirm his allegiance, Sanjar defeated and captured the Ghūrid ruler ʿAlā' al-Dīn Ḥusain, known as *Jahān-Sūz* {the World Incendiary}, in June 1152. Such successes were instantly swept away, however, when he was routed and captured near Balkh by his own kinsmen, the Oghuz led by Dinar, Tuti, Qorqut, Arslan, and other chieftains (Muḥarram 548/April 1153). Already an old man, the sultan remained in Oghuz hands for three years. Although he escaped in 1156, he was not able to reunite the Seljuk Empire, which was collapsing under the heavy blows of the Oghuz, and one year later, on 26 Rabīʿ I 552/9 May 1157, at the age of seventy-three, he passed away.[23] He was buried in the famous *türbe,* one of his artistic masterpieces, that he had previously built at Marv.[24] Sanjar had no sons. In 1155, ʿAlā' al-Dīn Jahān-Sūz declared himself sultan, and the Ghūrid state became independent. Beginning in the reign of İl-Arslan, the son of Atsız, the Khwārazm-Shāh also started to seek independence. Khurāsān, Sanjar's original country, had now lost its historical importance and was occupied by the Oghuz.[25]

In the Seljuk state of Iraq, the winner of the struggle (1152) between Masʿūd's son Malik-Shāh and his uncle Ghiyāth al-Dīn Muḥammad (1153–59) was the latter.[26] However, Muḥammad had to fight, on the one hand, Sulaimān-Shāh, the nephew of Sanjar who had entered Hamadān with the support of the Khwārazm-Shāh, and, on the other, the Caliph al-Muqtafī, who captured Ḥilla, Kūfa, Wāsiṭ, and Takrit and founded a caliphal state (1154). Muḥammad's siege of Baghdad failed (1155) and, with the encouragement of the caliph, the *atabeg* of Āzarbāījān, Eldigüz, who had married Toghrıl's widow, placed his stepson, that is, Toghrıl's son, Arslan-Shāh, on the throne in Hamadān (1161). Muḥammad died in 1159, the caliph died in 1160, and Malik-Shāh was poisoned and Sulaimān-Shāh put to death in 1161. With their removal from the scene, Shams al-Dīn Eldigüz was able to become the effective ruler of the Seljuk state of Iraq, but his authority was limited to ʿIrāq al-ʿAjam. Taking advantage of the troubles in Iraq, the Georgians drove back Sukmān II, the ruler of Akhlāṭ who had besieged Ani in 1161, and ʿIzz al-Dīn Saltuq, the ruler of Erzurum, and occupied Dvin, where they carried out a general massacre. However, with some of the *beg*s from eastern Anatolia, Shams al-Dīn Eldigüz delivered powerful blows against the Georgians (January 1163) and seized the

23. Köymen, *Büyük Selçuklu II,* pp. 219–36; idem, "Büyük Selçuklu imparatorluğunda Oğuz isyanı" [The insurrection of the Oghuz in the Great Seljuk Empire], *DTCF Dergisi* 5(1947):159–73; Kafesoğlu, *Harezmşahlar,* pp. 44–72.

24. See Yāqūt, *Muʿjam al-buldān,* IV, 144.

25. Köymen, "Büyük Selçuklu imparatorluğunda Oğuz istilâsı" [The Oghuz invasion in the Great Seljuk Empire], *DTCF Dergisi* 5(1947):546–616.

26. {The struggle for the throne was between Malik-Shāh and his brother Rukn al-Dīn Muḥammad. See C. E. Bosworth, "The Political and Dynastic History of the Iranian World (*A.D.* 1000--1217)," in *The Cambridge History of Iran* (Cambridge, 1968), V, 175, and idem, *The Islamic Dynasties* (Edinburgh, 1967), p. 115. Kafesoğlu's Seljuk genealogical chart has been so corrected.}

treasure of the fleeing Georgian king Giorgi III.[27] But the governors and *beg*s were not pleased with Eldigüz' oppression of Sultan Arslan-Shāh and his subordination of him to his sons Jahān-Pahlavān and Qızıl-Arslan, who were placed in charge of the capital. They therefore sought the help of İl-Arslan, which opened the way for the intervention of the Khwārazm-Shāh in the affairs of Iraq. Upon the death of Eldigüz in 1174 and the passing of Arslan-Shāh in the following year, Muḥammad Jahān-Pahlavān, the "*atabey-i âzam*" {the greatest *atabeg*}, became the absolute ruler, for the latter was succeeded on the throne by his seven-year-old son, Rukn al-Dīn Toghrıl. According to the contemporary historian Rāvandī, who describes Jahān-Pahlavān as "*hākān-i acem*" {the khān of the Persians or non-Arabs}, he brought peace and security to the country and also protected it from the attacks of the Georgians and Qıpchaqs.[28] When he died in 1185, conditions in Iraq became unsettled and confused. A struggle for power began between Toghrıl and Jahān-Pahlavān's brother Qızıl-Arslan ʿUthmān. This rivalry was strongly fanned by Caliph al-Nāṣir li-Dīn Allāh (1179–1225), who sought to expand the caliphal state. In 1187 the caliph demolished the sultan's palace in Baghdad and in 1188, under the command of his vizir, sent an army against Toghrıl in support of Qızıl-Arslan. In addition to this, the "servants" {"*bendeleri*"} of the *atabeg* Pahlavān had meanwhile all become *derebegs* {local despot} throughout the country.[29] During the struggle with the *atabeg* Qızıl-Arslan, Toghrıl heedlessly and inexplicably executed his leading commanders, men who were loyal to him like Ai-Aba and Boz-Aba. Toghrıl thus undermined his own position against him. Consequently, Qızıl-Arslan was able to enter Hamadān. He received from the caliph such titles as "al-Malik al-Muʿẓẓam" {the Great King} and "Nāṣir Amīr al-Mu'minīn" {the Helper of the Commander of the Faithful} and oppressed the people.[30] Although Qızıl-Arslan, who thus took the throne of Seljuk Iraq, was assassinated in October 1191, another of Toghrıl's opponents, Qutlugh Inanch, requested help from the Khwārazm-Shāh ʿAlā' al-Dīn Tekish, who already controlled all of Khurāsān. Tekish then advanced toward Iraq. In a battle near Rayy, the Khwārazm army routed the Seljuk forces. Sultan Toghrıl, who fought with great courage even though deserted at the last moment by all his men and left alone, was killed (29 Rabīʿ I 590/25 March 1194). The Seljuk state of Iraq thus passed from the scene and the region was absorbed by the Khwārazm-Shāhs.[31]

The Seljuks of Kirmān

The conquests in and around Kirmān by Qara-Arslan Qāvurt, the son of Chaghrı Beg, have been mentioned. In his last revolt against

27. Ibn al-Athīr, *al-Kāmil,* year 557; Matthew of Edessa, *Chronique,* continuation by Gregory the Priest, pp. 329--32, 335.

28. Rāvandī, *Rāḥat,* pp. 332 ff.

29. Ibid., pp. 335 f.

30. Sibṭ, *Mir'āt,* ed. Jewett (Chicago, 1907), fol. 181a.

31. For details, see Kafesoğlu, *Harezmşahlar,* pp. 63 f., 75 f., 79 f., 108--12, 116--19, 123--26.

Malik-Shāh, Qāvurt was defeated, taken prisoner, and put to death. But his family was left in place in the country and formed the Seljuk dynasty of Kirmān. In September 1074, Malik-Shāh carried out a campaign in Kirmān, which he had placed under the control of Sav-Tegin. At that time the sultan received the allegiance of Qāvurt's son Sultan-Shāh after receiving that of his other sons Ḥusain and Mirdān-Shāh.[32] When the empire began to break up after Malik-Shāh's death in 1092, another of Qāvurt's sons, Tūrān-Shāh (1085–97), who had been on the throne of Kirmān, occupied Fārs. He was followed by Īrān-Shāh and then Arslan-Shāh (1101–42), who recognized the authority of Sanjar. During the reign of Arslan-Shāh, the Seljuk state of Kirmān experienced a golden age. The reigns of his nephew Mughīth al-Dīn Muḥammad (1141–56) and then his son Muḥyī al-Dīn Toghrıl-Shāh (1156–69) were periods of peace. The latter's daughter married Ghiyāth al-Din Muḥammad, the Seljuk sultan of Iraq (Dhū 'l-Ḥijja 554/December 1159). But when the Seljuk state of Iraq collapsed in chaos, provoked by the *atabeg*s and commanders, the *malik*s of Kirmān also began to quarrel with each other. The country was weakened by the rivalry and struggles among Toghrıl-Shāh's three sons—Arslan-Shāh II, Bahrām-Shāh, and Tūrān-Shāh II—and for a while (after 1175) was subject to the Ghūrids.[33] Dinar Beg, one of the Oghuz chieftains who, as mentioned, invaded Khurāsān, took Kirmān from the last Seljuk *malik* Muḥammad-Shāh II, occupied it, and put an end to the Seljuk dynasty there. Although it survived for a rather long time, this family was not particularly dynamic.[34]

The Seljuks of Syria

After the death of Malik-Shāh, Tāj al-Dawla Tutush had declared himself sultan in opposition to Berk-Yaruq and marched as far as 'Irāq al-'Ajam before he was defeated and killed on 24 February 1095. At that time his sons Fakhr al-Mulūk Riḍwān and Shams al-Mulūk Duqaq were in Aleppo and Damascus respectively. Riḍwān assembled his brother, whom he had defeated at Qinnisrīn, and his brother's commanders and had his own name recited in the *khuṭba* in Aleppo. He cooperated with Yaghı-Sıyan, the Seljuk governor of Antioch, but when the two had a falling out, Yaghı-Sıyan supported Duqaq, and the ensuing struggle between the two brothers again led to war.[35] In the end, Syria was divided into two Seljuk states, one at Aleppo and the other at Damascus. In 1098, as a result of Kür-Bugha's failure, despite the heroic defense by Yaghı-Sıyan, the Crusaders, who had reached an agreement with the Fāṭimids to divide the Seljuk lands, captured Antioch. After defeating Riḍwān, they advanced toward the south.

32. {This sentence is somewhat confusing. Qāvurt was succeeded as the ruler of Kirmān by his sons Kirmān-Shāh (465/1073), Ḥusain (467/1074), Sulṭān-Shāh, and then Turān-Shāh (477/1085). Mirdān-Shāh never ruled Kirmān. See Bosworth, *The Islamic Dynasties,* p. 116; Erdoğan Merçil, *Kirman Selçukluları* (Istanbul, 1980), pp. 49--50, 60, 68--71. Kafesoğlu's Seljuk genealogical chart has been so corrected.}

33. {A fourth son, and the youngest, Terken-Shāh, also participated in these struggles but never reached the throne. See Bosworth, "The Political and Dynastic History," pp. 173–74; Merçil, *Kirman Selçukluları,* pp. 133–34. Bahrām-Shāh became ruler in 565/1170, Arslān-Shāh II in 570/1175, and Turān-Shāh II in 572/1176. Cf. Bosworth, *Islamic Dynasties,* p. 116, and Merçil, *Kirman Selçukluları,* pp. 371–72. Kafesoğlu's Seljuk genealogical chart has been so corrected.}

34. See Afḍal al-Dīn, *Badā'i',* idem, *'Iqd al-'ūlā li 'l-mawāqif al-a'lā',* ed. 'Alī Muḥammad 'Amīrī (Tehran, 1311/1932–33), pp. 7–16; Nāṣir al-Dīn Munshi' Kirmānī, *Simṭ al-'ulā li-'l- haḍrat al-'ulyā,* ed. 'Abbās Iqbāl (Tehran, 1328 *sh.*), pp. 17–21; 'Imād al-Dīn, *Zubdat,* p. 287; Rāvandī, *Rāḥat,* p. 270; Kafesoğlu, *Melikşah,* pp. 24 ff., idem, *Harezmşahlar,* pp. 87, 97, 107.

35. {In 488/1095, Riḍwān became the *malik* of Syria and Palestine with Aleppo as his capital, and Duqaq became *malik* of Damascus. Riḍwān tried twice to capture Damascus from his brother. In 490/1097, the two met in battle at Qinnisrīn, where Duqaq and his ally, Yaghı-Sıyan, were defeated. Duqaq was able to return to Damascus and Yaghı-Sıyan to Antioch. In both cities Riḍwān's name was then mentioned in the *khuṭba* before that of Duqaq. See Ali Sevim, *Suriye ve Filistin Selçukluları tarihi* (Ankara, 1983), pp. 171–73.}

There, real power was then in the hands of Duqaq's *atabeg* and step-father, Tugh-Tegin. Upon Duqaq's death in June 1104, the *atabeg* replaced him with another son of Tutush, the ten-year-old Bek-Tash. Although Duqaq, together with Janāḥ al-Dawla, had fought Baldwin and {Raymond of} Saint Gilles; Riḍwān had fought {Raymond of} Saint Gilles and Tancred (at Qinnisrīn and Acre); and Tugh-Tegin had co-operated with Sukmān b. Artuq, the ruler of al-Jazīra, and with Mawdūd, the *atabeg* of Mosul, there was mutual distrust and no definite agreement could be reached between Riḍwān and Tugh-Tegin. Consequently, it was not possible to stop the Crusaders who, with extreme zeal, immediately wanted to go to Jerusalem. When Riḍwān died in Aleppo in 1113, he was succeeded by his son Alp-Arslan, who was killed a short time later. He was replaced by his brother Sultan-Shāh (1114–17), but during his reign power was in the hands of Lu'lu', one of his father's slaves. When Lu'lu' was murdered by his own men, İl-Ghāzī b. Artuq, who had continuously and successfully fought the Crusaders, became ruler of Aleppo (1117) by the wish of its people. As for Damascus, because Tugh-Tegin had become the ruler, the Seljuk family was no longer in power there. He was killed in 1128. With his son, Tāj al-Dīn Böri, the branch of the Börids began.[36]

36. Ibn al-Athīr, *al-Kāmil,* years 490, 494–99, 502, 507–08, 511, 522; Matthew of Edessa, *Chronique,* pp. 185 f., 192 f., 250 ff., 257 f., 281–84, 287; Ibn Wāṣil, *Mufarrij,* I, 9, 40 f., 53; Ibn al-'Adīm, *Zubdat,* II, 100–180; Ibn al-Qalānisī, *Dhail,* pp. 175–92; Grousset, *Histoire,* pp. 250 ff., 257 ff., 265–80, 281–84, 287, 545–53, 565–73, 579, 614–18, 633 ff., 658.

The Seljuks of Anatolia

This branch of the Seljuk dynasty, which was founded by Sulaimān-Shāh—a grandson of Arslan Yabghu—and was continued by his family, established the most important and longest surviving Seljuk state. Sulaimān-Shāh made Iznik his capital in 1078. But when he went to Antioch in 1086, he died in a struggle with Tutush. For a while the Seljuk state of Anatolia was left in the hands of Abū 'l-Ghāzī {Dānishmend} but was then taken over by Qılıch-Arslan I, the son of Sulaimān-Shāh, who came to Iznik upon the death of Malik-Shāh. Although Qılıch-Arslan was the first sultan of Anatolia, there was no unified Seljuk state there because, in the time between his father's death and 1092, when there was no ruler in this region, the *beg*s in various areas of eastern Anatolia (the Dānishmendids in Sivas, Mangüjekids in Erzinjān, Saltuqids in Erzurum), and western Anatolia (Chakan in Izmir, the Tengribirmish *beg*s in Efes {Ephesus}), and then the Artuqids and Akhlāṭ-Shāhs, each set out to create independent states. Meanwhile, Byzantium had been launching attacks on Iznik. First Chakan Beg was eliminated (1094). As we have seen, Chakan Beg had threatened Constantinople with his powerful fleet, but Qılıch-Arslan was as pleased to be rid of him as Emperor Alexius I Comnenus, because

Chakan, even though he was his son-in-law, posed a potential danger to the sultan of Anatolia. Afterwards, the sultan set out for central Anatolia and laid siege to Malatya (1096), which had fallen into the hands of an Armenian prince. During the siege he learned of the approach of the Crusader armies and returned. Crusader bands composed of pillaging irregulars led by hermits were destroyed around Iznik by the sultan's brother Dā'ūd. But when the main Crusader army under the leadership of the counts, dukes, and knights advanced toward Iznik, it could not be stopped by Qılıch-Arslan when he arrived on the scene. Iznik surrendered to the Crusaders and was returned to Byzantine control (26 June 1097). The sultan decided on a war of attrition and when strengthened by the forces of Dānishmend Ghāzī and Ḥasan Beg, the ruler of Kayseri, he inflicted heavy losses on the Crusaders before they had reached Eskishehir {Dorylaeum} on the road to Syria. He then withdrew, fighting as he went, and destroyed the roads and all possibilities for provisions in the path of the enemy, who was not only in great number but also wearing armor against which Turkish weapons were ineffective. All areas inhabited by the Turks were evacuated. One section of the Crusader army, which advanced in the direction of Eskishehir-Akshehir {Philomelium}-Konya-Ereghli {Heraclea}, headed for Kayseri and clashed with Ḥasan Beg, who fought bravely. As this wing headed for Antioch via Marash {Germanicea} and the Turkish forces retreated, the Seljuk border in Anatolia receded to the Antioch-Eskishehir {sic} line. The Armenians in the Taurus mountains took advantage of the situation and succeeded in founding a kingdom in Cilicia. When Bohemond, the Crusader prince of Antioch, was taken prisoner by Dānishmend Ghāzī, a Crusader army set out on a campaign of revenge and destroyed Ankara, massacring the Muslim population. Numbering more than 100,000, it advanced along the Qızıl-Irmak River but was annihilated by Qılıch-Arslan near Amasya {Amasea}. Another Crusader army was also destroyed by him around Konya-Ereghli (1102).

About the time that Qılıch-Arslan was occupied with the Crusaders, he seized Malatya, which had passed to the Dānishmendids (1102). He thus broke their power, which had been increasing alongside him in Anatolia. He subsequently received the allegiance of the amīrs of Diyārbakr and also added to his territories Ḥarrān and Mayyāfāriqīn, which had until then belonged to Duqaq, the *malik* of Syria. Eventually he became the ruler of Mosul and its environs as well. However, after he lost the battle that he fought on the banks of the Khābūr against the amīr Chavlı, who had become ruler of Mosul by killing Chökermish and then had fled to Aleppo, and his allies, the Artuqid İl-Ghāzī and Riḍwān, the *malik* of Syria, he drowned in the river (1107). Sultan Qılıch-Arslan I had come to power at the most critical time in the history of the Turks in the Near East. He was the first real target of the fanatical Crusader armies and had hoped to unify the part of Anatolia that he succeeded in retaining.

Qılıch-Arslan's son Shahan-Shāh (or Malik-Shāh), who had been captured by Chavlı and sent to the sultan of Iraq, was released two years later and came to Malatya, where he became sultan. However, for many years he had to struggle against his younger brother Masʿūd, who challenged his claim to the sultanate. Finally, thanks to the support Masʿūd received from the Dānishmendid *beylik* {principality}, he ascended the throne in Konya, which he had taken back from the Byzantines with the help of his brother-in-law Amīr Ghāzī (1116). During Masʿūd's long sultanate, he continued to cooperate with Dānishmend Ghāzī (d. 1134). The latter had seized Malatya (1124) and taken possession of the districts of Kayseri, Ankara, Chankırı, and Kastamonu, which had belonged to Masʿūd's brothers. Dānishmend Ghāzī also gave refuge to Isaac, the rebellious brother of the Byzantine Emperor John II Comnenus, who claimed the throne. Upon Isaac's request, he set out for the Black Sea and drove out the invading Byzantine forces that had been sent to Kastamonu to counter him. With the successes that he won, he thus made his country the most powerful state in Anatolia. However, after the death of Dānishmend Ghāzī's son Muḥammad Beg (1142), who had defeated the Byzantine forces several times in western Anatolia, Masʿūd took back Ankara, Chankırı, Kastamonu and their surrounding areas in 1143 and tried to unify his country. He assigned his oldest son and heir apparent, Qılıch-Arslan, to Albistān, which he seized in 1144. At the same time that he began raids on the Gök-Su {Sanja, Singa} and Marash regions, which were under Crusader occupation, he also drove off a bloody attack on Konya made by the Emperor Manuel I Comnenus and took a great many prisoners. Near the Jeyhān {Pyramus} River, he inflicted a crushing defeat on the major part of the Crusader army under the leadership of the Holy Roman Emperor Conrad II (November 1147), which had set out on the Second Crusade (1147) in response to the loss of the Crusader state (Frankish county) of Edessa between 1144 and 1146 to ʿImād al-Dīn Zangī, the *atabeg* of Mosul and Aleppo, and his son Nūr al-Dīn Maḥmūd. While Conrad withdrew in confusion toward Iznik, the other Crusader army, under the command of the French king Louis VII, was defeated around Yalvach {west of Konya}, but was able to reach Acre by sea. Masʿūd received the allegiance of the Armenian Prince Stephen and in 1149 that of Marash and its environs. A year later he forced Joscelin, the count of Edessa, to become his subject and also acquired the submission of the Dānishmendid *beg* Yaghı-Basan. Just before his death (1156), he divided his country among his three sons.

Sultan Qılıch-Arslan II (1156–92) took the capital, Konya, and the surrounding area and, although his brothers held subordinate positions as *malik*s, he had his middle brother strangled in order to prevent a dispute over the throne. This caused his youngest brother, Shahan-Shāh, to flee toward Ankara-Chankırı, which in fact belonged to him, and to cooperate with Yaghı-Basan, who had heretofore been a rival of the Seljuks. The Armenian Prince Stephen consequently took advantage of the Dānishmendid-Seljuk antagonism to revolt but was punished by Qılıch-Arslan. Nūr al-Dīn Maḥmūd penetrated the border and was driven off. At the same time the forces of Emperor Manuel I Comnenus were also driven back near Eskishehir (1159). In 1162, in order to come to an understanding with Manuel, who sought to encircle Qılıch-Arslan with rival forces by spinning plots and following a policy of turning the Turks in Anatolia against each other, the sultan went to Constantinople, where he was received with extraordinary honor and a mutual assistance treaty was signed. With this agreement, which stopped the raids of the Turkmen forces on Byzantine territory, Qılıch-Arslan broke up the alliance that had been developing against him. After thus securing his western border, the sultan set out to establish unity in Anatolia: he took Albistān, Dārende and its surrounding area, Kayseri, the Zamantı {Karmalas} River region, and Malatya from the Dānishmendids. At the same time, Qılıch-Arslan also took Ankara and Chankırı from his brother Shahan-Shāh. After the death of Nūr al-Dīn Maḥmūd (1174), the *atabeg* of Mosul and Aleppo who had always been allied with the Dānishmendids against the Anatolian Seljuks, he seized Sivas, Niksar {Neocaesarea}, and Tokat. By thus occupying all the Dānishmendid lands, the sultan put an end to their *beylik* (1178). As his power increased, the Turkmen forces, which had been concentrated around Eskishehir, demolished the fortifications in the area and began to raid Byzantine territory. They pushed as far as Denizli, Kırk-Aghach {east of Bergama}, Bergama {Pergamum}, and Edremid {Adramyttium}. They carried out acts of destruction and attrition exactly as they had done on the eve of the battle of Malazgird. Manuel's perception of the danger, as well as his efforts to use the Dānishmendid Dhū 'l-Nūn, who had taken refuge with him, against the sultan around Amasya, impelled the Byzantines to settle accounts with the Turks once and for all. With an army exceeding 100,000 men—composed of Franks, Serbs, Hungarians, and Pechenegs in addition to the regular Byzantine forces—it appears that the emperor, who had rejected Qılıch-Arslan's requests for peace, had—like Romanus IV Diogenes—decided to destroy the Seljuk state whatever the cost. Thanks to the feigned retreat maneuver that the Turkmen forces skillfully executed, Qılıch-Arslan totally annihilated the Byzantine army (September 1176) that had succeeded in reaching the narrow and steep valley of Myriocephalum east of Denizli near Lake Hoyran. The emperor was allowed to return to Constantinople on condition that he remove the Byzantine fortifications in western Anatolia and pay heavy reparations. In addition to leaving to the Turks a valuable booty of jewels and the like—besides 5,000 carts full of weapons, equipment and stores—and at the same time putting an end to the crisis caused by the First Crusade, this victory completely destroyed the hope of retaking Anatolia, which the Byzantines had nourished during the century since the battle of Malazgird. It also confirmed that Anatolia, which until then had been regarded in the Christian world as a kind of "country under Turkish occupation," had become a truly Turkish homeland. The Byzantine Empire could thus no longer venture any attack on the Turks. As the immediate result of this victory, Ulu-Borlu {Sozopolis}, Eskishehir, Kütahya {Cotyaeum} and their surrounding areas were seized (1182) and the Seljuk border approached Denizli. In 1184, the Turkish forces reached the Aegean Sea and captured some seventy fortresses. One year later, the Byzantine Emperor Isaac II Angelus was forced to pay an annual tribute. Moreover, Turkmen forces completely overran the Armenian kingdom of Cilicia, took Silifke {Seleucia} in the name of Qılıch-Arslan, and from there spread toward Syria and al-Jazīra.

Around 1185, after a long and successful life of struggle, a tired Qılıch-Arslan II divided his country among his eleven sons. He himself lived in Konya, as the lord of these *malik*s, and had his vizir, Ikhtiyār al-Dīn Ḥaṣan, administer the state. But the division of the country increased the feelings of sovereignty of the brother *malik*s so that sometimes even armed clashes broke out against the aged sultan, causing the head of state great anxiety. Upon the capture of Jerusalem by Salāḥ al-Dīn al-Ayyūbī {Saladin} in 1187, another Crusader army, the third, set out again from Europe under the leadership of the German emperor and English and French kings, and approached the Seljuk state while it was in this difficult position. By making friends with Frederick Barbarossa and allowing the Crusaders to pass on to Syria, the sultan tried to render them as harmless as possible. However, after a fierce battle resulting in the defeat of the Turkmen at Akshehir, he could not prevent the Crusaders from entering Konya and causing great destruction and carnage. In the midst of this calamity, the ailing eighty-year-old sultan, who was under the tyranny of his son Quṭb al-Dīn Malik-Shāh in the capital, was forced to seek refuge with another son, Ghiyāth al-Dīn Kai-Khusraw, the heir apparent. He passed away at Ghiyāth al-Dīn's side (1192) while his sons were fighting each other.

Following the death of his father, and after seizing Konya from Malik-Shāh, Kai-Khusraw I, the *malik* of Ulu-Borlu and heir apparent, became the Seljuk sultan (1192–1211). During his first sultanate, which lasted five years, Kai-Khusraw fought his brothers, defeated the forces of the Byzantine Emperor Alexius III Angelus, and, at the same time, expanded his conquests toward the west. However, because of the pressure from his brother Rukn al-Dīn Sulaimān-Shāh, the *malik* of Tokat, who had asserted his military power and seized the area around Samsun and certain other coastal regions, he abandoned Konya and went to Constantinople, where he was well-received by the emperor. He even married a Comneni princess. But he was not able to obtain the support for which he had hoped. He had to fight Sulaimān-Shāh, who had taken his place as sultan, as well as the rest of his brothers, until his death in 1204. Because Sulaimān-Shāh's son Qılıch-Arslan III was still a child when he succeeded his father, Kai-Khusraw was summoned by the Turkmen on the frontier. While the emperor was establishing a new state (Pontus) at Trebizond as a result of the occupation of Constantinople by the army of the Fourth Crusade (1204), Kai-Khusraw reached an agreement with Theodore I Lascaris, who was trying to create another Byzantine state at Iznik, and returned to Anatolia. He imprisoned his nephew and once more became the head of the Seljuk state (1205). Kai-Khusraw sought to strengthen the unity established in Anatolia by Sulaimān-Shāh. He defeated Alexius III Angelus in the north and seized Antalya {Attalia} in the south (1207). He assigned Mubāriz al-Dīn Er-Tokush as the *sü-başı* of this city, which was a commercial center with the Venetians. Afterwards, he marched against the Armenian king Leo II, took some of his lands, defeated his son and took him prisoner (1209), and prevented the invasion of northern Syria and eastern

Anatolia by the Ayyūbid ruler al-Malik al-ʿĀdil. Finally, because Kai-Khusraw gave his protection to the Byzantine Emperor Alexius III Angelus, who had taken refuge with him, relations with Lascaris, the king of Iznik, deteriorated; and in the campaign that he launched against Lascaris, the sultan fell in battle around Ala-Shehir in 1211.

Although ʿIzz al-Dīn Kai-Kā'ūs, who took his place and spent his royal life in Malatya, was declared sultan on the decision of the leading officials of the Seljuk state, his younger brother Kai-Qubād, the *malik* of Tokat, claimed the right to the throne. He marched to Kayseri, where the coronation ceremonies were held, but was unsuccessful and the matter ended in favor of Kai-Kā'ūs (1211–19). After signing a favorable treaty with Lascaris and accepting gifts from the Armenian king, Kai-Kā'ūs renewed a {commercial} treaty with the king of Cyprus while continuing his father's economic policies in Anatolia. In order to secure his trade in the north, he marched to Sivas and from there, by way of Sinop, he captured Alexius I, the Greek king of Trebizond. Afterwards, he became the ruler of Sinop (1214) and received the allegiance of Alexius. On the other hand, the people of Antalya revolted at the instigation of the Latins of Cyprus (1216), and he had to take the city by applying pressure by land and sea. He also set out against the Armenian king who had taken Qaramān, Ereghli, and Ulu-Kishla {east of Ereghli} during the previous struggle with his brother. After a series of difficult battles and sieges, the sultan defeated the Armenians and, in addition to taking the aforesaid places, destroyed certain formidable Armenian fortresses. The Armenian king became subject to the Seljuks (1218) and was forced to provide an annual tribute and, when necessary, military assistance. The Turkmen on the frontier were informed that merchants were to be given freedom of movement by both sides. Meanwhile, Kai-Kā'ūs had become involved in domestic Ayyūbid affairs. Following the death of the Ayyūbid ruler of Aleppo, al-Malik al-Ẓāhir, who had sworn allegiance to him after the Armenian campaign, Kai-Kā'ūs, with al-Malik al-Afḍal {Ayyūbid prince of Samosata}, entered the territory of Aleppo against its new Ayyūbid ruler al-Malik al-ʿAzīz. He captured Manbij but had to retreat to Albistān because of al-Afḍal's treachery (1218). Al-Malik al-Ashraf, the Ayyūbid ruler of Edessa and Ḥarrān, followed him and recovered the fortresses that had passed to the Seljuks. Kai-Kā'ūs immediately prepared for another campaign, received the allegiance of Nāṣir al-Dīn Maḥmūd, the Artuqid ruler, and Muẓaffar al-Dīn Kök-Böri, the ruler of Irbil, and set out against al-Ashraf at the head of his army. When he reached Malatya he became ill and died. His death in 1220 was attributed to the crushing defeat he had suffered in Syria.

With the sultanate of ʿAlā' al-Dīn Kai-Qubād I (1220–37), the Anatolian Seljuk state enjoyed a great period of development. We have seen that he had unsuccessfully besieged Kayseri in opposition to Kai-Kā'ūs. He later took refuge in Ankara and was imprisoned for a while in a fortress near Malatya. Caliph al-Nāṣir li-Dīn Allāh sent a *manshūr* for the sultanate to Kai-Qubād. It was presented by the famous *ṣūfī* Shihāb al-Dīn Abū Ḥafṣ ʿUmar al-Suhrawardī. Kai-Qubād allied himself with al-Malik al-Ashraf because the latter had become a rival of the Ayyūbids of Egypt and needed a friend. Moreover, it was necessary to set his affairs in order at home and abroad, for in those years the Mongol invasion, which had brought the Khwārazmian Empire—then the largest Turco-Islamic political structure in the East—to its knees with one blow and was rapidly advancing toward the west, was scorching the Near East.[37] After strengthening his cities and fortresses, he besieged Kalon-Oros, a great castle of both military and commercial importance near Antalya, by land and sea. He was the first to build a Seljuk navy and used it for this purpose. He took the fortress from its Greek overlord with the intervention of Er-Tokush, the *sü-başı* of Antalya (1223). After rebuilding the city and its fortress, the latter was given the name ʿAlā'iyya, after the sultan, and became the winter residence of Kai-Qubād and his successors. He executed the great commanders Saif al-Dīn Ai-Aba, Zain al-Dīn Bashāra, Mubāriz al-Dīn Bahrām-Shāh, and Bahā' al-Dīn Qutlughja and exiled others because of their antagonism toward him. After thus strengthening the state, he ordered the frontier *beg* Ḥusām al-Dīn Choban in Kastamonu to set out on a naval expedition to take the commercial port of Sughdaq in the Crimea using the ships built at the shipyards that the sultan had established at Sinop (1226). This was done because the Mongol raids on Qıpchaq territory and the Crimea had broken down public order there, and upon the withdrawal of the Mongols from the north of the Black Sea, there was no authority in the Crimea—although it belonged to the Greek kingdom of Trebizond, a vassal state of the Seljuks—and the safety of the commercial vessels plying the Black Sea was threatened. In addition to taking Sughdaq, the Seljuks forced a number of Russian and Qıpchaq *beg*s to submit in connection with the same campaign. In the south, the ground forces under Mubāriz al-Dīn Er-Tokush and the naval forces under Mubāriz al-Dīn Chavlı were advancing at the same time and captured Anamur and all the fortresses as far

37. For details see Kafesoğlu, *Harezmşahlar*, pp. 229-85.

as Silifke. There were also forces coming from Marash that took a number of castles in that direction (1225). They forced the Armenian king Het'um I to sign a peace treaty according to which he had to provide the sultan with troops, double his annual tribute, and coin money in the name of Kai-Qubād. Turkmen were settled about that area and its control was given to Qamar al-Dīn (hence Qamar al-Dīn *ili,* the land of Qamar al-Dīn). Subsequently, in the time of the Qaramānids, this area took the name İch-İl {the land of the interior, hence the name of the province that is today called İçel}.

Because the Artuqid government in Diyārbakr, which was subject to the Seljuks, changed its allegiance to the Ayyūbid ruler of Egypt, al-Malik al-Kāmil, who seemed less dangerous to it, and also allied itself with Jalāl al-Dīn, the Khwārazm-Shāh, who had fled before the Mongols and was active on the Seljuks' eastern border, Kai-Qubād was compelled to march to the east (1226). While besieging and capturing the fortresses of Kahta, Ḥiṣn-Manṣūr (Adıyaman) and Chemishkezek, Kai-Qubād defeated the allied forces advancing upon him. He accepted the request of the Artuqid *malik* Masʿūd to remain his subject and later set out to reach an understanding with the Ayyūbids, for the Mongol danger was approaching. He married the daughter of al-Malik al-ʿĀdil {the former Ayyūbid ruler} and then annexed Erzinjān and Kemah, which belonged to the Mangüjekids, and Shebin-Qaraḥiṣār {Coloneia} in order to secure the eastern border of the state (1228). He assigned his son Kai-Khusraw to Erzinjān as *malik* and made Mubāriz al-Dīn Er-Tokush his *atabeg*. The appearance of Jalāl al-Dīn, the Khwārazm-Shāh, on the Seljuk border and the alliance of the *malik* of Erzurum, Jahān-Shāh, with the Ayyūbids of Akhlāṭ, which led Andronicus I, the king of Trebizond, to shed his allegiance and attack the ports of Samsun and Sinop, caused the sultan to prepare a naval expedition in the Black Sea. The army was under the direction of Er-Tokush and was strengthened by the forces of Kai-Khusraw. It reached Trebizond via Bayburt-Machka and laid siege to it in support of the fleet. But, because of a violent storm, this undertaking came to nothing. After the defeat of the Khwārazm-Shāh in 1230, however, Andronicus again proclaimed his allegiance to Kai-Qubād.

The good relations that were established between Jalāl al-Dīn, who struggled against the Mongols, and Kai-Qubād, who fought the Christians, were broken when the Khwārazm-Shāh took the Ayyūbid city of Akhlāṭ after a long siege, devastated it, and put the population to the sword. Brave but lacking political astuteness, the Khwārazm-Shāh was persuaded by the *malik* of Erzurum, whom he had taken under his protection, to turn against the sultan. At Erzurum, where the two armies met in the battle of Yassı-Chimen (August 1230), that of the Khwārazm-Shāh suffered defeat. Jahān-Shāh was taken prisoner and Erzurum surrendered.

After the death of Jalāl al-Dīn in 1231, the Seljuk state became the neighbor of the Mongols, who sometimes pillaged as far as the area around Malatya. A prudent ruler, Kai-Qubād sent an ambassador to Ögedei, the Mongol *qaghan* {supreme ruler}, and expressed his desire to reach an agreement. But in response, the *qaghan* sent a letter (dated 1236) with a command {*yarlık*} demanding that the sultan recognize the authority of the Mongols and send an ambassador and gifts every year. By regarding this as the customary exchange of ambassadors and gifts between two rulers, Kai-Qubād was careful not to break relations, and took precautions against future danger. He ordered Kamāl al-Dīn Qāmyār to seize the area around Lake Van and all the towns as far north as Tiflis. As these conquests progressed, troops were stationed in the castles and newly built fortified positions, and Turks were settled in those regions where the population had declined. The forces of the Khwārazm *beg*s, who had entered the service of the Seljuks after the death of Jalāl al-Dīn, were also sent there. Because the Seljuks occupied the great, militarily important city of Akhlāṭ in 1232, the Ayyūbid ruler of Egypt, al-Kāmil, went on the offensive and sent forces to invade Anatolia. But they were smashed (1234) by the Seljuks, lead by Kamāl al-Dīn Qāmyār, who held all the passes. In connection with this, Harput {Kharput, Khartpert} was occupied by Kai-Qubād (August 1234) and the Harput branch of the Artuqids became part of history. Afterwards, the districts of Edessa, Ḥarrān, and Raqqa came under Seljuk rule. However, because al-Kāmil took a fearful revenge of destruction and slaughter as far as Mārdīn, the army of Kai-Qubād assembled on the plain of Mashhad near Kayseri in preparation for a major campaign. During this mobilization, which was held just as a section of the Seljuk forces was laying siege to Diyārbakr, important decisions were reached concerning the future, appointments were made, and the ceremony for Rukn al-Dīn Qılıch-Arslan, as heir to the throne, was carried out. Meanwhile, the ambassadors who had come from Caliph al-Mustanṣir bi-'llāh, al-Malik al-Kāmil, and the Christian rulers expressed the need to unite against the Mongols, whose intensified raids had advanced as far as Mosul. Kai-Qubād was of the same mind. However, the sultan was poisoned during the banquet that he gave for these envoys (1237) and the great alliance could not be realized. Kai-Qubād had tried to create political unity in central, southern and eastern Anatolia. For this reason he had sought to complete the integration of the Turks and satisfy the political, geographical, and economic requirements of the country by annexing Aleppo and Northern Syria, most of whose population were Turks. He had also acquired the allegiance of the neighboring *beg*s and Ayyūbids. The death of this most distinguished figure of the Anatolian Turkish state, while only forty-five years old, therefore had grave consequences for the Seljuks.

As a result of the rivalries among the commanders and *beg*s, the *malik* of Erzinjān, Ghiyāth al-Dīn Kai-Khusraw II (1237–46), came to the throne after Kai-Qubād instead of Qılıch-Arslan, the crown prince. This inept ruler immediately fell under the influence of Saʿd al-Dīn Köpek. On his advice, he had the great Khwārazmian *beg* Qayır Khān put to death. This led to an uprising of the Khwārazmian forces that caused trouble for the head of state for a long time. Köpek had the great men of state, whom he considered to be his own rivals—in particular the famous *atabeg* Shams al-Dīn Altun-Aba—put to death on behalf of the sultan. But he himself nourished hopes of occupying the Seljuk throne. He took advantage of every opportunity and one by one eliminated the leading commanders from the reign of Kai-Qubād, including Kamāl al-Dīn Qāmyār. However, he lost his own life in 1239 when all of his plots were revealed. With the rise to prominence of statesmen like Muhadhdhab al-Dīn ʿAlī, Shams al-Dīn al-Iṣfahānī, and Jalāl al-Dīn Qaratay, who had played a role in this affair, the situation improved somewhat. Although the Diyārbakr region was taken from the Ayyūbids and annexed (1241), it was not possible to overcome the internal political and religious weaknesses of the Seljuk state. The "Bābā'ī" revolt, led by a Turkmen *shaikh* {elder} named Bābā Isḥāq, was suppressed with great difficulty and then the Mongols invaded. Under the command of Bayjū Noyan, the Mongol army inflicted a terrible defeat on the Seljuk forces at Köse-Dagh, east of Sivas (July 1243). This defeat dragged the country into captivity. For more than half a century, the Mongols exploited Anatolia, plundering it and putting it to the sword. The Seljuk sultans who succeeded Kai-Khusraw were neither free nor independent: ʿIzz al-Dīn Kai-Kā'ūs II (1246–49); Rukn al-Dīn Qılıch-Arslan IV (1248–49); Kai-Kā'ūs II, Qılıch-Arslan IV and ʿAlā' al-Dīn Kai-Qubād II (d. 1254; ruled jointly 1249–57); Kai-Kā'ūs II (second reign, 1257–59; jointly with Qılıch-Arslan IV, 1257–66); Ghiyāth al-Dīn Kai-Khusraw III (1266–83); Giyāth al-Dīn Masʿūd II (1283–98); ʿAlā' al-Dīn Kai-Qubād III (1298–1302);

and Ghiyāth al-Dīn Masʿūd II (second reign, 1303–8). From the battle of Köse-Dagh until the last Seljuk state sank into history in 1308, Anatolia was the scene of struggles among so-called sultans and princes, grasping and agitating statesmen and *beg*s, of assassinations, uprisings against the Mongols, Mongol campaigns of revenge, flights to the Byzantines, massacres, financial hardships and abuses, economic collapse and popular disorder. Among the important events that occurred in the Anatolian Seljuk state during this period were the following: the encouragement of struggles and fratricidal quarrels by Saif al-Dīn Toruntay, Jaja-oghlu ʿAlā' al-Dīn, Ḥusam al-Dīn Bīchār and other leading *beg*s; the rout of the Seljuk forces (1256) in a chastising military operation by Bayjū Noyan, the commander of the Mongol occupation forces in Anatolia; the division of the state into two sultanates, with the border along the Qızıl-Irmak, as the result of the actions of the ambitious Vizir Muʿīn al-Dīn Sulaimān Parvāna; the revolt of the Qaramānids and their march on Konya (1262); the incident of the Qaramānid Mehmed Beg Ghiyāth al-Dīn Siyāvush (Jimrī, 1277); the revolt of the Hatīrids against the Mongols (1276); and the invasion of Anatolia as far as Kayseri by Baybars, the Turkish sultan of Egypt (1277).

There was no longer any chance for Anatolia to pull itself together. Here and there toward the end of the thirteenth century, the Turkish *beg*s and the people stood up against the Mongol oppression, which was gradually weakening. As the Seljuk state was collapsing by degree under this oppression, the Anatolian *beylik*s (Pervānids, Ṣāḥib Atāids, Karasids, Germiyānids, Ṣārūkhānids, Aydınids, Menteshids, Ḥamīdids, Eshrefids, Inānjids, Jāndārids, Qaramānids, and others) slowly arose from its ruins. One *beylik* that began to develop in 1299 on the western frontier of the Anatolian Seljuk state was that of the Ottomans. With regard to its moral fiber and organization, this *beylik* acquired many values from Seljuk Turkishness. Moreover, it not only kept Anatolia as the Turkish motherland, but also succeeded in establishing one of the world's greatest empires.

5
The Reasons for the Rise of the Seljuk Empire

So far we have tried to present the main outline of Seljuk political history. We shall now focus on a number of points that were among the primary factors contributing to the outstanding success of the Seljuks in establishing a great political organization over the Near East; transforming Anatolia into a Turkish homeland, and thus giving a new direction to Turkish history; achieving a new orientation for the Islamic world within the framework of the Middle Ages; and, finally, acquiring an important place in world history by influencing the West.

The Settling of Khurāsān

When Seljuk decided to leave the country of the Oghuz with the groups that were loyal to him, he may have thought of going west, which was the traditional direction of previous Turkish migrations. Indeed, throughout the tenth century, it was to western countries that some of the Oghuz (Uzes), as well as the Pecheneg and Cuman Turks, had immigrated. But because of the serious obstacle presented by the dominion of the hostile Khazars in the west, Seljuk chose the southern direction that was open to him.[1] Moreover, Transoxiana, to which he turned, was not really foreign to the Turks. They constituted much of the population in the area stretching from the banks of the Jaxartes to the environs of Bukhārā. According to Maḥmūd Kāshgharī,[2] an important eleventh-century writer, this region had been composed of

1. Cf. Köymen, "Büyük Selçuklu," pp. 106 f.

2. *Dīwān,* III, 149 f.

Turkish countries but later, because of an increase in the Iranian population, became *ajem mülkü* {a Persian possession}. As we mentioned above, the existance of Turkish cities on the banks of the Jaxartes also confirms this report. For the Seljuk Turks, the Islam that they encountered in their new homeland was not a major obstacle. In fact, at the beginning of the tenth century, it was already known and accepted among the Itil (Volga) Bulgars who were north of the Oghuz.[3] Islam was no doubt not unknown among the Oghuz, who included the group later called the "Seljuks." Consequently, if one takes into consideration the environmental conditions and the religious views of the time, as well as the significance of the fact that all the leaders of the Seljuks later appeared as warriors for Islam, one must naturally assume that Seljuk established a homeland in the Jand region and converted to Islam with the forces in his company. Just when the Seljuks arrived on the scene, a very intense struggle for control of Transoxiana was taking place between the Sāmānids and Qarakhānids, the founders of the first Islamic Turkish state. Arslan Yabghu and the Seljuk groups, especially the Turkmen bound to him, took part in the battles on the side of the Sāmānids. Because the Seljuks assisted the rivals of the Qarakhānids, it is clear that they did not wish to come under the rule of the large and very powerful Qarakhānid state, even though they were descendants of the same family. Indeed, it was out of the question for the Seljuks to remain in Transoxiana in the face of the Qarakhānid pressure that led to the collapse of the Sāmānid state and was subsequently applied by the ruler of Samarqand. Accordingly, it was necessary to find a suitable place to settle by either going great distances (Chaghrı Beg's reconnaissance campaign) or establishing themselves in the region of nearby Khurāsān. Arslan Yabghu's Turkmen requested a homeland in Khurāsān from the Ghaznavid Sultan Maḥmūd, which reveals the importance of this area to the Seljuks. In fact, with respect to geographical conditions and climate, the vast territory of Khurāsān, which included such major settlements as Nīshāpūr, Sarakhs, Ṭūs, Marv, and Balkh, was a country that made a perfect place to live for the Turks, who followed a life of steppe-culture. Furthermore, the Turks who lived in the plains would complement the settled economy because the products they obtained from their great herds of sheep, cattle, and horses would meet the needs of the city and village and provide raw materials for local industry. Thus it would be possible for the Seljuk groups to satisfy their need for land and also improve their difficult livelihood. But the territory of Khurāsān was not only of great importance to the Turks, for the reasons that we have mentioned, but also had great significance as one of the major regions of medieval world commerce. With Baghdad as the focal point, the main trade

3. See Ibn Faḍlān, *al-Riḥla*, ed. A. Zeki Velidi Togan (Leipzig, 1939); K. Czeglédy, "Zur Meschheder Handschrift von Ibn Faḍlān's Reisebericht," *Acta Orientalia Hungarica* 1(1951):217–43.

routes stretched from Iraq and the Near East in general to Scandinavia and the West via the Volga on the one hand and to Central Asia and the Far East on the other. They thus passed through Khurāsān. Nīshāpūr, the leading city of Khurāsān, which was located at a junction of these various routes, served above all as one of the primary halting places where streams of caravan teams transporting the goods of the countries to the east, west, and south, spent the night. In addition to bringing lively commercial activity and economic affluence to this area, these roads were exceedingly convenient for dispatching troops. Khurāsān therefore had great strategic value.[4] Later, at the time of the Seljuks, this area nourished the greatest statesmen, administrators, and men of literature and science in the East and, for the reasons that we mentioned, became one of the scholarly centers of the Muslim world.[5] This region was the scene of the greatest rivalry between the Qarakhānids and the Sāmānids, who were later joined by the Ghaznavids. Its economic, military, and cultural importance made it the major object of the wars among these states.

In this regard one must naturally consider the efforts of the Seljuks to obtain the same goal, whatever the cost. Chaghrı Beg and Toghrıl Beg, who had to leave Khwārazm, which had more or less the same features but was of secondary appeal compared to Khurāsān, directly set about the business of founding a state in that region. There were various considerations that convinced the Seljuks to make this attempt even though their numbers were limited, as confirmed by the sources. In addition to the Turkmen of Arslan Yabghu, who had already been transferred to Khurāsān by Maḥmūd of Ghazna, there were other Turks in the region who had previously found its geographical and climatic conditions inviting. One indication that strongly supports the opinion that Turks from among the Seljuks had lived in eastern and northeastern Iran in earlier times is provided by al-Jāḥiẓ (d. 869), who reports that there was not a great distinction between the Turks and the people of Khurāsān in their way of life or in general. According to his testimony, the differences between the Turks and Khurāsānians was no more than those between an Arab from Medina and one from Mecca. And according to what al-Bīrūnī (d. 1051) states, the clearest point at which it was possible to draw a border between Iran and "Turan" was through Mashhad.[6] Thus the region of Khurāsān was the key element—economically, politically, and ethnically—that provided the Seljuks with the incentive and determination to found a state.

The Character and Structure of the Seljuk State

Despite the features described above, because the social and intellectual life of the settled areas of Khurāsān, namely, the cities and

4. See Bosworth, *The Ghaznavids: Their Empire in Afghanistan and Eastern Iran 994–1040* (Edinburgh, 1963), pp. 149 f.

5. Barthold-Köprülü, *İslâm medeniyeti tarihi* [The history of Islamic civilization] (Istanbul, 1940), pp. 82 f., 87.

6. Bosworth, *Ghaznavids,* pp. 205 ff.

towns, was dominated by eastern Islamic culture as represented by the ʿAbbāsid caliphate; and because this was an area where, at the same time, this culture had great potential for development, the concept of state and its legal meaning here were based on the ʿAbbāsid Islamic traditions that were of course also continued by the Ṭāhirids (821–73) and the Sāmānids. The Seljuk Turks, who brought with them the world view from the steppes, were able to establish a state in such a milieu by adapting to the new conditions required by Islamic and local practices. We have seen that the Seljuk commanders showed exceptional skill in this regard. Thus if we take into consideration the fact that these commanders, when they descended upon Khurāsān, already held a notion of sovereignty—because they were related to a family of *khān*s or *beg*s—and were neither adventurers nor upstarts, then the speed with which the Seljuk administrators, who had a tradition of founding states, adjusted to the new conditions should not be surprising. There are historical records which reveal that, even in the most difficult times, they did not lose their notion of sovereignty and that the goal of creating an independent state became their ultimate objective. In the famous meeting between the Qarakhānid ruler Yūsuf Qadır Khān and Maḥmūd of Ghazna in Transoxiana, the former referred in particular to this Seljuk mentality. After Arslan Yabghu was detained by Maḥmūd of Ghazna, he sent a message to the other Seljuk commanders, who had fallen into a very bewildering predicament, in which he reminded them that Sultan Maḥmūd was the son of a slave (*mavlā-zāda*); and, after declaring that a state should not be left to such men, wanted his *birāderler* {brothers} to continue the *taleb-i mülk* {search for sovereignty} and not give up hope.[7] Chaghrı Beg's campaign in eastern Anatolia was made with just this intention. The same subject was referred to in the letter that Toghrıl Beg sent to Caliph al-Qā'im in 435/1043 in which he made clear that he, as sultan, was superior to the Ghaznavid rulers and stated that "higher service should be rendered to him."[8] The concept of state among the Seljuks and the high value they placed on it can also be clearly seen in the talks held by Ibrāhīm Yınal, who came to Nīshāpūr in 1038 as Toghrıl Beg's ambassador and vanguard. According to Yınal the disturbances and disorder which had appeared there up to that time resulted from "inferior men," but now a state under the government of the "*ādil pādişāh*" {just ruler} Toghrıl Beg had been founded and no longer would anyone dare break the law or undermine public order.[9] Later, when Toghrıl Beg came to Nīshāpūr, he listened to the advice of the famous judge Ṣāʿid, whom he received with honor, and, because he did not know the local customs, asked the judge not to be sparing in his counsel. He also placed the management of state affairs in the hands of the commander

7. Rāvandī, *Rāḥat,* p. 91, Turkish trans., pp. 89 f.

8. Barhebraeus, *Tarihi,* I, 299.

9. Baihaqī, *Ta'rīkh,* pp. 551 f.; also Köymen, "Büyük Selçuklu," pp. 94–97.

of Būzjān, Abū 'l-Qāsim al-Kawbānī.[10] The fact that Abū 'l-Qāsim was Toghrıl Beg's first vizir[11] and the two who succeeded him up to the time of ʿAmīd al-Mulk were also Iranians[12] suffices to show how the Seljuk state acquired its character during its foundation and early development. Throughout its history in Khurāsān, the Seljuk Empire was administered as an Islamic state based on the *sharīʿa* {revealed law} and other Islamic principles and institutions. Indeed this was one of its dominant characteristics. However, because this state was rather far from the center of the caliphate, it was very different from the Iranian Muslim states like those of the Ṭāhirids, Ṣaffārids, and Sāmānids that had been created in the same area. As we have stated, the Seljuks, who had come from the steppes and had recently converted to Islam, were not really strangers to Khurāsān. It was natural that they would maintain the Turkish ideas of sovereignty that their ancestors had faithfully followed for centuries in the various states in this milieu and that they would continue their old ethnic traditions. As will be seen below, their usages and customs, concepts of justice and dominion, view of the position of the caliph, religious tolerance, and succession to the throne were apparent and were long evident as the dominant characteristics of the state. The Seljuk state was therefore a political entity born of a mixture of Turkish and Islamic thought, traditions, and institutions. Thanks to their traditional state-founding ability, the first Seljuk administrators knew how to reconcile these two separate elements—Turkish and Islamic—in a harmonious manner and placed the state on a very firm foundation. Consequently, all aspects of the new idea of state, concept of sovereignty, and world view that came into being in the medieval Islamic world with the Seljuk Empire later remained in effect in Muslim lands for centuries. In an environment where Turco-Islamic states had not been successful and were therefore supplanted without having had a great impact on history—for example, the Qarakhānids, because they maintained the old Turkish ideas and traditions too firmly; the Ghaznavids, because they were established on the eastern frontier of the Islamic lands and even more so because they were oriented toward India; and the Khwārazm-Shāhs, even though they came after the Seljuks, because they were not able to create a firm bond between the ruling group and the local subjects—the Seljuk Empire, the foundation of which was centered on Khurāsān and the most prominant feature of which was to weld together Turkish and Islamic elements, was founded in the middle of the Muslim world, had a policy which was directed within this world, delt with its material and moral problems, and bound the people to the state with a just government. These achievements appear to be the essential factors in the great political success of the Seljuk state and the high level of

10. Baihaqī, *Ta'rīkh*, pp. 553 f.; Köymen, "Büyük Selçuklu," pp. 96 ff.

11. Rāvandī, *Rāḥat*, p. 98, Turkish trans., p. 96; Ibn al-Athīr, *al-Kāmil*, year 436.

12. See H. Bowen, "Notes on some early Seljuqid viziers," *BSOAS* 20(1957):105–10.

socio-intellectual development that it reached. Furthermore, with regard to its structure, the Seljuk state was not centralized like the old Sasānid or ʿAbbāsid empires. Although the government arose by subordinating the powers of the *malik*s, who were members of the Seljuk family, Turkmen *beg*s, heads of local dynasties, and tributary rulers directly to the person of the great sultan, it was never unified under the direct authority of the great council of state {*dīwān*} in the capital even when the empire was at the height of its power. This government constituted a continuation of the old Turkish state tradition born of the nature of steppe culture (e.g., the empires of the Asian Huns, European Huns, Gök-Turks) and was in accord with the old Turkish concept of sovereignty and idea of world dominion. For this reason, the usual claim that the Seljuk Empire could not escape from its tribal identity and could not establish a centralized administrative system—a claim like that based on the mistaken but common approach of analyzing the empire from the point of view of a settled state merely because it was founded in Iranian territory, but unsuitable to the Turkish state system—indicates that the Turkish reality of the empire has escaped notice. Although the local vizirs, led by Niẓām al-Mulk, made various attempts to mold this state in the Sasānid and ʿAbbāsid fashion, the Seljuk sultans and Turkish administrators had very little sympathy for such efforts to limit the Turkish idea of worldwide sovereignty. Toghrıl Beg's pursuit of certain Turkmen units (e.g., by Ibrāhīm Yınal) had nothing to do with the idea of centralization but resulted from the concern for ensuring public order and preventing harm by forcing them to submit. The lack of centralization, which prevailed in all Turco-Islamic states throughout the Middle Ages, took a different direction however at the time of the Ottoman Empire, thanks to the radical changes of Fatih Sultan Mehmed.[13]

13. Cf. Halil İnalcık, "Osmanlı hukukuna giriş" [An introduction to Ottoman law], *AÜSBF Dergisi* 13(1958):102–07.

Ethnic Characteristics

In the Seljuk Empire, most of the population was composed of non-Turkish peoples like Persians and Arabs. The traditions of state, customs, and practices peculiar to the Turks—and above all Turkish, the mother tongue that the Turkish masses very jealously maintained—assured that the Turks would always retain their identity as an ethnic element within the empire, and formed an obstacle to any forces that would undermine the prominence of the ruling group of this empire, founded and developed as it was in the Islamic world, by insulating them from government positions that degenerated in foreign environments and cultures. Consequently, these characteristics helped the Turkish consciousness to be forever alert with regard to keeping control

control of and advancing the state. This consciousness thrived at the very top, in the Seljuk dynasty, the family of the ruler. In this Turkish state, as appears to be generally the case in other empires ruling various countries, the domestic administration was run by local bureaucrats. Although it was necessary to use Persian and Arabic in correspondence between the government and its subjects in order to govern the state, Turkish was the language spoken by the rulers and their families in the palace. It was also the language spoken everywhere by the Turkish population and the Turkish military forces, which had spread throughout the empire and were in great number. Although the Turks had previously had their own writings and had developed a literary language, because of the influence of Islam Turkish did not become as common as Arabic, which was widespread at that time because it was the language of the Qur'ān, and Persian, which mainly developed under the patronge of the Turkish sultans. But because Turkish arose from the very nature of the empire, it of course had to be accepted. Moreover, this situation did not hamper the historical function of Turkish, which consisted of maintaining the Turkish element of the ruling group, as we just mentioned, and drawing it together. Seljuk Turkishness did not suffer the consequences of, for example, the Tabgach in China and the Hungarians and Danube Bulgars in the Christian environment who forgot their original languages. On the contrary, thanks primarily to the great masses of Turkmen who were driven to the western border of the Seljuk Empire, Turkish gradually became the only major spoken and literary language in Anatolia (see below).

There are also documents showing the importance of Turkish at the time of the Great Seljuk Empire. One of them was the *Dīwān Lughāt al-Turk,* written in 1074 in Baghdad by the Turkish lexicographer Maḥmūd Kāshgharī.[14] The author records that he wrote this book to meet the needs of non-Turks who wanted to learn Turkish. Kāshgharī heard and seized upon the tradition of the Prophet (*ḥadīth*) transmitted by the two scholars Bukhārī and Nīshāpūrī, who both specialized in this subject, which stated in effect "learn the language of the Turks for they have had a long rule." This *ḥadīth* reveals a noteworthy view of that period.[15] Kāshgharī says that Turkish speech had reached "the age of maturity."[16] The superiority he felt as a Turk while writing this was part of the prevailing spirit of Turkish society at that time and can also be easily seen in the remarks of statesmen like the foreigner Ibn Ḥassūl and poets like al-Thaʿālibī and al-Ghazzī.

Furthermore, many old Turkish traditions, customs, and usages continued among the Seljuks. For example, just as the tale of the dog-like animal that led the Turks who came to Anatolia was based on the Oghuz and Gök-Turk gray-wolf legend, which was current among the

14. See Köprülü, *Türk dili ve edebiyatı hakkında araştırmalar* [Research on Turkish language and literature] (Istanbul, 1934), pp. 33–44; Kafesoğlu, *Melikşah,* p. 188.

15. *Dīwān,* I, 4.

16. Ibid., I, 363.

Turkmen,[17] the *tughra* {monogram} of the sultan found on official Seljuk documents; and the bow and arrow, which were used as a common symbol of sovereignty by the Seljuk dynastic family,[18] depicted on coins,[19] and pictured on the *chetr* {tent, umbrella}, which was also a symbol of sovereignty,[20] had a long history revealing the continuity of a venerable tradition that went back to the Gök-Turks, and even the Tabgach Turks, and was reflected in the epic of Oghuz Khān. Moreover, on the request of Toghrıl Beg, who liked to play with a bow and two arrows that were always in his hands,[21] signs of the bow and arrow were carved symbolically on the *miḥrāb* {niche indicating the direction of Mecca} of the mosque that the emperor had repaired in the Byzantine capital.[22] Although it appears that these signs were used above all during the imperial period of the Seljuks, there are also references to their existence as symbols of allegiance and sovereignty among the Anatolian Seljuks.[23] The institution of the *atabeglik,* which occupied an important place in the organization of the Seljuk Empire, also came from an old Turkish tradition (see below). According to the testimony of the Orkhon inscriptions,[24] showing respect to women and giving them a place in society and a role in state affairs on equal footing with men were practices whose roots were deep in the ancient Turkish lands. These were among the social innovations brought to the eastern Islamic world by the Seljuks. Among the early Turks, a woman could have the status of a queen or empress. The sources tell us that the wife of Toghrıl Beg had influence over this great Seljuk sultan and in matters of state.[25] The wife of Malik-Shāh, the famous Terken Khātūn,[26] held the second position in the empire after the sultan because of her immense prestige. She even had a separate *dīwān* where the vizir was Tāj al-Mulk Abū 'l-Ghanā'im, a rival of Niẓām al-Mulk, the vizir of the empire. Eventually, in her lust for power, this woman, to whom many political matters were referred, joined those who plotted the death of Malik-Shāh.[27] Despite the negative recommendations of Niẓām al-Mulk, who did not approve of women having such influence and power in state and social life,[28] women had a say in Turkish palaces and Turkish women were also seen in society. Moreover, Turkmen women in particular went on campaign with the men and joined them in battle.[29]

In the army, the creation of a massive cavalry class, the division into right and left wings, and steppe battle tactics ("*Turan taktiği*"),[30] which were seen in the major battles (Dandānqān, Malazgird, Chaghrı Beg's Caucasus campaign), were all traditions of early Turkish steppe culture which were alive at the time of the Seljuks. With some differences, but basically unchanged, they also appeared in the Ottoman period. Other early Turkish customs and usages which continued among the Seljuks were *yogh,*[31] marrying the wife of one's dead brother or a

17. Michael the Syrian, Fr. trans. J.-B. Chabot, *Chronique de Michel le Syrien* (Paris, 1905), III, 153, 155.

18. Rāvandī, *Rāḥat,* p. 98; Barhebraeus, *Tarihi,* I, 298.

19. Ahmed Tevhîd, *Meskûkât-i kadîme-i islâmiye kataloğu* [Catalogue of old islamic coins] (Istanbul, 1321), pt. 4, pp. 58 ff.; *Monnaies antiques et orientales* (private collections) (Amsterdam, 1913), nos. 1054–57; G. C. Miles, *The Numismatic History of Rayy,* ANSNS, vol. 2 (New York, 1938), nos. 239–44; D. Sourdel, *Inventaire des monnaies musulmanes anciennes du Musée de Caboul* (Damascus, 1953), pp. 85 ff.

20. See Turan, "Eski Türklerde okun," p. 315.

21. Barhebraeus, *Tarihi,* I, 298.

22. Ibn al-Athīr, *al-Kāmil,* year 455.

23. Turan, "Eski Türklerde okun," p. 315.

24. H. N. Orhun, *Eski Türk yazıtları* [Ancient Turkish inscriptions] (Istanbul: TDK, 1936–41), I, 34, 44, 50, 110.

25. Barhebraeus, *Tarihi,* I, 315.

26. See Turan, "Türkān değil, Terken" [Not *Türkān* but *Terken*], *Türk Hukuk Tarihi Dergisi* [The journal of the history of Turkish law], 1(1944):67–73.

27. See Kafesoğlu, *Melikşah,* pp. 52 f., 96 f., 121, 149, 182, 201 ff., 205–10.

28. See *Siyāsat-Nāma,* chap. 43.

29. See, e.g., Sibṭ, from the text in Ibn al-Qalānisī, *Dhail,* p. 109.

30. See J. Darkó, *Turáni hatások a görög-Római hadügy fejlödésében, Hadtörténelmi közlemények* (Budapest, 1934), XXXV, 3–40, and his "Influences touraniennes sur l'évolution de l'art militaire des Grecs, des Romains et des Byzantins," *Byzantion* 10(1935):443–63.

young widowed stepmother,[32] and the strangling of members of a noble family with a bowstring in order not to shed their blood.[33] In addition, the sultans would give regular banquets (*toy, şölen*) for the prominent men of the state and for the public. At the end of these banquets, there would be a rush for the eating utensils—plates, spoons, and the like (in Persian *khvān-i yaghmā*).[34] This too was related to the early Turkish view of sovereignty. As stated in the Orkhon inscriptions, the Turkish ruler was obliged to feed his people.[35] There were certain places to sit for those who came to the feasts and certain things for them to eat. This was arranged according to protocol,[36] for these banquets, being of an official nature, reflected inferior and superior relationships. Every morning Toghrıl Beg opened his table to the public and gave feasts in the field.[37] During his campaign in Transoxiana in 482/1090, Malik-Shāh did not give a feast for the Chighilids, who lived in that area. This Turkish subtribe therefore claimed they were insulted and complained.[38] Niẓām al-Mulk says in his famous work, the *Siyāsat-Nāma,* that one of the obligations of being a ruler was to have a table prepared for one's subjects. He further stated that there was no objection if high officials and notables known for their loyalty to the sultan did not participate in his meal,[39] but other people, such as tribal leaders, who did not accept an invitation should be considered to have repudiated their allegiance. The banner (*tugh,* horsetail);[40] large hunting drives, which were essentially military exercises; the ball (*kurra, gûy*) and stick (*çöğen*) game;[41] Turkish dancing and the like, in which Toghrıl Beg participated in Baghdad at his last wedding while Turkish songs were sung[42] and which, according to Barthold,[43] passed, along with military costume, to the Russians; and all other Turkish elements and customary laws that were followed according to certain rules and regulations,[44] all came to the Seljuk Empire from Central Asia. These things were to last for centuries in the Turco-Islamic world.[45]

The Concept of Sovereignty

In the case of the former Iranian emperor or the Muslim caliph, who was the representative of the Prophet, who in turn was the spokesman of God, sovereignty signified unconditional authority. In contrast to this meaning of the concept, there existed in the Turkish state a certain implied contract between the ruler and his subjects. In return for the obedient and loyal devotion of the people under his authority, the ruler was customarily obligated to nourish, cloth, and enrich them.[46] An important source in this regard is the *Kutadgu Bilig*.[47] This work states that in order for one to become a *beg* (ruler), he must provide a service. This created the best relationship between the Turkish ruler and his

31. Kāshgharī, *Dīwān,* III, 143; Orhun, *Yazıtları,* I, 70; 'Imād al-Dīn, *Zubdat,* p. 24.

32. E.g., Toghrıl Beg's marriage to the widow of Chaghrı Beg. For this reason Chaghrı Beg's son, Sulaimān, who was born by her, became Toghrıl Beg's heir apparent. See Ibn al-Athīr, *al-Kāmil,* year 455; on Qāvurt Beg's marriage to the widow of Alp-Arslan, see Barhebraeus, *Tarihi,* I, 325 et passim.

33. Köprülü, "Türk ve Moğol sülâlelerinde hânedan âzasinin idâmında kan dökme memnûiyeti" [The prohibition among Turkish and Mongol families against shedding the blood of members of a royal dynasty who were to be executed], *Türk Hukuk Tarihi Dergisi* 1(1944):1–9.

34. See Kafesoğlu, *Melikşah,* pp. 137 f.

35. Orhun, *Yazıtları,* I, 26, 42, 66, 102.

36. See Abdülkadir İnan, "'Orun' ve 'ülüş' meselesi" [The question of 'place' and 'gift' {in tribal protocol}], *THIT Mecmuası* 1(1931):121–33.

37. Niẓām al-Mulk, *Siyāsat-Nāma,* Paris ed., chap. 35, Tehran ed., chap. 36.

38. Ibn al-Athīr, *al-Kāmil,* year 482.

39. *Siyāsat-Nāma,* Paris ed., chap. 35; see also Kafesoğlu, "Selçuklu vezîri Niẓām al-Mulk'un eseri Siyâsetnâme ve türkçe tercümesi" [The Seljuk vizir Niẓām al-Mulk's work the *Siyāsat-Nāma* and its Turkish translation], *TM* 12(1955):250.

40. Kāshgharī, *Dīwān,* III, 127.

41. Niẓām al-Mulk, *Siyāsat-Nāma,* chap. 17.

42. Barhebraeus, *Tarihi,* I, 315.

43. *Dersler,* p. 97.

44. R. Giraud, *L'Empire des Turcs céleste* (Paris, 1960), p. 71.

45. For more on Turkish legal traditions, see Köprülü, "Ortazaman Türk hukukî müesseseleri. İslâm âmme hukukunda ayrı bir Türk âmme hukuku yok mudur?" [Medieval Turkish legal problems. Was there not a separate Turkish public law within Islamic public law?], *Ikinci Türk tarih kongresi zabıtları* [Communications of the Second Congress of Turkish History] (Istanbul, 1943), pp. 387–96, 411 {cf. *Belleten* 2(1938):39–72}.

46. See Orhun, *Yazıtları,* IV, index.

47. By Yūsuf Khāṣṣ Ḥājib. Turkish trans. G. R. Rahmeti Arat (Ankara: TTK, 1959), p. 550.

subjects. Although the *Kutadgu Bilig* was written in the country of the Qarakhānids, it generally reflected the Turkish world view and, given the time when it was composed (462/1069–70), would doubtless have incorporated the prevailing ideas of the Seljuks. The *Kutadgu Bilig* was also representative of the ruler's "law" and showed that benevolence and correct behavior were the foundation of *beg*ship.[48] In short, according to this important work, benevolence meant to feed and nourish others while correct behavior meant the application of justice. Furthermore, the declaration in a book having such a political philosophy that "the best *beg*s in the world are Turkish *beg*s"[49] has special significance, for it is possible to find proof of this among the Seljuks. In the Islamic world before the coming of the Seljuks, each state sided against the other: we have, for example, the Sāmānids in Transoxiana and part of Khurāsān, the Ṣaffārids in Sīstān, the Shabānkārids in Fārs, the Simjūrids in the rest of Khurāsān and around Gurgān, the Bāvandids in Māzandarān, the Bāduspānids in Rustamdār, the ʿAlawīs in Ṭabaristān, the Ziyārids in Gurgān, the Ḥasanveyhids in Nihāvand, the Kākūyids in Iṣfahān and Hamadān, the Shīrvān-Shāhs in Shīrvān, the Shaddādids in Arrān, the Hāshimids in Darband, the Ḥamdānids in northern Syria, the ʿUqailids in Mosul, the Marwānids in Diyārbakr and Mayyāfāriqīn, the Mirdāsids in Aleppo, the Mazyādids in Ḥilla and the Būyids in Baghdad itself and ʿIrāq al-ʿArab. Because of the political division and confusion in the Near East created by some twenty local rulers and above all resulting from the havoc wrought by this political disorder, the cities and towns became fortified places. They suffered from such hardships as lack of public order, the cutting of the highways and breakdown in communications, and an absence of security for life and property. Because of the disorder, villagers and townsmen could not lead normal lives and everyone was forced to look after himself. In addition to all this, the people contended with each other over various religious creeds and heretical doctrines.[50] In contrast to this, the foundation of the Seljuk state and expansion of the empire present a picture of political unity, an end to religious discord, popular affluence, economic progress, public order, and tranquility. This clearly conforms to the description of the "Turkish ruler" in the *Kutadgu Bilig*. By bringing peace and security to the inhabitants of the empire, "the ruler was at the service of his subjects." In this way, the Seljuk administrators truly presented the Turkish idea of the state to the Islamic world, and for this reason most of the sultans were called "*al-Sulṭān al-ʿĀdil*" {"the Just Sultan"} while they themselves were described as merciful, congenial, and kind. At the same time, these administrators affirmed the former state structure, being content to bind the local rulers in this domain, whom we have listed above, to the authority of

48. Ibid., pp. 36, 68 ff., 112 f., 126.

49. Ibid., p. 31.

50. See M. Şemseddin Günaltay, "Selçukluların Horasan'a indikleri zaman İslâm dünyasının siyasal, sosyal, ekonomik ve dinî durumu" [Political, social, economic, and religious conditions in the Islamic world at the time of the Seljuk invasion of Khurāsān], *Belleten* 7(1943):59–99.

the Seljuk state. They left those who offered allegiance in their positions and did not interfere in their internal affairs but dealt severely with those who would not. Their goal was not to oppress and exploit the people but simply to maintain justice and "the law." Thus the new state, which was administered under the guidance of the Seljuk sultan, secured the loyalty of the masses without interfering in their personal occupations, religions, customs, and usages. The peoples who held various faiths and doctines and spoke various languages were thus left in complete freedom and safety in their daily lives. As for certain military actions that took place within the empire, it is known that they did not result from social or economic causes but from political ambitions; and the vast majority of the people were far from interested in such matters (on the uprising of the Bābā'īs in Anatolia, which was partially social and religious, see below).

The Change in the Concept of Public Law

The Turks were known as state founders, that is, for their habit of establishing public laws, from the moment they appeared on the scene of history. In their early periods, especially at the time of the Gök-Turks, Uighurs, and Khazars, they followed the principle of separating religious from worldly affairs. This was a new kind of legal doctrine of state that appeared in the Islamic world with the Seljuks and must be considered one of the primary factors that assured the rise of the empire. When the Seljuks came to the area of Iran, that region was already composed of a number of independent Islamic states. The Muslim Turkish states there, like those of the Qarakhānids and Ghaznavids, usually preserved Turkish customs and followed Turkish traditions. However, these entities, whose rulers were described as "Muslim commanders subject to the caliph,"[51] always zealously recognized the high authority of the caliph, carried out all activities within the framework of religious prescriptions, and, as far as possible, conducted their affairs according to the *sharīʿa*. These states, which developed on the far frontiers of the Muslim world, moreover, did not have an intellectual principle connected with the concept of secularism. The Seljuk state, however, was founded in the center of the eastern part of the Islamic world and included Baghdad, the center of the ʿAbbāsid caliphate, within its area of authority. The Seljuks regarded the seat of the caliphate as a province of the Turkish Empire and the second largest city after the capital. The sultans considered the caliph, whom they always respected, to be an honored fellow countryman. This idea of secularism, which was first pointed out

51. Barthold, *Dersler*, p. 95.

by Barthold,[52] was put into practice when Toghrıl Beg entered Baghdad in 1055 and was content simply to increase Caliph al-Qā'im's annual allowance of funds and provisions while keeping worldly affairs to himself. (It should be mentioned that, at the time of the Būyids, the caliph was also essentially kept from worldly affairs. However, this was not related to the principle of secularism. Rather, it was done by an oppressive Shīʿī government to prevent Sunnī laws from being carried out.) Later, the caliphs gained their income and livelihood from the lands that the Seljuk sultans granted to the caliphate as *iqṭāʿ*s.[53] This state of affairs brought about an important change in the Islamic state with respect to public law. Accordingly, the sultan and caliph each came to have a separate but equal area of authority, one worldly and the other religious. Furthermore, the Seljuk ruler was not just "a Muslim commander subject to the caliph," but the real possessor of power and the only person responsible for worldly affairs. This was so to the extent that sometimes the caliph had to be recognized by the sultan himself. Consequently, while the civil law of the empire was carried out according to the canonical decisions of the Sunnī *qāḍī*s, the great Sultan Malik-Shāh was able to call together a committee of great legal experts and issue laws confirming new provisions concerning civil law.[54] For example, he was able to give Sulaimān-Shāh a patent of sovereignty over Anatolia while the caliph only participated in the confirmation of his authority with regard to its Islamic bases. At the time of Sultan Sanjar, when the laws of Malik-Shāh were in force, the situation was still no different.[55] Under these conditions, which began with Toghrıl Beg, worldly affairs were entrusted to *shiḥna*s and *ʿamīd*s {high administrative official}, dispatched from the seat of the sultanate, that is, the military and civil administration of Baghdad, while the duties and authority of the caliph were simply restricted to solving Islamic legal problems and performing heretofore customary ceremonies like receiving visitors, confirming governments, and giving robes of honor and numerous titles to the sultan and tributary rulers. This highest representative of the Muslim faith was thus cut off from worldly affairs.[56] On the one hand, secularism prepared the ground for the free development of science, thought, and literature, which made it possible for the Seljuk period, especially at the time of the empire, to enjoy a brilliant age; and, on the other, it lightened the obligations to which the non-Muslim elements (*dhimmīs*) in the state were subjected by Islamic legal prescriptions, and this assured winning their confidence. Religious tolerance, which derived from the principle of secularism, helped in great measure to

52. See ibid., pp. 95, 98.

53. Ibn al-Jawzī, *al-Muntaẓam,* VIII, 284; Sibṭ, *Mir'āt,* XII, 14b.

54. For a six-part section from *al-Rasā'il al-malikshāhiyya,* see Muḥammad Ibn al-Niẓām al-Ḥusainī, *al-'Urāḍa fī 'l-ḥikāyat al-saljūqiyya,* ed. K. Süssheim (Egypt, 1326 {Leyden, 1909}), pp. 69 ff.; *MTM* 2(1331):249 ff.; Köprülü, "Ortazaman Türk hukukî muesseseleri," p. 410.

55. See Köymen, *Büyük Selçuklu II,* pp. 60, 74 f., 88, 286 f., 300–03.

56. See Kafesoğlu, *Melikşah,* pp. 153 f.

provide peace and security in those lands within the borders of the vast empire where the majority of the population were Christians (Georgians, Armenians, Assyrians, etc.) and also helped obtain the loyalty of the numerous subjects of various religions to the state. For this reason it is not very difficult to explain why the death of a Malik-Shāh or Qılıch-Arslan, for example, aroused profound anxiety among the non-Muslim masses. It is known that those caliphs who wished to reestablish their former worldly power by taking advantage of the weakness of the state during the fratricidal struggles which led to the dismemberment of the empire played a negative role in the collapse of the Seljuk state of Iraq. Al-Nāṣir, in particular, was instrumental in the collapse of the state of the Khwārazm-Shāhs and the subjection of Islamic countries to the Mongol invasion and slavery. Despite all this, the principle of secularism that the Seljuks brought to the Muslim world, namely, the idea that above all else the state authority was obliged to protect the public welfare and maintain its vitality, was in contrast to the theories—which were limited and often without practical value—that did not recognize the possibility of freedom of action in a state placed under the influence of Islamic religious law. Henceforth the caliphs in Baghdad and Cairo were kept from interfering in worldly affairs and eventually, in the sixteenth century, this matter was really closed when the Ottoman ruler Yavuz Selim took upon himself the duties and authority of the caliph.

The Concept of Universal Dominion

The goal of universal dominion meant uniting the world under the authority of a single ruler. This concept formed the philosophical basis for the early Turkish conquests[57] and was alive among the various Turkish societies in the eleventh century.[58] It was a basic concept that also had to be applied in the milieu of the Seljuk sultans whose unquestioned membership in Turkish society and adherence to the Turkish tradition of dominion we have mentioned. Nobility, which was necessary for universal dominion, and the idea that sovereignty was granted by God, which formed the basis of this nobility,[59] were inherent within the Seljuk family (see below). Maḥmūd Kāshgharī, who reflected the attitude of that time, says "God made the sun rise from the zodiac of the Turks; made the states, which resemble the spheres in the heavens, revolve within the circle of their authority; and made the Turks the masters over the face of the earth."[60] He also cited a *ḥadīth* the essence of which stated; "I {God} have an army. I have given it the name

57. Cf. Anonymous, *Oğuz Kağan destanı* [The epic of Oghuz Kaghan], ed. and trans. W. Bang and G. R. Rahmeti Arat (Istanbul, 1936), pp. 17, 31; Orhun, *Yazıtları*, I, 29; Szász Béla, citing Priskos, *A Húnok története, Attila nagykiraly* (Budapest, 1943), pp. 238 f.

58. See Yūsuf, *Kutadgu Bilig*, p. 31.

59. Ibid., pp. 147 f.; Orhun, *Yazıtları*, I, 34 f., 41, 43, 56, 58, 64; M. Weber, *Wirtschaft und Gesellschaft* (Tübingen, 1925), pp. 124, 140; L. Ferenc, "A Kagan és családja," *KCA* III, 9–12; J. Deér, *Magyar Müvelödés története* (Budapest, 1940), pp. 30–50.

60. *Dīwān*, I, 3; Köprülü, *Türk dili*, p. 36.

Turk. When I am angry with a nation, I send the Turks upon it."[61] Although this *ḥadīth* was spurious, it was still important for expressing the dominant view of the age. Kāshgharī thus records and confirms the idea that the Seljuk rulers and the Turkish nation were appointed by God to govern the world. In this light, Toghrıl Beg's girding himself with the sword as "the ruler of the East and West" in the caliphal palace in Baghdad, and Malik-Shāh's being girded with two swords by the caliph as "the ruler of the East and West" on his first visit to the seat of the caliphate in 1087,[62] acquire a clearer meaning. Indeed, on his last visit to Baghdad, Malik-Shāh held a war council, in which the leading commanders participated, and planned to capture Egypt[63] and the lands of North Africa.[64] He thus sought to establish world dominion. According to Sanjar, who declared that his *cihandārlık* {universal sovereignty} was passed down from his father, God had allotted certain ranks and had entrusted him with a *cihan pādişāhlığı* {universal empire} by placing the world under his authority.[65] The concept of universal dominion was an ideal throughout history for all great Turkish rulers, including the Ottoman sultans (for example Yavuz Selim). When it is placed in perspective with the idea of sovereignty and the principle of religious tolerance that we have described above, it can well be appreciated that it was not without practical effect. In the event, the necessary conditions for bringing about the realization of such a concept existed in the Seljuk Empire and were particularly manifest in Seljuk diplomacy.

61. *Dīwān,* I, 351.

62. ʿImād al-Dīn, *Zubdat,* pp. 81 f.

63. Ibn al-Qalānisī, *Dhail,* p. 121.

64. Ṣadr al-Dīn, *Akhbār,* p. 65.

65. See Köymen, *Büyük Selçuklu II,* pp. 219, 222.

The Nature of Seljuk Diplomacy

From the very moment they entered Khurāsān, the Seljuk administrators were not slow to understand which directions to follow in order to establish a state in Iranian territory. First of all, as we tried to explain above, they had to put an end to political divisions by eliminating the small local governments whose existence left the entire country in turmoil. And this was done. But in addition to this action, which was not anything out of the ordinary since it arose from the need to establish political unity where virtually every petty state was sovereign, Seljuk diplomacy pursued two basic objectives which were unique unto themselves. Up to now we have considered these diplomatic objectives to be of equal importance with regard to the speedy development and rise of the empire. One of them was to struggle against Shīʿism and the other was to control the Turkmen nomads. It is first necessary to state that being anti-Shīʿī did not mean taking a position in conflict with the idea of secularism in the Seljuk state, for the Shīʿī movement, although religious and partially social, acquired a political orientation from its very beginning. In the eleventh century the Egyptian Fāṭimids gave Shīʿism the administrative and financial support of their empire and used it as their most powerful weapon in an attempt to destroy the Sunnī Muslim countries by provoking rebellions. Even long before the Seljuks, the Shīʿī Būyids (932–1055), who founded a state in Iraq and southern Iran, brought Baghdad under their control and subjected the ʿAbbāsid caliphs to their oppression, dismissing and appointing them as they wished. This situation left the inhabitants of the eastern Muslim world, the great majority of whom were Sunnīs, in a state of unease. Indeed, the enormous mass of Muslims, who were loyal to the ʿAbbāsid caliphs, were gravely afflicted by this. Moreover, profiting from the power Shīʿism had gained, its proponents intensified their efforts to spread it in the same countries. This greatly increased the anxiety that already existed in Sunnī circles, for it was impossible for them to reconcile their dogma with that of the Shīʿīs. As we saw at the beginning, Arslan al-Basāsīrī, the famous commander of the Būyids, was a zealous Shīʿī who cooperated with the Fāṭimids. Furthermore, a great many *rāfiḍīs* were active under various names almost everywhere in Iran. According to ʿAbd al-Qāhir al-Baghdādī (d. 1037), who wrote in the second quarter of the eleventh century, there were more than seventy such sects.[66] Consequently, when the Seljuk leaders, each of whom was a sincere Sunnī and was enthusiastic about the religion he had recently embraced, came to Khurāsān, the ʿAbbāsid caliphs greeted this with pleasure and sought means quietly to make contact with them. According to the sources, in the year that Toghrıl Beg first entered Nīshāpūr (1038), before the Seljuk battle for independence, the ambassador from al-Qā'im to the Seljuks carried out the task of warning them not to be destructive. However, at a time when destructive activities in fact continued throughout the realm, the purpose of the caliph's haste in sending him is clear. Because of the great respect that Chaghrı Beg and Toghrıl Beg showed the ambassador as the representative of the caliph, it is certain that al-Qā'im was pleased. As the Seljuk conquests advanced and the power of the new state became manifest throughout the territory of Iran, the Būyids were extremely concerned and increased their oppression. Al-Qā'im therefore did not hesitate to invite the Seljuk sultan to Baghdad. After Toghrıl Beg entered the city at the head of his army, erased the Shīʿī Būyids from history and inflicted major defeats on Arslan al-Basāsīrī, which resulted in his death, he forced the Fāṭimids to

66. See Günaltay, "Selçukluların," p. 79.

fall back to the Syrian border and considered eliminating them entirely.[67] By forcing the Fāṭimids to withdraw from the eastern Islamic world, Toghrıl Beg brought about a complete victory for Sunnism. Thus, except for North Africa, the Seljuks created Islamic unity in all those countries where they rallied the inhabitants to Sunnism and so rejuvinated the Muslim world. After Toghrıl Beg, during the time of the empire, this Seljuk policy was strictly enforced. It was said of Alp-Arslan that he brought peace and prosperity to the Islamic countries, which he defended with the sword, by extinguishing the flame of Shīʿī propaganda, which had created such strife and drowned Muslim society in a sea of discord. For example, on the one hand, he put an end to the Fāṭimid call to prayer and *khuṭba* in Mecca—having the latter read in his own name and that of al-Qā'im (461/1069)[68]—and, on the other, laid the foundation for the overthrow of the Fāṭimids by strengthening science and thought in the Sunnī world by means of the Niẓāmiyya *madrasas* {law schools} (see below) that he established in Baghdad and other important centers. Indeed, on the eve of the great battle of Malazgird, he was before Aleppo on his way to Egypt. Malik-Shāh also ordered the Turkmen forces in Syria to continue to move forward. In this case they were thrown into a fierce struggle against Ḥasan al-Ṣabbāḥ, who tried to undermine the Seljuk Empire by resorting to terroristic underground activity based on the *bāṭinism* that he had spread with the creed of *davet-i jedīde* {the new call}, which was also connected with Fāṭimid propaganda, in Qazvīn, Gurgān, Kūhistān, and its environs.[69] Malik-Shāh had the *khuṭba* read in his own name and that of the ʿAbbāsid caliph in both Mecca and Medina (468/1076)[70] and, as we saw in the previous section, had planned shortly before his death to annex Egypt to the empire. This Seljuk policy aiming at the total destruction of *bāṭinism,* which was composed of a network of Shīʿī and Shīʿī-related assassins, was of as vital importance to the Islamic world as it was to the Seljuk Empire. With regard to its conception, organization, and political objective, this policy was followed and brought to fruition by the Ayyūbids, who represented a continuation of the Seljuks. It was Ṣalāḥ al-Dīn al-Ayyūbī who overthrew the Fāṭimid state (1171), which had shown absolutely no interest in the Muslims who were defending their homeland from the invading Crusaders, and founded a Sunnī state in its place.

The Turkmen Migrations and Their Consequences

We have stated that the second major thrust of Seljuk diplomacy

67. Ibn al-Athīr, *al-Kāmil,* year 447; Barhebraeus, *Tarihi,* I, 306.

68. Ibn al-Athīr, *al-Kāmil,* year 462.

69. Juvainī, *Ta'rīkh,* III, 190 f., 194, 196–99, 201 ff.; Qazvīnī, *Guzīda,* I, 514, 517 ff.; Ibn Isfandiyār, *Ta'rīkh,* p. 240; anonymous, *Sīstān,* p. 386; Kafesoğlu, *Melikşah,* pp. 128–35.

70. Sibṭ, *Mir'āt,* XII, fol. 28a.

was to control the Turkmen nomads. Since *Turkmen* was another name for the Oghuz, Seljuk and his sons, the state founders Chaghrı Beg and Toghrıl Beg, Qutalmısh and Ibrāhīm Yınal, were all in fact Turkmen *beg*s. However, as indicated by the Iranian vizirs, who headed the civil administration in a Muslim milieu where the state borders expanded with increasing conquests, the Seljuk Empire's administrative, financial, and military organization acquired an Islamic character. When it began to develop beyond the Oghuz state into a Muslim Turkish Empire, the Seljuk sultans became "sultans of Islam," relying on many different elements rather than just on Turkish commanders. They therefore had to relegate the Oghuz, who had until then constituted their sole source of support, to a position of secondary importance. This was to the extent that when the forces charged with serving the sultan in the capital of the empire were selected from the various subject peoples, the lack of any group of Turkmen attracted the attention of Vizir Niẓām al-Mulk. Taking into consideration their great services at the beginning and their relationship to the ruling dynasty, he felt it necessary to recommend that 5,000–10,000 Turkmen be brought into the palace service, despite the difficulties they had caused the state.[71] From the victory at Dandānqān until the empire reached its greatest extent, it was essentially the Turkmen who had the largest part in the establishment of the Great Seljuk Empire and the fame that it won. They did so by conquering, with endless self-sacrifice, Iran, Kirmān, Oman, Sīstān, ʿIrāq al-ʿAjam, ʿIrāq al-ʿArab, Āzarbāījān, eastern Anatolia, al-Jazīra, Bahrain, the Ḥijāz, Yemen, Syria, and finally central and western Anatolia under the direction of the *beg*s and chiefs whose names we have listed above. The "difficulty that the Turkmen caused the state" arose from the fact that they searched for a homeland and summer and winter pastures for themselves in this state that belonged to their kinsmen, and they continuously immigrated to it en masse from Central Asia, from the steppes of the Oghuz which were {nevertheless} a source of manpower for the Seljuks. There is a very strong likelihood that the newcomers were impelled by the desire to escape from the distress in which they had fallen because of over population and a lack of grazing lands, which were exactly the reasons why the Seljuks descended upon Transoxiana and Iran. In order to do this, the Turkmen became Muslims and moved in a westerly direction. Furthermore their own safety was assured under the protection of the state system found in the Seljuk area. Indeed, the immigration of these masses, who were newly converted to Islam in Central Asia and Transoxiana, toward Khurāsān

71. *Siyāsat-Nāma*, chap. 26.

and their advance from there to Iran is sometimes explained in this manner in the sources.[72] The Seljuk government encouraged these teeming Turkish masses—the great majority of whom were Oghuz—who continuously filled the regions of the empire that were suitable for them, to move toward Anatolia and the Byzantine frontier with a very specific purpose in mind. In this way, the Seljuks wanted, on the one hand, to stop the material damage and turmoil that the Turkmen had caused in different regions of Iran and Iraq; and, on the other, they wanted to prepare the ground for undermining Anatolia, whose geography and climatic conditions were particularly attractive to the Turks of the steppes, so that it could be easily conquered in the future. At the same time a most important opportunity was seized to bring down the old unconquered enemy of the Muslim world, the Byzantine Empire, under the continuous blows of the daring Turkmen masses, who had reached the point where they could no longer turn back with their families and possessions and were motivated by the need to settle and establish a homeland. The Turkmen gathered in Āzarbāījān and because of the gap in the Byzantine defenses, which were open from Lake Van to Georgia following the victory at Malazgird, spread into Anatolia like a fan. There were also other conditions that facilitated their speedy successes in this region which had suffered from much destruction because of the continual struggle between Byzantium and Islam as far back as the time of the ʿAbbāsid Empire. First, Anatolia was much neglected because of Byzantine domestic strife. In the second half of the eleventh century, the oppression and plundering by the great {Greek} feudal lords {*beg*s} distressed the people; the villagers were helpless and tired of constant warfare and being forced to pay heavy taxes;[73] and the population had declined. Byzantine forces stayed in the garrisons of the large cities, were not composed of the local people, and were under the command of generals each of whom wished to declare himself emperor at the first opportunity.[74] Faced with this, the Byzantine emperors tried to put a stop to the Turkish raids mainly with Frankish mercenaries. Furthermore, the Armenian, Assyrian, and Paulician populations living primarily in eastern Anatolia were not content with Byzantine rule. In addition to its well-known policy of annexation in the East, Byzantium subjected the Gregorian Armenians, heretical Christian Paulicians, and Assyrian Christians to religious pressure and used force to try to make these groups accept the Orthodox doctrine.[75] This facilitated the occupation movement of the Turks who recognized freedom of religion. Finally, because the Byzantine Empire was preoccupied in the Balkans,[76] it was

72. Ibn al-Athīr, *al-Kāmil,* years 435, 440, 447; Barhebraeus, *Tarihi,* I, 300, 302.

73. See Bryennius, *Historia,* pp. 531–37.

74. See Laurent, *Byzance,* pp. 61 ff.

75. See Michael the Syrian, *Chronique,* III, 163, 169; Matthew of Edessa, *Chronique,* pp. 72 f., 80 f., 85 f., 98 f., 111 f., 123 f., 128 ff., 141; Laurent, *Byzance,* pp. 67 f., 70 ff., 74 f., 78.

incapable of resisting Seljuk pressure from the East. When all resistance was broken at Malazgird, Emperor Michael VII Ducas transferred to the Balkans a significant part of the Greek population that had stayed behind in Anatolia, whose population anyway had declined.[77] As a result of this, Anatolia became almost devoid of people, except for the Greeks and some of the Armenians who took refuge in formidable castles and walled towns. After the foundation of the Seljuk state by Sulaimān-Shāh, the number of Turkish nomads who headed for Anatolia began to increase. The Oghuz carried out raids from the steppes toward Anatolia because of the presence of the Iraqi Seljuks in the west. Sultan Sanjar had wanted to put an end to these raids by closing the border stretching from the Jand region to Khwārazm and Manqıshlaq but was not successful. Upon his defeat and capture by the Oghuz, the immigration of the Turkmen resumed en masse. In the first quarter of the thirteenth century, another wave of immigration to Anatolia was caused chiefly by the Mongol invasion of the eastern Muslim countries. As they continued to arrive in this manner, the Turkmen nomads, to whom the Seljuk Empire began to apply a policy of transfer and settlement, consequently assured the Turkization of Āzarbāījān, al-Jazīra, northern Syria, and especially Anatolia. Thanks to the Turkmen forces, which made up the army of the Anatolian Seljuks, the Byzantine Emperor Manuel I Comnenus, whom we saw mobilize to take advantage of the destruction caused by the Crusades, suffered a decisive defeat at the hands of Qılıch-Arslan at Myriocephalum (1176). This led to the complete transformation of Anatolia into a Turkish homeland and from that time onward it took the name Turkey.[78]

Because the great majority of the Turkmen migrated to the Seljuk Empire, only a small number remained in present-day Turkmenistan. According to the list of Oghuz tribes recorded by Maḥmūd Kāshgharī,[79] the following Turkish groups were driven toward, and were settled in, Anatolia: the Qınıqs, to whom the Seljuk dynasty was related;[80] Kayıs;[81] Bayındırs;[82] Baraks, who were supposedly a branch of the Bayındır tribe;[83] Yıvas;[84] Salurs; Avshars;[85] Beghds;[86] Büghdüz;[87] Baya'uts;[88] Yazırs;[89] Qara-Bölüqs;[90] Alka-Bölüqs;[91] Yüreghirs;[92] Dodurgas;[93] Alayunds;[94] Döghers;[95] Ighdirs;[96] Pechenegs;[97] Chavuldurs (Chavdırs, the tribe of Chakan, *beg* of Izmir);[98] Chepnis;[99] Charuks;[100] and the other Oghuz tribes, namely, the Karkıns;[101] Kızıks;[102] Yapars;[103] and Eymirs;[104] plus certain Qıpchaqs, Qarluqs, and the Khwārazm-Shāhs. Some branches of these tribes, which brought about the Turkization of Anatolia with their languge, customs, usages, and traditions, also went to the Balkans.

76. Kurat, *Peçenek tarihi*, pp. 143–60.

77. Michael the Syrian, *Chronique*, III, 172.

78. Τούρκια, Turcia, Lebeau, *Histoire*, XV, 185; Joseph De Guignes, trans. H. Cahid, *Hunların, Türklerin . . . tarih-i umûmîsi* [A general history of the Huns, Turks . . .] (Istanbul, 1923–24), IV, 9; L. Rásonyi, *Dünya tarihinde türklük* [Turkism in world history] (Istanbul, 1942), p. 185; Moravcsik, *Byzantinoturcica*, II, 269.

79. *Dīwān*, I, 55 ff.

80. Sümer, "Osmanlı devrinde Anadolu'da yaşayan bazı Üç-oklu Oğuz boylarına mensup teşekküller" [Entities related to some of the Üç-ok clans of the Oghuz who lived in Anatolia in the Ottoman period], *IÜİF Mecmuası* 11(1950), 474–79, 505–08.

81. Köprülü, "Osmanlı imparatorluğunun etnik menşe'i mes'eleleri" [Problems of the ethnic origin of the Ottoman Empire], *Belleten* 8(1943):246–54, 284–303; F. Demirtaş [Sümer], "Osmanlı devrinde Anadolu'da Kayılar" [The Kayıs in Anatolia in the Ottoman period], *Belleten* 12(1948):575–615.

82. Idem, "Bayındır, Peçenek ve Yüreğirler" [The Bayındırs, Pechenegs, and Yüreğirs], *DTCF Dergisi* 11(1953):317–22, 335–40.

Among them were those who went to Dobruja with the Turkmen *shaikh* Sarı Saltuk Dede. The Christian Gagauz, who presently live in the same area and speak Turkish, are probably the descendants of the Turks who were sent to Rumeli with Sultan Kai-Kā'ūs II, who took refuge in Byzantium.[105]

When they first came to Anatolia, the Turkish tribes occupied the plains, valleys, and sumer pastures. Later, they gradually took possession of fortresses and then various walled cities and centers of military and economic importance around which arose independent *beylik*s. The Turkmen states that were founded in eastern Anatolia in the years after the victory at Malazgird and that long disturbed the sultans of the Anatolian Seljuks who were trying to establish political unity in the new homeland, were the following: the Artuqids of Jerusalem, Ḥiṣn Kaifā, Mārdīn, and Harput (1098–1234); the Dānishmendids of Sivas and Malatya (1092–1178); the Mangüjekids of Erzinjān, Kemah {Kamakh, Camacha}, and Divriği (1118–1252); the Saltuqids of Erzurum (1092–1202); the Akhlāṭ-Shāhs (1100–1207); the Inalids and Nisanids of Diyārbakr (1103–83); the *beylik* of Izmir (1081–97); and the *beylik* of Efes,[106] all from the Kayı or Dögher tribe of the Oghuz.[107] Beginning in the second half of the thirteenth century, when the Anatolian Seljuk state was on its way to extinction under Mongol oppression, a number of other *beyliks* were established in central, northern, and western Anatolia with the support of various groups of Turkmen. There were the Pervānadids at Sinop (1265–1322); the Ṣāḥib Atadids at Afyon-Karahisar (1277–1341); the Karasids from the Dānishmendid family at Balıkesir {Palaeocastro/Achyraus} (1293–1359); the Germiyānids at Kütahya (1302–1429); the Aydınids[108] at Aydın {Tralleis} (1308–1425); the ṣārūkhānids, who were probably from the Khwārazm Turkmen, at Manisa {Magnesia} (1313–1410); the Menteshids[109] at Mughla (1282–1424); the Ḥamīdids[110] at Eghridir and Antalya (1300–1423); the Eshrefids[111] at Beyshehir (1284–1325); the Inanchids[112] at Denizli (1277–1390); the Jāndārids[113] at Kastamonu (1309–1462); the Dulghadirids {or Dhū 'l-Qadr} at Marash (1337–1521); the Ramaḍānids[114] at Adana (1353–1608); the *beylik*s founded by Qāḍī Burhān al-Dīn,[115] namely those of the Eretna or Ertana tribe in Kayseri (1343–81) and those of the Salur tribe in Sivas (1381–98); the Qaramānids,[116] founded by the Qaramān Turkmen from the Avshar tribe, in Qaramān {Laranda} and Konya (1256–1483); and the states of the Akkoyunlu, established by the *beg*s of the Bayındır tribe, and the Karakoyunlu, whose founders were probably related to the Yıva tribe.[117]

As we have seen, the Turkmen masses continuously played a

83. See Cahid Tanyol, "Baraklar'da örf ve âdet araştırmaları" [Research on the customs and usages of the Baraks], *Sosyoloji Dergisi* [Journal of sociology], 7(1952): 71–108.
84. Sümer, "Yıva Oğuz boyuna dâir" [On the Yıva clan of the Oghuz], *TM* 9(1951):151–66.
85. Sümer, "Avşarlara dâir" [On the Avshars], *Fuad Köprülü armağanı*, pp. 453–78.
86. Idem, "Boz-oklu Oğuz boylarına dâir" [On the Boz-ok clans of the Oghuz], *DTCF Dergisi* 9(1953):78–86, 95–105.
87. Idem, "Osmanlı devrinde," pp. 473 f., 505.
88. Köprülü, "Oğuz etnolojisine âit notlar" [Notes on the ethnology of the Oghuz], *TM* 1(1925):198–205.
89. Kafesoğlu, *Harezmşahlar*, pp. 171, 270; Sümer, "Boz-oklu," pp. 68 ff., 90.
90. Ibid., pp. 67 f.
91. Ibid., p. 66.
92. Ibid., pp. 329–34, 344.
93. Ibid., pp. 71 ff., 91–94.
94. Idem, "Üç-oklu," pp. 466–69, 500 ff.
95. Idem, "Döğerlere dâir" [On the Döğers], *TM* 10(1953):149–58.
96. Idem, "Üç-oklu," pp. 469–73, 502 ff.
97. Idem, "Boz-oklu," pp. 322–29, 341–44.
98. Idem, "Üç-oklu," pp. 438–80.
99. Köprülü, "Oğuz etnolojisine," pp. 206–9; Sümer, "Üç-oklu," pp. 441–53, 480–85.
100. Idem, "Boz-oklu," pp. 77 ff.
101. Ibid., pp. 86–89, 101 ff.
102. Ibid., pp. 74–77, 94 ff.
103. Ibid., pp. 73 f.
104. Idem, "Üç-oklu," pp. 459–66, 492–500.
105. P. Wittek, "Les Gagaouzes—les gens de Kaykaūs," *RO* 17(1951-52):12–24.
106. See Kurat, *Çaka, Izmir ve yakınlarındaki adaların ilk türk hâkimi* [Chaka, the first Turkish ruler of Izmir and its nearby islands], (Istanbul, 1936).
107. See Sümer, "Döğerlere dâir," p. 149.
108. Himmet Akın, *Aydınoğulları tarihi hakkında bir araştirma* [Research on the history of the Aydınıds], (Istanbul, 1946).
109. Wittek, Turkish trans. O. S. Gökyay, *Menteşe beyliği* [The Menteshid *beylik*], (Ankara: TTK, 1944).
110. Bahriye Üçok, "Hamîd-oğulları beyliği" [The Ḥamīdid *beylik*], *AÜİF Dergisi* 1(1955):73–80.
111. See Halil Edhem, "Beyşehir'de Eşref-oğulları kitâbeleri" [Inscriptions of the Eshrefids of Beyshehir], *TOEM*, year 5; Yusuf Akyurt, "Beyşehir, Eşref-oğlu câmii" [The Eshrefid mosque in Beyshehir], *Türk Tarih, Arkeologya, Etnografya Dergisi* [The journal of Turkish history, archeology, and ethnography], 4(1944):104–12.
112. See Köprülü, "Anadolu beylikleri tarihine âit notlar" [Notes on the history of the *beyliks* of Anatolia], *TM* 2(1928):13 f.
113. See M. Şâkir, *Sinop'ta Candar-oğulları zamanına âit eserler* [Monuments from the time of the Jāndārids in Sinop] (Istanbul, 1934).
114. Sümer, "Çukur-ova tarihine dâir araştırmalar" [Research on the history of Chukurova], *DTCF Tarih Araştırmaları Dergisi* [Journal of historical research of DTCF], 1(1963):1–98.
115. See 'Azīz b. Ardashīr al-Astarābādhī, *Bazm u razm*, ed. Kilisli Rifat (Istanbul, 1928).
116. Köprülü, "Anadolu beylikleri," pp. 14–32.

major role on the frontier (*uc*) of the Seljuk Empire when it was expanding and when it reached its greatest extent. When necessary, they also founded states and, above all, courageously undertook and carried out a task that was as important as it was dangerous, that is, opening new countries to Turkish rule. The Seljuk attempt to direct these Turkmen systematically toward their western borders thus clearly became the second distinguishing characteristic of Seljuk diplomacy. This policy was the most significant and continuous, and therefore historically the most important, in its consequences for the empire. This great historical process culminated when the Ottoman dynasty, which was related to the Turkmen Kayı tribe, used extremely skillful diplomacy to eliminate one by one the *beyliks* and states that we listed above in Anatolia and to unify their lands. The Ottomans then established one of the greatest empires in world history with Anatolia and the areas to which the Oghuz and other Turkmen spread as the mother country.[118] Just as the present-day people of Anatolia are the descendants of these Turkmen and the other Turkish clans who came with them, as revealed by the villages, towns, regions, and the like throughout Turkey bearing Oghuz and other Turkish names,[119] other descendants of these various groups are also living today in western and southern Iran, the Caucasus, al-Jazīra, Iraq, and Syria where they went upon the establishment of the Seljuk Empire and later continued to immigrate.[120]

117. Minorsky, "The Clan of the Qara Qoyunlu Rulers," *Fuad Köprülü armağanı*, pp. 391–95; and on the history and remains of these *beyliks* and states, see I. H. Uzunçarsılı, *Anadolu beylikleri ve Akkoyunlu, Karakoyunlu devletleri* [The Anatolian *beyliks* and the Akkoyunlu and Karakoyunlu states] (Ankara: TTK, 1937); idem, *Anadolu türk tarihi vesikalarından: kitâbeler* [Historical documents of the Anatolian Turks: inscriptions], 2 vols. (Istanbul 1927–29); on the ruins of Kastamonu, Sinop, Chankırı and vicinity, see Ahmed Gökoğlu, *Paflagonya gayr-i menkul eserleri ve arkeolojisi* [The archeology and standing ruins of Paphlagonia], vol. 1 (Kastamonu, 1952).

118. For details, see Köprülü, *Osmanlı devletinin kuruluşu* [his *Les origines de l'Empire ottoman*], (Ankara: TTK, 1953).

119. See *Köylerimiz* [Our villages], Ministry of the Interior (Istanbul, 1928).

120. Details are given on the places where the aforesaid Turkmen tribes were found in the Ottoman period, the units in which they participated, and the new tribes that they formed in Sümer's aforementioned articles and his "XVI. asırda Anadolu, Suriye ve Irak'ta yaşayan türk aşiretlerine umûmî bir bakış" [An overview of the Turkish tribes living in Syria, Iraq, and Anatolia in the sixteenth century], *İÜİF Mecmuası* 11(1949- 50):509–22.

6
The Reasons for the Collapse of the Seljuk Dominion

In the Middle Ages the Seljuks brought new ideas, a new value system, and a new organization to the eastern Muslim world. Although this new orientation would last for centuries, it is noteworthy that the Seljuk dynasty was relatively short-lived. It appears that the early collapse of Seljuk rule resulted mainly from internal causes. It is possible to summarize them around several points.

The Problem of Succession

Among the Seljuks, exactly as it was among the founders of earlier Turkish empires, the state was considered to be the common property of the dynasty. According to this view of sovereignty, which was based on the belief that the ruler was of divine origin, sovereign power (charisma),[1] and the ability to govern,[2] which were granted by God, were transferred by blood from father to son. Thus all members of a dynasty were qualified and had a right to be the ruler. Whenever the position of the sultan weakened, the sons embarked on a struggle to occupy the throne based on this quality and right. In the Turkish milieu, it was accepted that the one who was successful was therefore endowed with the greatest divine strength and was recognized as ruler. Niẓām al-Mulk was opposed to this Turkish concept of sovereignty. As he stated, "the state and its subjects belong to the sultan"[3] and "the sultan is the steward of the universe, all of the people are his family and servants."[4] Despite his suggestions and recommendations that the ear-

1. See Weber, *Wirtschaft*, pp. 124, 140.
2. Yūsuf, *Kutadgu Bilig*, pp. 147 f.
3. *Siyāsat-Nāma*, chap. 5.
4. Ibid., chap. 29.

lier Oriental and Islamic view be adopted, and despite the efforts of the Seljuk sultans themselves to appoint a legal heir apparent and even have the state notables and commanders swear allegiance to him for added security, the Turkish principle of succession never lost its influence as long as the dynasty endured. Because it caused incessant quarrels, this principle undermined the Seljuk Empire and its successor states. Not only were the countries whose conquest would later be decided divided among the members of the dynasty, but even the lands possessed by the Seljuks of Anatolia were parceled out among the princes. Since they and the other members of the dynasty lived with freedom of action with forces under their own command in the countries, provinces, or governorates alloted to them, the struggles for the throne were the most important reason for the dissolution of the Seljuk states.[5] It can be said that fighting over the sultanate occupied about half of Seljuk history.

5. Cf. İnalcık, "Osmanlılarda saltanat verâseti usûlü ve Türk hâkimiyet telakkîsi ile ilgisi" [The method of inheriting the sultanate among the Ottomans and its relationship to the Turkish view of sovereignty], *AÜSBF Degisi* 14(1959):69–94.

The Struggle Between Caliph and Sultan

As we have seen, from the time of Toghrıl Beg the caliphs were not allowed to interfere in worldly affairs. But when the power of the Seljuk sultans declined during the struggles for succession, the caliphs set about reestablishing their own worldly power and this became the second source of violent domestic strife that ruined the Seljuk state. The caliphs were able to assemble considerable forces, establish armies, and capture various cities. Moreover, millions of Muslims had feelings of deep respect for the caliphs so that when the sultans were forced to meet them on the battlefield this naturally had negative consequences for both the sultans and the future of the state.[6] While the western part of the Sunnī Islamic world was preoccupied with the frightful turmoil caused by the Crusader invasion—and the sultans made every attempt to equip and send armies to stop it—the caliphs were {completely} unconcerned about protecting the Muslim countries from this danger. Indeed, they devoted themselves to practicing fine penmanship or writing poetry in their palaces in Baghdad as they made plans to undermine the Seljuk government.[7] It is worthy of note how Ibn Wāṣil described the mood of that time when he praised Caliph al-Muqtafī, who had taken possession of Iraq after the death of Masʿūd, the sultan of that province, by saying "he resurrected the grandeur of the ʿAbbāsid state."[8] The grave results of the ʿAbbāsid caliphs' ambition to found a universal state were touched on above.

6. For details see Köymen, *Büyük Selçuklu II*, pp. 91–113, 255–300.

7. On al-Mustaẓhir and al-Mustarshid, see Ibn al-Athīr, *al-Kāmil*, year 512; Ibn Wāṣil, *Mufarrij*, I, 51.

8. Ibid.

The Oppression of the Atabegs

When the sultans were strong, the *atabeg*s were the most trustworthy men of the state. They trained the "heir apparent" in the capital or the princes in the provinces, where they were assigned as *maliks,* and above all served in the defense of the empire. When the dynasty began to decline, the *atabeg*s oppressed the members of the Seljuk family and later placed their own families in power. This resulted in the creation of many local governments and was the third reason for the dissolution and collapse of the empire. Among the well-known *atabeg* families that established local dynasties were the following: the Salghurids in Fārs (1147–1286); the Tughteginids or Börids in Damascus (1104–54); the Zangids in Mosul (1127–1233), Aleppo (1146–81), and Sinjār (1170–1220); the *atabeg*s of al-Jazīra (1180–1227); the Begteginids in Irbil (1144–1233); and the Eldigüzids in Āzarbāījān (1146–1225).[9]

9. For brief information on all of them, see Halil Edhem, *Düvel-i islâmiye* [The Islamic dynasties], (Istanbul, 1927), pp. 230–36, 247–50.

Foreign Intervention

If we exclude the Qara-Khitai War, which shook the Seljuk Empire, and the rebellion of the Arab amirate of Ḥilla,[10] which did not have a significant political effect within the empire, intervention from abroad first came in the form of the Oghuz invasion, which brought down the Seljuk Empire, and then came in the form of the destruction of the Seljuk state of Iraq by the empire of the Khwārazm-Shāhs, albeit both {the Oghuz and the Khwārazm-Shāhs} were Turkish. As for the Seljuk state of Anatolia, it was destroyed by neither the Crusades nor the Mongol invasion, which occurred when the Seljuk dynasty was confined to Asia Minor. Despite both these invasions, the Turkmen frontier *begs,* as we have seen, arose at the end of the Seljuk era and succeeded in founding various states there by eliminating the Mongol oppression.

10. Ṣadaqa and his son Dubais, see Köymen, *Büyük Selçkulu II,* pp. 28 ff., 35–40, 49–63, 75–85, 116–48.

7
Seljuk Institutions

It was natural for the military, administrative, and financial institutions of the Seljuk state to follow Islamic traditions, for this state was established in Khurāsān and organized by Iranian vizirs in a Muslim milieu. From the names of the offices, positions, and ranks, and the contents of Niẓām al-Mulk's *Siyāsat-Nāma* concerning the organization of the state, it can be seen that the Ghaznavid Turkish Empire, whose political structure represented a continuation of early Iranian and ʿAbbāsid features, was the primary model for the Seljuks. The need for conformity to the conditions, constraints, and customs of the local inhabitants formed the basis of Seljuk institutions. Above all, the Seljuks maintained the system they found. This is clearly seen when their administration is studied in the light of the spirit that we tried to outline above. It was most effective during the reigns of Alp-Arslan and Malik-Shāh, who both had Niẓām al-Mulk as their vizir. Moreover, just as there were also Turkish vizirs in the Seljuk government,[1] the presence of such terms as *ağacı* (*ḥājib*),[2] *çavuş* (*sarhang*), *tuğra, ulaġ* and *cufġa,*[3] *atabeg, sü-başı,* and so forth, reveal that Turkish words were used in the administrative and military organization and in the state postal bureau.

1. See, e.g., Rāvandī, *Rāḥat,* p. 167.

2. See Köprülü, "Bizans müesseselerinin Osmanlı müesseselerine te'siri hakkında bâzı mülâhazalar," *THİT Mecmuası* 1(1931):209n. 3.

3. Kāshgharī, *Dīwān,* I, 122, 424.

The Ruler

During the reign of Malik-Shāh, when state organization reached its highest level, the Seljuk sultan held the title of "al-Sulṭān al-Aʿẓam"[4]

4. Niẓām al-Mulk, *Siyāsat-Nāma,* Paris ed., p. 7.

in his capacity as the sovereign of the Ghaznavid and Anatolian Seljuk states, whose rulers held the title of sultan at the same time and where there were *maliks,* subject governments, and *begs*. The *khuṭba* was read and money was minted in his name in all countries. In the place for the signature on edicts {*fermans*} and decisions of the grand *dīwān,* a *tuğra,* which constituted the name of the Great Sultan, was inscribed; his signature (*tevkīi*) was written; and the order was henceforth in force. Each sultan took a Muslim name in addition to his Turkish name.[5] After the sultan ascended the throne, the caliph gave him a *kunya* and *laqab* {and title?} while confirming his authority.[6] On campaign and when traveling with his staff, an umbrella (*çetr*) made of satin or velvet embroidered with gold was held over the sultan's head as a symbol of sovereignty. A band of military musicians (*navbat*) always accompanied him and played each day at the five prayer times. Members of the dynasty who were sent to rule different regions of the empire with the title *malik* had the right to have such a band play three times a day. On certain days of the week the sultan gave an audience for the leading men of state and commanders and held consultations with them. At the same time he also listened to the complaints of the people.[7] In addition, he distributed *iqṭā*'s, appointed judges, confirmed the authority of the heads of subject states, and presided over the high court concerned with crimes against the state.

5. Toghrıl Beg, Muḥammad; Chaghrı Beg, Dā'ūd; Alp-Arslan, Muḥammad; Sanjar, Aḥmad, and so forth.

6. Toghrıl Beg: Abū Ṭālib, Rukn al-Dīn, Yamīn Amīr al-Mu'minīn; Alp-Arslan: Abū Shujāᶜ, ᶜAḍud al-Dawla, Burhān Amīr al-Mu'minīn; Malik-Shāh: Abū 'l-Fatḥ, Muᶜizz al-Dīn, Qasīm Amīr al-Mu'minīn; Sanjar: Abū 'l-Ḥārith, Muᶜizz al-Dīn, Burhān Amīr al-Mu'minīn, and so forth. See anonymous, *Mujmal,* pp. 429 f.; Rāvandī, *Rāḥat,* pp. 85 f. Only the great Sultan Malik-Shāh held the highest title of Qasīm Amīr al-Mu'minīn, which meant "the partner of the caliph in all matters," see al-Qalqashandī, *Ṣubḥ al-aᶜshā* (Cairo, 1915), VI, 113.

7. *"Bār dādan-i khāṣṣ u 'āmm,"* Niẓām al-Mulk, *Siyāsat-Nāma,* chap. 28.

The Palace

The palace, which was also known by such terms as *dergāh* {court of the sultan} and *bārgāh* {audience chamber}, was comprised of the following personnel who were directly responsible to the person of the sultan: *ḥājib* (*ḥājib al-ḥujjāb* or *ḥājib-i buzurg* {chamberlain}), *çūbdār* ("*değnekci*" {usher with staff}), *ṣilāḥdār* (warden or chief of the armory, which was called the *zered-hāne,* who carried the sultan's weapons), *amīr-i 'alam* (standard bearer), *jāmedār* {keeper of the wardrobe}, *ṣarābdār* {butler}, *taṣtdār* (or *ābdār* {valet in charge of the after-meal wash basin and ewer}), *amīr-i çaṣnigīr* {chief taster}, *amīr-i āhūr* {chief of the stable}, *vekīl-i hās* (overseer of the people in the sultan's apartment), *sarhang* {yeomen of the guard}, courtiers, and companions. Those who held these positions were chosen from among the sultan's most trusted men, and each had military units under his command.[8]

8. Ibid., chaps. 16, 17, 29.

The Government

The government (*dīwān al-salṭanat*) was composed of five *dīwāns* (*nezāret* {ministries}). At the top was the *dīwān al-wizāra*. It was headed by the vizir, who was called *ṣāḥib dīvān-i salṭanat* or *khwāja-i buzurg* (prime minister). He was the ultimate representative of the ruler (*vezāret-i tefvīz*).[9] The other four *dīwāns* were subordinate to the *dīwān al-wizāra*. These were the *dīwān al-tughra* (its minister, the *tughrā'ī*, was in charge of foreign affairs);[10] *dīwān al-'arḍ wa 'l-jaish* (its minister, the *'āriḍ*, was in charge of the military); the *dīwān al-ishrāf* (its minister, the *mushrif*, was in charge of general investigations); and the *dīwān al-istīfā'* (its minister, the *mustawfī*, was in charge of financial affairs). With regard to the last ministry, the lands of the empire were placed in three catagories: *khāṣṣ* {the sultan's private domain}, *iqṭā'*, and *kharājī* {taxable}. The *dīwān al-istīfā'* was responsible for determining and recording the population to be taxed on these lands, from large city to village. It also recorded the tax-assessable property of everyone,[11] and collected canonical (*sharī'a*) and customary (*'urfī*) taxes by means of "agents." Furthermore, it managed government expenses (*maṣraf*) and the sultan's private account (reserve) of taxes obtained from the *khāṣṣ* lands and subject states. It is also worth mentioning here that, except for military and judicial matters, all officials and transactions of the empire were subject to inspection by an "oversight" (*ishrāf*) department, which was completely independent from the ministries concerned.[12] In the provinces, as we have seen, there were minor rulers called *malik*s who had different-colored banners and umbrellas and, when given permission, minted coins. These men, military commanders (called the *shiḥna*) and governors general all had their own vizirs and *dīwān*s, but on a smaller scale than those in the capital (for example, Niẓām al-Mulk was first the vizir of *malik* Alp-Arslan, and Ḥasan b. Ṭāhir Shahrastānī was the vizir of Sulaimān-Shāh. In Kirmān, the vizir was Mukarram b. al-'Alā' Tūrān-Shāh. Qasīm al-Dawla Aq-Sonqur had a vizir named Zarrīn-Qamar). Alongside the princes and *malik*s were *atabeg*s, who were entrusted with their military, administrative, and political training (Niẓām al-Mulk served as the *atabeg* of prince Malik-Shāh). This institution, the roots of which go back to the Gök-Turks,[13] was a Turkish innovation in organization and in state government. As noted, the *atabeg*s founded many states at the time of the demise of the empire. In addition, in the provincial centers subordinate to the grand *dīwān* there were leaders (*'amīd*s) responsible for the civil administration, chiefs (*ra'īs*es) selected from among the people, and inspectors (*muḥtasib*s) of the marketplace as well as the military commanders called *shiḥna*. In short, the representatives, agents, secretaries, tax collectors, and the like, bound to the ministries and offices that we have mentioned, were active throughout the empire in great number.

9. See Köprülü, "Bizans müesseselerinin," pp. 186–90; 'Abbās Iqbāl, *Vizārat dar 'ahd-i Saljūqiyyān-i buzurg* (Tehran, 1327 *sh.*)

10. This position was created by the Seljuks, see Barhebraeus, *Tarihi,* I, 305, but was found in other Islamic states like that of the Ghaznavids. It was considered to be superior to the *dīwān al-rasā'il,* which also developed among the Seljuks and had more or less the same responsibilities, see Köprülü, "Ortazaman Türk hukukî müesseseleri," p. 408; Cahen, "La Tuġrâ Seljukide," *JA* 239(1943–45):167–72.

11. See Köprülü, "Anadolu Selçukluları tarihinin yerli kaynakları," pp. 406, 408.

12. Niẓām al-Mulk, *Siyāsat-Nāma,* chaps. 9, 21, 48, 50.

13. See N. Kozmin, Turkish trans. A. Caferoğlu, "Orhun âbideleri muharriri Atısı lekaplı Yollug Tigin" [Yollig Tegin, the author of the Orkhon inscriptions who had the byname Atası], *TM* 5(1936):367 ff.

The Military

In the reign of Malik-Shāh, which was the golden age of the Seljuks, the greatest military force of the Middle Ages was created. The Seljuk armies, which served as an example to later Turco-Islamic states, were composed of (1) the *ghulāmān-i sarai,* who were selected from various peoples, brought to the palace where they were given special training, learned the principles of ceremony and protocol, and were under the direct command of the sultan; (2) the special corps that was drilled and trained under the most distinguished commanders and was ready for action at a moment's notice; (3) the troops of the *malik*s, *ghulām* {slave} governors, and state officials like the vizirs; and (4) the forces of the subject governments. Members of the *ghulāmān-i sarai,* whose names were recorded in the *dīwān* registers, received their pay (*bīst-gānī*) four times a year. The special corps, which participated with its commanders, the sultans, in the great campaigns or was sent on punitive operations and which was also assigned to the regular military commanders {*şiḥnelik*} and had members serve as governors general, was also salaried. Furthermore, there was a great number of cavalry dispersed throughout the empire and they were always prepared to go on campaign. They received their livelihood from the *iqṭā*ʿ lands set aside for them. However, they were not able to take more in taxes (*māl-i ḥaqq*) from the subjects (farmers, villagers) living on their *iqṭā*ʿs than certain amounts specified by the grand *dīwān*. Moreover, if an *iqṭā*ʿ holder interfered with a villager's property or violated the sanctity of the family, the villager could go directly to the grand *dīwān* and complain to the sultan. Those who were not pleased with their *iqṭā*ʿ holder could move to another place.[14]

With regard to military organization, this military *iqṭā*ʿ was one of the most important innovations in the Seljuk Empire. On the one hand, this system made it possible to maintain rather large armies without placing a burden on the state and, on the other, helped the country to prosper. It was not, as has been believed to date, a direct creation of Niẓām al-Mulk, but apparently resulted from the adaptation of an old Turkish land law to new conditions.[15] This system formed one of the sturdiest pillars of the empire, administratively and legally as well as militarily. The breakdown of order in the Seljuk state of Anatolia as a result of the Mongol invasion turned productive *iqṭā*ʿ lands into private domains (*mulk*). In this way the state land system deteriorated and the Seljuk army dissolved. Insurrections of cavalry {*sipāhīs*} who had no *iqṭā*ʿs compounded the oppression of the Mongols and were the main reason for the collapse of the state.[16]

Furthermore, when necessary, mercenary troops, *ḳaşer* {?}, were

14. Niẓām al-Mulk, *Siyāsat-Nāma,* chaps. 5, 6, 33.

15. Köprülü, "Bizans müesseselerinin," p. 240n. 1; Turan, "Türkiye Selçuklularında toprak hukuku" [Land law among the Seljuks of Turkey], *Belleten* 12(1948):549, 566–71.

16. Ibid., p. 554.

also raised from among the people. The units in the army had different banners. The Seljuk army had mobile hospitals and the Anatolian armies had mobile baths (*çerge*). If we add to the Seljuk armies the Turkmen led by their *begs,* whose major service from the beginning of the Seljuk state, and especially on the frontiers, was as a genuine strike force, we will have an even greater appreciation of the army and military organization.

The Administration of Justice

The Seljuk administration of justice was divided between the *sharīʿa* and customary law. The *qāḍīs* in each country were responsible for decisions concerning the *sharīʿa*. In Baghdad there was a chief *qāḍī* (*qāḍī al-quḍāt*) who was a scholar of *fiqh* {Islamic jurisprudence}. He served as the head of the law court in the capital as well as the supervisor of the other *qāḍīs*. In addition to settling lawsuits related to the *sharīʿa* among the people, these judges were also responsible for matters concerning inheritance, charitable works, and *waqfs* {pious endowments}, which were an important social assistance institution in medieval Turco-Islamic states.[17] The *qāḍīs* {generally} acted according to Ḥanafī *fiqh,* to which most Turks adhered, and sometimes according to Shāfiʿī *fiqh*. Their decisions were final and inviolable. However, if a judge issued a biased ruling, it could be referred to the sultan after being signed on the bottom by other *qāḍīs*. In the *Siyāsat-Nāma,* great importance was given to the education and morals of these judges "to whom Muslims entrusted their lives and property" (chap. 6). In addition to the *sharīʿa* courts, there were separate courts charged with settling questions of custom and other legal problems. This system was usually concerned with such matters as crimes of a political nature, disobedience to the orders of the state, and various kinds of disturbances. At the head of it was the *emīr-i dād*. In the provinces, officials of this system looked after the same kinds of cases. *Sharīʿa* lawsuits concerning those in the army were within the purview of the *qāḍī ʿaskar*s. Above all, it should be noted here that the people responsible for the administration of justice under the Seljuks were independent of the grand *dīwān* and the provincial *dīwāns,* i.e., the government. It was thus possible to carry out justice free from any political or government influence.

The Seljuks had a speedy intelligence-reporting system, which made use of birds as well as messengers, a secret service whose members were called "informants" {*münhīler*},[18] a regular postal service, a system of police stations on the major strategic commercial roads, and *ribāṭ*s {fortified retreat} at places which needed constant watch.[19]

The Seljuk organization of the palace, *dīwān,* army, and financial

17. See Köprülü, "Vakıf müesseseleri ve vakıf vesikalarının tarihî ehemmiyeti" [The historical significance of *waqf* institutions and *waqf* documents], *VD* 1(1938):1–6.

18. For details see Kafesoğlu, *Melikşah,* pp. 143–66; A. K. S. Lambton, "The Administration of Sanjar's Empire as Illustrated in the ʿAtabat al-Kataba," *BSOAS* 20(1957):367–88.

and judicial matters, which we have tried to describe briefly to this point, was maintained with minor variations, despite the change in certain names (e.g., *al-dīwān al-ʿālī, nāʾib al-ḥaḍra, dīwān al-maẓālim, ḥisba, shurṭa, beyler-beyi, sü-başı*), in the states of the *atabegs*, the empire of the Khwārazm-Shāhs, among the Ayyūbids, the Turkish and Circassian military slave states of Egypt and Syria, among the Artuqids, Dānishmendids, and to some extent the other Anatolian *beyliks*, in the ʿAbbāsid state in the second half of the twelfth century, and finally in the Ottoman Empire. The Seljuks thus set an example for organizing an administrative cadre that lasted for almost eight hundred years in the eastern Islamic world.[20]

19. See Köprülü, "Vakfa ait tarihî ıstılâhlar: Ribât" [Historical terms concerning the *waqf:* Ribāṭs], *VD* 2(1942):267–78.

20. For details see Köprülü, "Bizans müesseselerinin," pp. 165–309; Uzunçarsılı, *Osmanlı devleti teşkilâtına medhal* [Introduction to the organization of the Ottoman state] (Istanbul: TTK, 1941).

8
Social and Intellectual Life

Social Conditions

Except for the Turkish element among the high palace officials and their assistants who controlled the country, commanders, the military forces and the like, the Seljuks did not directly interfere with the lives and occupations of the people. The social conditions under the Seljuks, which were shared by all medieval Muslim Turkish states, thus generally maintained the traditions of earlier periods. State positions became almost hereditary.[1] Even changes in power usually took place within the same family. In various provinces and cities a great many local conditions and traditions prevailed with regard to financial matters. The families of great influence, which came into being by seizing the opportunity to acquire economic wealth or to attach themselves to the administrative authority in the cities, were able to preserve their positions.[2] The *dihqāns* {minor feudal nobility} in the villages were from such families. Another large group that had great influence over the people were men of religion. They along with *saiyids* and *sharīfs* {both of whom were descendants of the Prophet} and members of the Ḥanafī and Shāfiʿī *madhhabs* {schools of law}, who held positions throughout the country, were in the forefront of the struggle against the adherents of Shīʿism, especially around Baghdad, Baṣra, and Bahrain. Merchants who carried on medium and small-scale business in the cities and towns, various tradesmen {*esnef*}, shopkeepers, and craftsmen in the minor arts formed different guilds {*lonca*}. The pop-

1. On Niẓām al-Mulk's family for example, see Khwāndamīr, *Dastūr al-wuzarā'*, ed. S. Nafīsī (Tehran, 1317 *sh.*), pp. 149–67, 178–88.

2. For the city of Baihaq, see Ibn Funduq, *Ta'rīkh*.

ulation generally congregated about Ḥanafī and Shāfiʿī *raʾīses* and Shīʿī *naqībs* {headman}. In the large cities there were also organized bands of vagrants. These groups, which had previously formed armies of volunteers during the campaigns of Maḥmūd of Ghazna in India, followed a *ṣūfī* way of life and were known by such names as *rind* {vagabonds}, *ʿayyār* {rogues}, and *sattār* {veilers}.[3] As for the peasants who worked in the plains, fields, vineyards, and gardens, they made their living under government protection on either royal {*khāṣṣ*} or *iqṭāʿ* lands, as mentioned above, and paid taxes. Legally they were as free as the people in the cities. As long as they were able to cultivate the lands in their possession, which they owned by hereditary right, they did not have to work just to keep alive. As for economic development, in Anatolia where there were few exceptions to these general conditions and the great majority of the population were essentially settled Turks,[4] the people worked as laborers, tradesmen, artisans, and transporters of goods in all the aspects of commercial and economic life that we shall discuss below. Thus, because of peace, security, and prosperity, the towns, which had previously consisted of little more than fortresses, expanded and developed. Konya, Kayseri, Sivas, Erzurum, Erzinjān, Harput, Amasya, Tokat, Aksaray, and Ankara grew into major Turkish cities inland while Sinop, Samsun, Antalya, and ʿAlāʾiyya did so on the coast. Certain cities like Aksaray,[5] Kırshehir,[6] ʿAlāʾiyya, Kubādiyya, and Kubād-ābād[7] and others with Turkish names were founded by the Turks.

3. For extensive details, see Cahen, "Mouvements populaires et autonomisme urbain dans l'Asie Musulmane du moyen-âge," *Arabica* 5(1958):225–50, 6(1959):25–56, 233–65.

4. See Sümer, "Anadolu'ya yalnız göçebe Türkler mi geldi?" [Did only nomadic Turks come to Anatolia?], *Belleten* 24(1960):567–94.

5. M. Zeki Oral, "Aksaray'ın tarihi önemi" [The historical importance of Aksaray], *VD* 5(1962):223–40.

6. See A. Saim Ülgen, "Kırsehir'de Türk eserleri" [Turkish monuments in Kirshehir], *VD* 1(1942):253–61.

7. See Oral, "Kayseri'de Kubâdiye sarayları" [The Qubādiyya palaces in Kayseri], *Belleten* 17(1953):501–17; idem, "Kubâd-âbâd nasıl bulundu?" [How was Qubād-ābād found?], *AÜİF Dergisi* 2(1953):171–79.

Economic and Commercial Conditions

We have described the excellent economic and commercial location of Khurāsān where the Seljuk state was founded. Because of the political unity that the Seljuks created in Iran and Iraq, and the regular administration and complete public security established there under the control of a powerful army, which kept the commercial routes under constant supervision and the like, the existing commercial activity between the Near East and Central Asia and between the Near East and Eastern Europe—where their Mediterranean ports on the Syrian coast played the roles of intermediaries with India—increased in every respect and provided a firm financial foundation for the Seljuk states.[8] One of the factors which assured such continuity to Seljuk administration and organization was this economic prosperity. During the period of the empire, dispatching the largest army in the Middle Ages with proper clothing, supplies, equipment, and military transport; the splendor and great expense of the luxury and affluence to which our sources testify on the occasions of the sultans' banquets, holidays,

8. See W. Heyd, *Histoire du Commerce du Levant au moyen-âge* (Paris, 1923), I, 164–68; Jean Aubin, "La Ruine de Sîrâf et les routes du Golf Persique aux XIe et XIIe siècles," *Cahiers de Civilisation Médiévale* 2(1959):295–301.

merrymaking, victory celebrations, and wedding feasts; and, at the same time, the lack of any action on the part of the subjects caused by a life of poverty are evidence of the existence of an economic balance. In this respect, Ḥamd Allāh Mustawfī Qazvīnī, who provides valuable information on the reign of Malik-Shāh,[9] of whose coins in our possession sixteen of twenty-two are gold and the rest silver, tells us[10] that the annual revenue of the Seljuk countries was 21,500 *tūmāns* {a Persian coin} of red gold (*zer-i surkh*) and the yearly taxes received as *kharāj* were 20,000 *mithqāls* {a standard of weight} of gold (*ṭalā*).[11] In today's {1965} figures the total would be in excess of an average of 225 billion liras {one dollar was then equal to about nine liras}. If we take into consideration the differences in market prices and purchasing power since then, this would amount to about 500 billion liras. In addition to Malik-Shāh, others, such as Toghrıl Beg, Alp-Arslan, and Sanjar, also struck gold coins.[12] Economic conditions under the Seljuks of Kirmān progressed as well, and the coinage that was struck, above all in the time of Qāvurt, maintained its value for a long time. According to Afḍal al-Dīn Kirmānī, an eyewitness, a century and a half later the *naqd-i Qāvurt* still held great value.[13] As for the Anatolian Seljuks, the subject of commerce was one of the major considerations that determined the main policies of the state. First of all, the political disorder that occurred in the Near East, especially Syria, because of the Crusades and then the economic blockade encouraged by the pope, which was applied at sea in order to undermine the trade of Egypt, paralyzed the intense commercial activity {in the eastern Mediterranean}. Moreover, the Mongol invasion struck a blow to the exchange of goods between the Mediterranean and Central Asia and the northern shore of the Black Sea. While world trade thus fell into a severe depression, the Seljuk sultans, beginning chiefly in the last years of Qılıch-Arslan II, who recognized the potentially great importance of Anatolia in this respect, succeeded in making Seljuk Turkey an intercontinental transit center. It was then, when the Seljuks entered international commercial relations, that comprehensive measures for public security were put into effect on the roads that were built. The state guaranteed the lives and property of foreign merchants. Even a kind of state insurance was placed on merchandise for the purpose of indemnifying the losses of merchants against possible ambushes by brigands in the country, pirate attacks at sea, and shipwreck. In the important centers, which had large inns and marketplaces, *khāns* and covered markets were established. And as we stated above, sections of the Black Sea and Mediterranean coasts were conquered for purely commercial and economic reasons. In order to provide for the comfort of merchants and the protection of their property, caravansaries, which

9. See Kafesoğlu, *Melikşah*, p. 146.

10. See Qazvīnī, *Guzīda*, which cites the *Risāla-i malikshāhiyya* written in the time of Malik-Shāh, I, 449; idem, *Nuzhat al-qulūb*, ed. {*The Geographical Part*} G. Le Strange (Leiden, 1915), p. 226a.

11. On the value of the *tūmān*, *dīnār*, and *dirham* at different times, see Barthold, "İlhanlılar devrinde mâlî vaziyet" [Fiscal conditions in the Ilkhānid period], *THİT Mecmuası* 1(1931):143, ff.

12. Sourdel, *Inventaire*, p. XVI, 82–94; İbrahim Artuk, "Selçuklu sultanı Mahmud bin Melik Şah'a âit bir dinar" [A dinar belonging to the Seljuk sultan Maḥmūd b. Malik-Shāh], *Istanbul Üniversitesi Edebiyat Fakültesi Tarih Dergisi* [The journal of history of the Istanbul University Faculty of Literature], 6(1954):141–44.

13. *Badā'i'*, p. 4.

first began to be constructed by Qılıch-Arslan II—some of which are individual architectural masterpieces (e.g., the sultan *khāns*)—multiplied under later sultans and a series of them were built along the main roads. Qılıch-Arslan II was also the first Anatolian Seljuk ruler to strike gold coins.[14] Anatolia thus experienced its most prosperous period in history and its wealth became legendary in Europe.

14. See Artuk, "Abbasi ve Anadolu Selçukîlerine ait iki eşsiz dinar" [Two rare dinars belonging to the ʿAbbāsids and Seljuks of Anatolia], *İstanbul Arkeoloji Müzeleri Yıllığı* [Annual of the Istanbul archeology museums], 8(1958):45 f.; on the gold and silver coinage of the Anatolian Seljuks, see Tevhîd, *Meskûkât-i kadîme*, pt. 4; Behzad Butak, *XI. XII. ve XIII. yüzyıllarda resimli Türk paraları* [Pictorial Turkish coins from the eleventh, twelfth, and thirteenth centuries], *Ek* [Supplement], 1–2 (Istanbul, 1950); idem, *Ġiyās al-Dīn Kayhusrav II.'in görülmemiş iki sikkesi* [Two unknown coins belonging to Ghiyāth al-Dīn Kai-Khusraw II] (Istanbul, 1950); Şeraffeddin Erel, *Nâdir bir kaç sikke* [A few rare coins] (Istanbul, 1963), pp. 4–8.

Industrial life in Anatolia, like that in other countries in the Middle Ages, was based on guilds that adhered to strict rules according to the type of goods made. By inculcating in those who worked in every branch of craft the belief in the spiritual sanctity of its "patron saint" {*pīr*}, these institutions made the "apprentice" {*murīd*} faithful to the demands of the profession, and completely bound him to all its rules. The professions were monopolized by the guilds. According to a given number of stores or workshops, there were a certain number of masters and workmen whose names and patronymics were registered. Those who wanted to advance from apprenticeship to being a master craftsman had to pass a special examination in the presence of the masters and, if successful, were ceremoniously given the rank of "master of a craft." The most skilled and respected member of the institution became the head of the guild and had the title of *akhī*. In addition to the *akhī*, who was exacty like the *shaikh* of a religious order {*ṭarīqa*} with respect to influence and power, there was a second administrative official called the *yiğit-başı*, or *server*, who was responsible for carrying out his orders. The craftsmen and apprentices who were members of the guild were called *fityān* (youths). In addition, the head of the *akhī*s in a city was called *akhī bābā*. Consequently, in cities where there were a great many *akhī*s (*ikhwān*), *yiğit-başıs* (*serverān*) and *fityān*, they had a voice in administrative and political affairs because they were the dominant group in the economy of the country. This was so to the extent that, when the Seljuk state broke up, they established a kind of popular government through their own efforts in the principle centers that we mentioned above and thus saved society from disintegration. They successfully maintained this state of affairs until the foundation of the Ottoman Empire. We learn from the traveler Ibn Baṭṭūṭa that each guild also occupied a rather important position as a kind of religio-military order among the Anatolian *beyliks*. The foundation of these organizations was based on the *futuwwa* ("youth") order that the ʿAbbāsid Caliph al-Nāṣir li-Dīn Allāh (1180–1225) had proposed as a means of securing the spiritual unity of the Islamic countries. Al-Nāṣir succeeded in inducting all the Muslim rulers into this order and conferred upon them the distinction of *rāmī al-bunduq* {crossbowman}. Ghiyāth al-Dīn Kai-Khusraw, Baybars the Turkish sultan of Egypt, and others wore special *futuwwa* clothing according to certain protocol.

This religio-military order later became particularly useful for the caliph's objective when a great many professionals and artisans joined its ranks. The *akhī* organization was subsequently applied to the economic sphere. As can be seen from the *futuwwat-nāma*s written at various times, the Ottoman Empire continued to maintain this organization and devoted considerable attention to problems of the trades and their interests {*dava*}. Even after the guilds were abolished, the tradition of mutual respect that they had established continued the feeling of cooperation among the different trades.[15] The *futuwwa* order rested on a religious foundation and had special lodges where each guild met on certain days and discussed its affairs. An important characteristic of the *akhī* organization that should be mentioned was that Christians were not admitted. This gave the Muslim Turkish professionals a priviliged position in society, for Muslims were able to control both the crafts and professions. Thus the Turks gradually came to dominate the urban economy. Moreover, because they were not included in the guilds, the non-Muslims who worked in various professions and crafts naturally encountered certain difficulties. They were thus encouraged to convert to Islam. Consequently, this institution also contributed in great measure to the Islamization of Turkey.[16] Just as there was no persecution, oppression, massacres or the like during the Turkization of Anatolia, there also appears to have been no political and administrative pressure on non-Muslims during the Islamization of Anatolia. They therefore converted to Islam en masse for other reasons {i.e., economic and social}.[17]

Religious Life

Of the four Sunnī *madhhab*s, Ḥanafism, and to a much lesser extent Shāfi'ism, were adopted by the Seljuks. In Transoxiana, Ḥanafism developed through the preaching of Abū Manṣūr al-Māturīdī of Samarqand (d. 944),[18] who was probably of Turkish origin. His teachings emphasized free will. Because this *madhhab* used reason and logical arguments to prove the existence of God and, above all, because its legal content included Turkish usages and traditions, it was the most widespread school of law among the Turks, who had a realistic world view.[19] Moreover, because Ḥanafism determined the lawfulness of judgments according to circumstances and need, it was thus possible for the Turkish state to adapt this Islamic legal system to the requirments and conditions of the times, and it became the official *madhhab* first of the Seljuks and then of the other Turkish dynasties. Because the 'Abbāsid caliphs adhered to the same law school, the bond between these

15. Tevhîd, "Ankara ahîleri" [The *akhīs* of Ankara], *TOEM*, 1329, 1200 ff.; M. Cevdet, *Dhail ᶜalā faṣl "al-Akhiyya al-fityān al-turkiyya" fī Kitāb al-Riḥla li-Ibn Baṭṭūṭa* (Istanbul, 1932); F. Taeschner, "Beitrage zur Geschichte der Achis in Anatolien (14.–15. Jhdt)," *Islamica* 4(1931); idem, "Futuwwa-Studien, die Futuwwabünde in der Türkei und ihre Literatur," *Islamica* 5(1932); idem, "Der Anteil des Sufismus an der Formung des Futuwwaideals," *Der Islam* 29(1937); idem, "Islâm orta çağında fütüvvet teşkilâtı" [The *futuwwa* organization in the Islamic Middle Ages], *İÜİF Mecmuası* 15(1954):1–32; A. Gölpınarlı, "İslâm ve Türk illerinde fütüvve teşkilâtı ve kaynakları" [The organization of the *futuwwa* in Islamic and Turkish lands and its sources], *İÜİF Mecmuası* 11(1950):3–354; Köprülü, *Osmanlı devletinin kuruluşu*, pp. 89–93; Cahen, "Sur les traces des premiers Akhis," in *Fuad Köprülü armağanı*, pp. 81–92; M. Akdağ, *Türkiye'nin iktisâdî ve içtimâî tarihi* [The economic and social history of Turkey], (Ankara, 1959), I, 1–18.

16. Cf. G. Vernadsky, *The Mongols and Russia* (New Haven, 1953), p. 304.

17. See Turan, "Les Souverains Seldjoukides et leurs sujets non-musulmans," *Studia Islamica* 1(1953):65–100; idem, "L'Islamisation dans la Turquie du Moyen-Âge," *Studia Islamica* 10(1959):137–52.

18. See also M. Tanci, "Abū Manṣūr al-Māturīdī," *AÜİF Dergisi* 4(1958):1–12.

19. See H. Z. Ülken, *İslâm düşüncesi* [Islamic thought] (Istanbul, 1946), pp. 68, 92 f.

two powers was greatly strengthened. Shāfiʿism, a moderate law school that later tried to reconcile Ḥanafism with the Mālikī and Ḥanbalī *madhhab*s, both of which took a more literal view of Islamic dogma, also became popular in the Seljuk Empire and among the Turks in general, thanks to the efforts of Niẓām al-Mulk.[20] He put an end to the policy of ʿAmīd al-Mulk al-Kundurī, the vizir of Toghrıl Beg, of anathematizing the ʿAshʿarīs and persecuting Shāfiʿīs, and assured the return of the great Shāfiʿī scholars and jurists who had been forced to leave the country. Furthermore, because the Seljuk government, which was the standard-bearer of Sunnism, combined the Islamic idea of *ghazā* {military expedition} with the Turkish view of conquest, it had considerable incentive to combat the Fāṭimids, after gaining sovereignty over the other Muslim countries, and was successful in opposing the Crusaders.

20. M. Şerefeddin, "Selçuklular devrinde mezâhib" [The *madhhabs* in the Seljuk period], *TM* 1(1925):101–18.

Many of the greatest men of *fiqh, kalām* {scholastic theology}, *tafsīr* {Qur'ānic exegesis}, and *ḥadīth* in Muslim history lived during the time of the Seljuk Empire. They included the great *ṣūfī* Abū 'l-Qāsim al-Qushairī (d. 1072), who wrote *al-Risāla al-qushairiyya,* which was translated into Turkish at the same time, and his son Abū Naṣr ʿAbd al-Raḥīm, the author of the *tafsīr* work entitled *al-Taisīr;* Abū Isḥāq al-Shīrāzī (d. 1083), a Shāfiʿī jurist and teacher in the Baghdad Niẓāmiyya; Abū 'l-Maʿālī al-Juwainī (d. 1085), who wrote many works; the *kalām* specialist al-Ghazzālī (d. 1111), who was one of the greatest thinkers in the Muslim world and rector of the Baghdad Niẓāmiyya; Fakhr al-Islām ʿAbd al-Wāḥid (d. 1108), who was called the second al-Shāfiʿī and was a teacher in the Āmul Niẓāmiyya; the great Ḥanafī jurist and chief *qāḍī* al-Khaṭībī (d. 1079) {not otherwise identified}; the Ḥanbalī jurist, *ḥadīth* specialist, and famous *ṣūfī* ʿAbd Allāh al-Anṣārī (d. 1108); the great *tafsīr* specialist and grammarian, ʿAlī al-Wāḥidī (d. 1076), whose works were read as handbooks in the *madrasas;* the great Ḥanafī jurist and *tafsīr* specialist from Transoxiana and author of the well-known *Kanz al-wuṣūl,* al-Pazdawī (d. 1089); al-Sarakhsī (d. 1090), who was of Turkish origin and gained great fame among the Ḥanafīs with his book entitled *al-Mabsūṭ;* the jurist, philosopher and poet, ʿAin al-Quḍāt al-Hamadānī (d. 1130), some of whose works were translated into Turkish; Muḥammad al-Shahrastānī (d. 1153), who specialized in the history of the law schools during the reign of Sanjar and wrote the *Kitāb al-Milal wa 'l-niḥal;* and al-Baghawī (d. 1116), the author of *Maṣābiḥ al-sunna.* All these men were influential figures in Islamic science and intellectual life for centuries after their own time.

Although the Crusader and Mongol invasions brought about a

stagnation in religious instruction in Anatolia, by the end of the thirteenth century scholars writing important works had reappeared there. For example, Qāḍī 'l-Baidāwī (d. 1291), the famous *tafsīr* specialist and author of *Anwār al-tanzīl;* Sirāj al-Dīn al-Urmawī (d. 1283), who wrote *Maṭāli' al-anwār,* one part of which concerns logic and the other *kalām;* and Quṭb al-Dīn al-Shīrāzī (d. 1310), who revived the philosophical *kalām* movement and was an astronomer at the same time, all began a tradition which they passed to future generations. It should be mentioned here that although the Seljuks were all sincere Muslims who avidly defended Sunnism and were absolutely committed to the need for traditional training and education, they were also open-minded. Alp-Arslan and Malik-Shāh behaved paternalistically toward non-Muslims. Religious and philosophical discussions were held in the presence of Sanjar. Qılıch-Arlsan I, who always showed tolerance to Assyrians and Armenians; Qılıch-Arslan II, who decorated the gardens of some of his houses in Konya with marble statues and was magnanimous to Christians, and even debated the Bible with the Assyrian patriarch of Malatya; Kai-Qubād I, who adorned the gates and walls of his palaces with reliefs and pictures of men and women and embellished the walls that he built for Konya with statues;[21] and Kai-Khusraw II, who struck coins with images on them, were all freethinkers and devoid of any religious fanaticism. Apart from certain cities where the great influence of the *madrasas* resulted in pedantic religious pressure, the people in the empire were generally freethinkers in the Seljuk period. The Turkish villagers in particular were not even very interested in the Ḥanafī *madhhab.* They more often held heretical beliefs related to Ṣūfism. This is one of the major subjects of Turco-Islamic history, especially in Seljuk times.

It can be said that Khurāsān, where the Seljuk state was founded, definitely played a significant religious role in that state, just as it had done with regard to politics, economics, and government. Khurāsān was considered to be the focal point of intellectual currents coming from the west, that is, the 'Abbāsid area of Baghdad, Kūfa, and Baṣra, which was acquainted with ancient Greek science and philosophy, and from India, where there were concepts that were basically monistic. Muslim thinkers combined these two currents with their own views of the cosmos in a manner that suited the usages and customs of the area in which they lived. One consequence of this was the birth of Islamic mysticism. The significance of Khurāsān can be appreciated when we take into account the fact that, when the Turks appeared there, Ṣūfism was experi-

21. See Mehmed Önder, *Mevlānā şehri Konya* [Konya the city of Mawlānā] (Konya, 1962), pp. 58–66.

encing a vigorous period. In the eleventh century, when various *ṣūfī* brotherhoods began to appear in the Islamic world, the *shaikh*s {*ṣūfī* masters} who lived in a spiritual milieu with *ṣūfī* novices and dervishes and gathered at seances (*tezkir muhiti*), lodges, and retreats—which were very widespread in Khurāsān, where the above ideas were welded together—claimed that reality could not be understood from the book (the Qur'ān), but by the senses. For this reason they were opposed to those belonging to the *madrasa*s and emphasized dancing and music, which were religiously proscribed. These *shaikh*s naturally had a great influence on the Turkmen masses who had been nourished on the shamanistic beliefs of the northern steppes and could not adjust very well to the dogmatic precepts of Islam. Many of the outstanding personalities of that period, like those we listed above, were also *ṣūfī*s. The famous authority on *kalām,* al-Ghazzālī, publicly allied himself against Greek philosophy and made the new Islamic mysticism, which he brought about by reconciling—with great erudition and a keen mind—the science of *kalām* with the *ṣūfī* world view, the prevailing form of Islam for centuries. As for the great brotherhoods of the Muslim world, they were the Qādiriyya, which was founded by ʿAbd al-Qādir al-Jīlānī (d. 1166) and spread to India, Anatolia, and as far as Spain; the Kubrāwiyya, established by *shaikh* Najm al-Dīn Kubrā al-Khwārazmī (d. 1221); and the Akbariyya, founded in the thirteenth century. The latter in particular, together with the ideas of the Malāmiyya, which included elements of the old Turkish "Alpiyya," held to the simplicity and ethical and aesthetic principles proper to Turkish spiritualism with regard to beliefs, rituals, and music played during worship, and, by establishing the rules and conditions of the Turkish religious *samāʿ* {a *ṣūfī* seance held with music and dancing}, which was inspired by shamanism, laid the foundation for the Mawlawiyya in Anatolia. The fourth great brotherhood, the Yasawiyya, was founded by Aḥmad Yasawī (d. 1116), who was himself a Turk. In order to spread Islam among the Turks, this brotherhood in particular adopted a great many Turkish usages and customs and used the Turkish language (the *Hikmetler* of Yasawī {i.e., his *Dīwān-i Ḥikmet,* a collection of religious poems}). The Yasawiyya differed from the other brotherhoods by being clearly characterized as popular Ṣūfism. It spread to Turkistan, Afghanistan, the area of the Golden Horde, and northern Iran. It also prepared the way for the spread of other brotherhoods, such as the Naqshabandiyya (fourteenth century) in Central Asia and the Bektashiyya, which found very fertile ground in Anatolia. One can in fact discover its success in the difference between the Iranian and Turkish understanding of Ṣūfism. This was primarily a difference between art and ultimate goal. In contrast to the Iranian view, which considered the *ṣūfī* state of mind to be a means of seeing the world artistically and directed this frame of mind toward a state beyond man and time, the Turkish view considered the goal of Ṣūfism to be strictly one of moral and spiritual purification. Furthermore, because of its contact with early Turkish thought, the *ṣūfī* state of mind appears to have been combined with the concepts of motherland and country. Consequently, when adherents of Turkish Ṣūfism came to Anatolia, their followers could be found performing important services along the border. Thus under the leadership of Turkish *shaikh*s called "heros, *bābā*s, and *abdal*s," who were all essentially the old Turkish *alp* of Central Asia, "heroic men" {*alp-erenler,* dervishes} imbued with the spiritual atmosphere of Khurāsān carried out their national duty as *ghāzī*s in the country of battle, Anatolia. At the time of the Ottoman Empire, they also carried out the same function on the Rumeli frontier. Indeed, this is how the Bektashiyya, which derived from the Yasawiyya, became the official brotherhood of the warrior class.[22]

On the other hand, while it was very natural for pre-Islamic Turkish concepts to have an influence on the rise of Turco-Islamic brotherhoods and to leave traces in Turkish Ṣūfism, it was just as natural for the Shīʿī movement, which appeared in the guise of a quasi-*madhhab,* by becoming identified with the beliefs of such early religions as Zoroastrianism, Manichaeism, and Mazdakism (which were wrapped in Islamic garb in Iran when it was the main center for the struggle for power), to make an impression on Turkish ideas because both Shīʿism and Ṣūfism were nourished by common sources and held the same views in such matters as having a deep affection for the family of the Prophet and being opposed to the intolerant strictness of Sunnī dogma. In fact, the popular saints who began to appear in the eleventh century were strongly perceived in the same way as the Turkmen *bābā*s. Those who held these heretical views came on the scene like the old Turkish shaman-wandering minstrel (sorcerer-popular poet) and, rather than being regarded as strangers, were respected and greatly loved by the Turkmen. Not just the great popular masses, but even the Turkmen rulers (the Seljuk sultans), each of whom, as we have seen, set out to defend the Muslim world as a Sunnī Muslim and in this respect mercilessly fought against heretical movements like Shīʿism and its various branches, were tolerant of the *ṣūfī*s who spread ideas that were full of Shīʿī teachings. Famous *ṣūfī*s like Bābā Ṭāhir ʿUryān and Abū Saʿīd b. Abī 'l-Khair,[23] for example, were highly

22. See Köprülü, *Osmanlı devletinin kuruluşu,* pp. 83–102; Wittek, "Deux chapitres de l'histoire des Turcs de Roum," pt. 2 "Les Ghazis dans l'histoire Ottomane," *Byzantion* 11(1936):302–19; Ülken, *İslâm düşüncesi,* pp. 104–08, 175–81, 185.

esteemed figures during the reigns of Toghrıl Beg, Alp-Arslan, and Malik-Shāh. These *ṣūfīs* who represented the people, as well as the great *ṣūfīs* we mentioned above who addressed the intellectuals, helped their movement to develop on two fronts, both of which were active in Anatolia.

Asia Minor became a land of leading *ṣūfī* personalities. These *ṣūfīs* were in fact exceptional people having great knowledge, keen intellect, and a refined aesthetic sense and literary ability. Indeed, it suffices to state that Seljuk Turkey was a country having a moral and spiritual milieu favorable to the work of a systematic religious philosopher of such rare attainment as Muḥyī 'l-Dīn Ibn al-ʿArabī (d. 1240). Of Spanish origin, Ibn al-ʿArabī studied the Islamic sciences and then began to make "discoveries" by entering the mystical and philosophical atmosphere of his homeland. He made the pilgrimage to Mecca and there profited from the works of ʿAbd Allāh al-Anṣārī,[24] and al-Ghazzālī. When he later came to Anatolia, he was received with honor. He won the favor and generosity of the sultans and settled in Konya. Ibn al-ʿArabī's literary production reached the unprecedented level of some 250 books and treatises, the most important of which were *al-Futūḥāt al-makkiyya, Fuṣūṣ al-ḥikam, Ishārāt al-Qur'ān,* and *Jawāhir al-nuṣūṣ*. According to him, the highest and most authentic knowledge is not that perceived by the mind, but only the "knowledge" that God imparts to those ("the perfect man," *al-insān al-kāmil*), who have received genuine and thorough *ṣūfī* training. Ibn al-ʿArabī's greatness derives in considerable measure from his ability to reconcile in one unifying concept, by means of the theory that he developed of the unity of his own being (*waḥdat al-wujūd* {monism}), the various and contradictory metaphysical views that came from different sources and had not been harmonized up to that time. According to his theory, there is only one true existence and that consists of God. The world and the cosmos are nothing but a temporary manifestation and shadow of Him, and mankind is nothing but the external appearance of Him. In other words, everything, all matter, represents and expresses different aspects of God. Also related to this idea was the concept of "the perfect man" which derived from Ibn al-ʿArabī's famous theory of the *al-haḍarāt al-khamsa* (five stages, *beş kat*). Because he was something that existed, and thus himself reflected God, his "knowledge" {*ʿilm*} was therefore God's "knowledge." By advancing through various stages of essentially mystical exercises, eventualy slipping completely away from the flesh and fusing with the true reality that was identical with oneself, the "perfect man" attained a state of illumination "lost" in God. For

23. See *Asrār al-tawḥīd,* ed. Ḍ. Ṣafā (Tehran, 1332 *sh.*).

24. See also Tahsin Yazıcı, "ʿAbd Allāh al-Anṣārī'nin Kanz al-sālikīn'i" [ʿAbd Allāh al-Anṣārī's *Kanz al-sālikīn*], *ŞM* 1(1956):59–88; Ahmed Ateş, "ʿAbd Allāh al-Anṣārī'nin Zam al- kalām va ahlih adlı eseri" [ʿAbd Allāh al-Anṣārī's work entitled *Dhamm al-kalām wa ahlihi*], *ŞM* 5(1964):45–60.

him, nothing unknown was left in the eternity of the past and future. He could predict the future, divine a man's fate, and magically make objects obey him. The reason that we are describing Ibn al-ʿArabī and his contributions here in some detail is to emphasize the enormous influence this great *ṣūfī* of the Seljuk period had in the Islamic world and, indeed, continued to have in Turkey until recent times. The ideas that he committed to writing as a first-class stylist in Arabic literature were continued by the famous *ṣūfī* Ṣadr al-Dīn al-Qūnawī (d. 1234),[25] his student and spiritual heir, who founded a brotherhood called the Akbariyya, after the title of his master "al-Shaikh al-Akbar" (the Greatest Shaikh). Despite being accused of unbelief by judges who were *ahl al-kitāb* {adherents of a revealed religion}, he trained many *ṣufī*s, some of whom wrote important books. They included Fakhr al-Dīn al-ʿIrāqī (d. 1287), Muʿayyad al-Jandī (d. 1291), and Saʿd al-Dīn al-Farghānī (d. 1299). Moreover, the Akbariyya spread to Iran, India, and as far as Yemen in Arabia. The most renowned *ṣufī*s who lived between the fourteenth and eighteenth centuries, like Davud of Kayseri, Kutbeddin of Iznik, Yazıcıoğlu Mehmed, Jāmi, Ibrāhīm Gülshenī, Shaʿrānī, and ʿAbd al-Ghanī al-Nābulusī, followed in his footsteps. Commentaries were written on Ibn al-ʿArabī's works in virtually every part of the Muslim world, and a great many contradictory things were said about him. In Turkey his influence can still be felt in such works as M. Ali Aynī's *Şeyh-i ekberi niçin severim?* [Why do I love the Great Shaikh?] (Istanbul, 1926) and in the *Muhyiddin Arabī tābir-nāmesi tercümesi* [The translation of Muḥyī 'l-Dīn ʿArabī's *Taʿbīr-Nāma*]. Although the latter work is spurious, that is, no such book was written by this outstanding *ṣūfī,* this reveals that the Akbariyya, *ṣūfī* movements that were greatly inspired by it like the Malāmiyya and Bektashiyya, and the practical aspects of it which took the place of a genuine philosophical view in the popular brotherhoods were in demand. Miracles were attributed to *shaikh*s or dervishes everywhere. Claims of soothsaying, predicting the future, and revealing various mysteries, which were easily fostered in the simple popular mind, deprived people of the faculty for positive thought and at the same time had a negative effect on religious instruction. All this kept the people from reality and the scientific mentality based on observation and experience.

Coming to the Mawlawiyya {or Mevleviye}, which was founded by the other great *ṣūfī* of Anatolia, Mawlānā {or Mevlana} Jalāl al-Dīn al-Rūmī (d. 1273), it can be described as placing the strongest emphasis on art, ethics, and science. It was based on the

25. See also Osman Ergin, "Ṣadr al-Dīn al-Ḳonavī ve eserleri" [Ṣadr al-Dīn al-Qūnawī and his work], *ŞM* 2(1958):63–90.

Malāmiyya ideas from Khurāsān and differed from the Akbariyya, which frequently even considered the Old and New Testaments as vehicles for its purposes. In addition to accepting the idea of the "unity of being," the Malāmiyya can be characterized as being very truthful in its thought and well-mannered in behavior while giving no importance to attire, appearance, or ceremony. About the time of the appearance of the Seljuks, it was widespread in Transoxiana and Khurāsān. Turkmen Malāmī *shaikh*s came on the scene like Muḥammad Maʿshūqī, whom al-Ghazzālī respected. The Malāmiyya held such principles as avoiding hypocrisy, pride, boastfulness, and greed; sincerely believing in God and imitating the Prophet; and not believing in the miracles of the saints. It was also open to ideas that were removed from human affectation, such as not being bound to formal ceremonies like prayer and *dhikr* {*ṣūfī* seance}. Because the Malāmiyya accepted the concept of "heroism" {*alplık*} and had a realistic spirit that thrived on simplicity, the Turks were strongly attracted to it. By adding the spirit of a love of fighting and a number of shamanistic beliefs to these sincere feelings, and giving priority to love and ecstasy, the Turkish Malāmīs were a factor in the rise and development of a number of brotherhoods, both esoteric {*bāṭīnī*} and conforming to Islamic law. The Turkish Malāmīs were given the title *Erenler* {those who have arrived at the divine truth, dervish} of Khurāsān, which was later used by every *shaikh* and dervish, whether or not from Khurāsān, who held Malāmī ideas. Shaikh Najm al-Dīn Kubrā, who laid the foundation of the Kubrāwiyya brotherhood at the beginning of the thirteenth century, was a practical man and did not ignore the customs and tendencies of the time, such as the *samāʿ,* which was a dance accompanied by music, and the *mujāhada,* namely, the love of battle and fighting for the faith. A number of the students whom he trained came to Anatolia because of the Mongol invasion. One of the most important of them was Najm al-Dīn Dāya (d. 1256). He wrote a book entitled *Mirshād al-ʿibād,* which he dedicated to ʿAlā' al-Dīn Kai-Qubād I. Another was Bahā' al-Dīn Valad, the father of Mawlānā. The latter came to Anatolia with his father and settled in Konya, where he performed his novitiate steeped in Mawlawī {*sic*} concepts in which were found, of course, traces of Malāmī ideas and old Turkish rites of worship with regard to aesthetics. Mawlānā had received a strong *madrasa* education, but easily passed from being a scholar {*ilm ehli*} to a mystic {*hal ehli*}, because he was, above all, a man of the heart and an excellent poet. Most important, imbued with *ṣūfī*-Malāmī ideas after conversations with Shams-i Tabrīzī, who had come to Anatolia from

Tabrīz, he devoted himself completely to the spiritual world and with great literary ability began his inspired teaching. His famous *al-Dīwān al-kabīr,* and especially his *Mathnawī,* which was highly esteemed in literature, masterfully helped him to address directly the feelings of the people with enchanting poetic strength. Mawlānā's basic idea, which could be summarized as an expression of humanitarianism, was of a universal nature. Differences in religion, creed, and race were of no consideration. The significance of this concept is found in a statement by ʿAlam al-Dīn, one of the commanders of Kai-Khusraw III, who said, "every people loves its prophet but people of every religion and state love Mawlānā." This view describes the great tolerance of the Turks in general, and the Seljuk government in particular, and held an attraction for non-Turks and non-Muslims, such as Greeks, Armenians, and Jews, that was impossible to resist. For this reason the death of this great Turk was truly mourned by all the people, Muslim and non-Muslim, in the Seljuk state of Anatolia. His humanistic idea continues to live as a concept leading men to well-being and equality. His *Mathnawī,* which contains this idea, was regarded in many circles as a "second Qur'ān." Mawlānā succeeded in providing the guidelines for the complete ecstacy and submission of the human soul that he brought to a state of spiritual unity (with respect to the Supreme Being, God) and mystical love, which he considered to be an expression of an unrequited love of God. He did so in the performance of the *samāʿ,* in which he created a harmonious blend of poetry, music, and dance—three important branches of the fine arts. Moreover, as is known, Mawlānā did not give much emphasis to fighting and warfare. While even Ibn al-ʿArabī advised that one should take up arms to defend Islam against nonbelievers, the peace-loving and conciliatory Mawlānā did not interfere in political or administrative affairs. He even sought ways to get along with the Mongols and was on good terms with Muʿīn al-Dīn Parvāna, who cooperated with the invaders. Because his inspired message was addressed to the more enlightened upper class, it was not of great interest to the masses, especially the Turkmen. But by always cooperating with those in power, the Mawlawiyya showed that it had the ability to guarantee its future in later centuries. And because Mawlaism, all of the principles and rules of which were not established until the fifteenth century, was on a level above the great masses and its language was Persian, it was identified until recent times as a brotherhood composed exclusively of sultans, vizirs, and leading families. After Mawlānā passed away, the third person to succeed to his position in the order was his son Sultan Valad (or Veled, d. 1312) who shaped Mawlānā's Ṣūfism with such works as his *Dīvān, Ibtidā-Nāma, Valad-Nāma,* and *Rabāb-Nāma,* and assured the establishment of a learned {*çelebi*} dynasty by limiting the succession to his own family. But he also accused Turkish of being inadequate for refined speech, even though it was his native language. Yunus Emre, however, who was the real representative of the Turkish milieu in Anatolia, was able to express the most subtle ideas and religious and mystical concepts in this supposedly inadequate language with great ease and created poems that became immortal masterpieces of Turkish literature. For Yunus knew the great Turkish masses and so represented the people.

In addition to the Mawlawiyya and Akbariyya, there were in fact other movements in the Seljuk state of Anatolia. Indeed, the divisions among various currents of thought that began in Khurāsān also continued here. At the time of the very first migrations, a great many Turkmen *bābās* came to Anatolia, which was considered the *dār al-jihād* {abode of Holy War}, with the Turkmen tribes, and {together with} Yasawī dervishes and *erens* from Khurāsān settled in places that slowly began to be Islamized. Those among them who played the most important religious role were not the *ṣūfī*s who wrote poetry and commentaries in Arabic and Persian in the palaces, which were unquestionably inclined toward Iranian culture under the patronage of the rulers and other state officials, but the *bābā*s who, by possessing strange powers and an aura of sanctity passed down from the old shamans and wandering minstrels, and living lives of mystical contemplation, maintained a link with the old shamanism in Muslim form and addressed the Oghuz tribes in their own language. They inspired a form of Islam that was reduced to Ṣūfism, which was compatible with old Turkish traditions. This form of Islam was understood by the people but was consequently rather corrupt and much different from the Sunnī creed officially accepted and defended by the Seljuk states. Because of the Mongol invasion, there was a great migration to the west. This was a factor in filling Anatolia with members of the Qalandāriyya, who had ties to Central Asian ideas and the Malāmiyya, and had no permanent homes or established way of life and ignored formal religious rites and the social niceties of the age; and the devotees of the Ḥaidariyya, which was founded by the famous Turkish *shaikh* Quṭb al-Dīn Ḥaidar at the end of the twelfth century and was inspired by the Yasawiyya. Both of these brotherhoods were found among the immigrant groups and had a great influence on them. Thus Qalandārī and Ḥaidarī Turkmen *bābā*s, like Shaikh Arslan and Bābā Merendi, who spread Shīʿī beliefs and *bāṭinī* ideas among the great masses of Turkmen, prepared the way for the famous Bābā'ī uprising (1239) during the reign of Sultan Ghiyāth al-Dīn Kai-Khusraw II. It occurred just before the Mongol invasion—at a time when the Seljuk government appeared to be disintegrating and the Khwārazmians were disruptive—and shook the state to its very foundations.

At the head of this movement was a *shaikh* named Bābā Isḥāq, who lived like a saint in a cave in the neighborhood of Amasya and was recognized by the Turkmen as a prophet (*Bābā rasūl Allāh* {Bābā is the prophet of God}). The populous Turkmen masses, including women and children, were thrown into a state of emotional excitement by him and, after defeating the forces of the state one after another, took control of the areas around Amasya, Tokat, and Malatya. They were crushed only with great difficulty after Bābā Isḥāq and his leading disciples were captured and executed. After this first Turkmen uprising of such a religio-political nature, a great many saints and dervishes with *bāṭinī* beliefs appeared among the Turkmen supporters of Bābā, who were scattered in all directions. They were the cause of numerous rebellions in Anatolia. Just as Nūra Ṣūfī, the founding father of the Qaramānids, who were the enemies of the Seljuks, had been connected with the *bābā*s, Jimrī, whom the Qaramānid Mehmed Beg placed on the throne in Konya, also behaved, at least outwardly, like a *bābā shaikh* who was considered to be holy. In the early Ottoman period, there were rebellions instigated by Börklüce Mustafa and Shaikh Badr al-Dīn Simāvī. Their activities, like those of such famous men as Sarı Saltuk Dede, who took a number of *bābā'ī* Turkmen into his service and went as far as Dobruja in the Balkans (1264); Buzaghı Bābā, said to be the *shaikh* of Qılıch-Arslan IV; Geyikli Bābā; and Barak Bābā (d. 1307), who was one of Sarı Saltuk's disciples; as well as the successes won by the Iranian Safavid ruler Shāh Ismā'īl in his political propaganda against the Ottomans, were all related to Bābā'ism. Indeed, this creed was continued by the *tahtacı, çepni,* and *kızıl-baş* groups in a great many places in Anatolia.

There was also a very close relationship between the Bektashī brotherhood and Bābā'ism. The founder of the Bektashiyya, which was the largest brotherhood that was clearly opposed to Sunnism and the scholasticism of the *madrasas* and which spread Shī'ī-*bāṭinī* ideas, was Ḥājjī Bektash Veli, who belonged to the *eren*s of Khurāsān. He was one of the successors of Bābā Isḥāq in the fourteenth century. Because he was attached to the Twelver branch of Shi'ism, his brotherhood immediately spread among those people who were of the same mind, like the Ḥaidarīs, Qalandārīs, and Abdals. And because the *eren*s of Khurāsān had a reputation as fighters, it took hold among the warriors for the faith and military classes, thus spreading its influence as far west as the Turkmen reached. The main feature of Bektashism was essentially its reliance on positive interpretations and its spirit of tolerance, as can be seen throughout Bektashī literature. It therefore had a great number of supporters among the people. By incorporating over time many elements of the Ḥurūfiyya {a Shī'ī sect}, the Nuqṭawiyya {another Shī'ī sect}, and even the Naqshabandiyya, which was a Sunnī brotherhood, it became a kind of union of brotherhoods. Its principles and rules were established in the fifteenth century by the chief {*post-nişīn*} *bābā*s in Ḥājjī Bektash's home town, and above all by Balım Sultan (d. 1516) at the beginning of the sixteenth century, and has survived until recent times.

Meanwhile, western Anatolia in particular presented a rather different picture in the Seljuk period. Religious personalities and *ṣūfī* leaders who came to Anatolia from among the Khurāsānian *erens* and provided moral support on the frontiers, the areas of conquest, also participated in the fighting. In the words of 'Āshıq Pasha, they were known as *alp-erenler*. The *alp-erenler,* who were land-owning cavalry soldiers and who had connections with the *akhī* organizations which, as we have seen, extended to the frontiers, differed from the other Muslim *ghāzī*s in the Middle Ages in that they preserved Turkish national traditions. In the thirteenth and fourteenth centuries, they constituted the core of the military forces on the frontiers and in the western Anatolian *beylik*s and provided inestimable services. Later, as a result of growing urbanization and the increasing influence of Sunnī Islam, they began to be known as *ghāzī*s, although their activities did not change. This name continued in use throughout Ottoman history.[26]

26. See Köprülü, "Anadolu'da islâmiyet," *Darülfünün Edebiyat Fakültesi Mecmuası* 2(1922):281–311, 385–420, 456–86; idem, "Anadolu Selçukluları tarihinin yerli kaynakları," pp. 445–56; idem, *Osmanlı devletinin kuruluşu,* pp. 93–102; Gölpınarlı, *Melâmîlik ve melâmiler* [The Malāmiyya and the Malāmīs] (Istanbul, 1931); Cahen, "Notes pour l'histoire des Turcomans d'Asie Mineure au XIIIe siècle," *JA* 239(1951):335–54; A. İnan, "Müsülman Türklerde şamanizm kalıntıları" [Vestiges of shamanism among the Muslim Turks], *AÜİF Dergisi* 5(1952):19–30; Akdağ, *Türkiye'nin iktisâdî,* I, 54–65; Kafesoğlu, *Melikşah,* pp. 172–85.

Science, Literature, and Art

It is known that the period of the Seljuk Empire marked a turning point in the teaching of religious sciences in the Islamic world. Religious instruction, which that era considered a science, had previously been disorganized, irregular, and of a completely private nature. It was systemized for the first time in the reign of Alp-Arslan and brought under state patronage. The Seljuk Empire pursued this important cultural program under the direction of Niẓām al-Mulk, who was responsible for the civil administration. The main reason for this was the need for a fundamental policy to combat Shīʿism and other schismatic beliefs. At first they sought to create a strong spiritual front that was loyal to the state by setting aside appropriations for the Sunnī jurists and legal scholars of the time and by opening soup kitchens {*imāret*} for ascetics. With the establishment of *madrasa*s, the great scholarly fraternities were finally made part of a teaching system that was staffed throughout the empire. This was not the *madrasa* that was known to have had certain precedents and merely indicated a "place where a *dars* {lesson in Islamic law} was given."[27] Rather, the first *madrasa,* as the highest institution of learning in the Muslim world, which brought together, as teachers and preachers, the most famous scholars, jurists, and intellectuals of the time and made them salaried professors; provided students with a monthly allowance and provisions; gave free instruction; set up programs of study; and was equipped with a rich library, was founded by Alp-Arslan (1066). It was built next to the Tigris in Baghdad and, with all its facilities and annexes, reputedly cost 60,000 dinars (gold) in the money of the time. This *madrasa* was endowed with markets, *khāns,* baths, and agricultural lands. Because Niẓām al-Mulk's name was written on the front of the building, it became known as the Niẓāmiyya. The Niẓāmiyya in Baghdad provided religious instruction according to Ḥanafī and Shāfiʿī *fiqh*. It played a major role in scientific and intellectual life and trained scholars of high quality. *Qāḍī*s and religious officials were generally sent from there to every corner of the empire. Because they were the most competent, young Niẓāmiyya graduates occupied high positions in the country. Around the same time, sister institutions of this *madrasa* were established in such centers as Iṣfahān, Nīshāpūr, Balkh, Herāt, Baṣra, and Āmul. The subjects of study and programs in the Niẓāmiyya were basically followed and applied for centuries in all Muslim countries and by all Islamic Turkish dynasties, including the Ottomans.[28]

27. See Tāj al-Dīn al-Subkī, *Ṭabaqāt al-shāfiʿiyya al-kubrā* (Cairo, 1299), III, 136; Ibn Khallikān, *Wafayāt,* I, 6, 35.

28. See Asad Talas, *L'Enseignment chez les arabs: La Madrasa Nizamiyya et son histoire* (Paris, 1939).

Because not only the religious sciences but also the hard sciences, such as mathematics and astronomy, were taught at the same time in the Niẓāmiyya *madrasa*s, and because similar institutions were not founded in Europe until much later, the Baghdad Niẓāmiyya is considered to be the world's first university.[29] As is known, countless *madrasas* were later founded on the same basis by sultans, state officials, and important women throughout the Seljuk Empire and in all Seljuk states. *Madrasas* were also very important with regard to training officials for the state's bureaucratic and judicial staff.

29. Cf. Ülken, *İslâm düşüncesi,* p. 357.

In the Seljuk period, the science of mathematics reached a high level. During the reign of Malik-Shāh, its outstanding representatives were men like the famous ᶜUmar al-Khayyām (d. 1131), who was better known for literature, and Muḥammad Baihaqī. They wrote important works on algebra, conics, and geometry as well as astronomical tables. In addition, in 476/1074-75 an observatory was built and research was carried out in it. A scientific committee composed of leading astronomers like ᶜUmar al-Khayyām, Abū Ḥātim al-Muẓaffar al-Isfizārī, and Maimūn b. Najīb al-Wāsiṭī created a new calendar called *ta'rīkh-i malikī, ta'rīkh-i jalālī,* or *taqwīmī Malik-Shāh*. This calendar, which was based on a knowledge of higher physics and optics, relied on more accurate calculations than the Christian (Gregorian) calendar that we currently use. In chemistry, the paint industry was well developed and paper production was advanced. Great doctors and Arabic linguists and rhetoriticians were trained.[30] Above all, new facilities were created for developing the medical and health professions in Anatolia. Hospitals were built at that time in Kayseri (1205), Sivas (1217), Konya, ʿAlā'iyya, Divriği (1228), Chankırı (1235), and Kastamonu (1273).[31] At the very least, physicians were trained in the manner of master and apprentice. In the Seljuk period, historiography apparently took a very different approach from that of the old Arabic biographies and books of campaigns {*megāzī kitapları*}. The Seljuk sultans, who had a love of history like all Turkish rulers, encouraged the development of this field. Among the products of the Seljuk era that we have used as sources are the *Malik-Nāma* (ca. 1058), which mentions the origins of the Seljuks; Ibn Ḥassūl's history; the important work entitled *Risāla-i Malik-shāhiyya;* the *Ta'rīkh-i āl-i Saljūq* by the poet Abū Ṭāhir-i Khātūnī; the *Siyar-u futūḥ-i sultān Sanjar* by the poet Amīr Muʿizzī; the *ʿUnwān al-siyar* by Hamadānī; the *Mashārib al-tajārib* and *Zīnat al-kuttāb* by Ibn Funduq; the *Kitāb Mafākhir al-atrāk* by ʿAlī al-Qā'inī on behalf of Sultan Sanjar; and other works by such authors as ʿImād al-Dīn al-Iṣfahānī, Ibn al-Jawzī, Sibṭ b. al-Jawzī, and Rāvandī. Unfortunately, much of the work of these latter writers was lost in the destruction caused by the Mongol invasion. In the reign of Toghrıl III, the sultan of Iraq, a geographical work called *ʿAjā'ib al-makhlūqāt* was composed by Aḥmad al-Ṭūsī. Rāvandī dedicated his famous Seljuk history, *Rāḥat al-ṣudūr,* to Ghiyāth al-Dīn Kai-Khusraw I (1207). The most outstanding history of ʿAlā' al-Dīn Kai-Qubād I, who was interested in astrology just like Qutalmısh, the son of Arslan Yabghu,[32] was written by Ibn Bībī. It was called *al-Awāmir al-ʿalā'iyya* and covered the events of the years 1192-1280.[33] Later, in the time of the Mongols, Karīm al-Dīn al-Aqsarāyī composed his *Musāmarat al-akhbār* (1323), a

30. See Kafesoğlu, *Melikşah,* pp. 185–89.

31. A. S. Ünver, "Büyük Selçuklu imparatorluğu zamanında vakıf hasta-hânelerin bir kısmına dâir" [On a number of endowed hospitals during the time of the Great Seljuk Empire], *VD* 1(1938):17–23.

32. Ibn al-Athīr, *al-Kāmil,* year 456.

33. Photocopy ed. (Ankara: TTK, 1956).

major source of Seljuk history.[34] In addition to these works, there were some in verse like the great Seljuk epic {*shāh-nāma*} by the poet Aḥmad Qāniʿī, the *Selçuklular şeh-nāmesi* written in 20,000 couplets by the Khurāsānian Turkish poet Khwāja Dehhānī, and undoubtedly many others that have not come down to us.

As for the literature of Seljuk times, very great progress was made in poetry and prose just as we have seen in every other field. In the empire period, this was above all to the benefit of Persian literature. Thanks to the material and moral support of the Turkish sultans, outstanding figures in Iranian literature appeared at that time. They included Lāmiʿī-i Jurjānī, Abū 'l-Maʿālī al-Naḥḥās, Abū Ṭāhir-i Khātūnī, Abīwardī, and the famous satirical poet Ibn al-Habbāriyya. In addition, there were, above all, Amīr Muʿizzī; ʿUmar al-Khayyām; the renowned poet of odes, Anwarī; Azraqī who was patronized by Malik Tughan-Shāh; Niẓāmī who lived in the country of the Eldigüz *atabeg*s, who continued the traditions of the Seljuks; Saʿdī-i Shīrāzī, who flourished among the *atabeg*s of Fārs; and others.

Persian had risen to such a high level at the time of the Seljuks that it also had an effect on Anatolia. The works that we mentioned above were written in that language. However, in the struggle that took place in this land, on the one hand between Turkish and Arabic, which maintained its position and spread because it was the language of the Qur'ān and was the medium of the *madrasa*s, and, on the other, between Turkish and Persian, which was cultivated as the literary language, Turkish finally triumphed by confining Arabic within the walls of the *madrasa*s and displacing Persian as the every-day language. Thus, although the palace circles in particular took Iranian names instead of Turkish names, had *shāh-nāma*s composed and assumed Persian and Arabic titles, the battle among the Arabic, Persian, and Turkish cultures ended in a victory for the latter thanks to the great masses of Turkmen who were very closely attached to their traditions. In Anatolia, Turkish culture and Turkish literature had a remarkable number of representatives. We saw the first political sign of this in the *ferman* (1277) issued by the Qaramānid Mehmed Beg, who put Ghiyāth al-Dīn Siyāvush (Jimrī) on the throne in Konya in an attempt to overthrow the Seljuk dynasty. It stated that "from this day forward no language but Turkish will be spoken in the government, court, audience chamber, or in public." In the years after the battle of Malazgird, these representatives of Turkish culture and literature were the popular poets of the Turkmen who played the *kopuz* {an old Turkish stringed instrument} and sang the old Oghuz legends

34. Ed. Turan (Ankara: TTK, 1944).

and heroic stories embellished by poetic gusts from the steppes. The tales that arose about Abū Muslim al-Khurāsānī, Ḥaḍrat-i Ḥamza, and Ḥaḍrat-i ʿAlī formed the subjects of their stories and were in complete accord with the *ghāzī* psychology of twelfth- and thirteenth-century Anatolia. There is no doubt that exuberant Turkish poetic stories like that of Abū Muslim, whose memory had not been forgotten after the great ᶜAbbāsid revolt, in which Turks had also participated, and whose legends were known to have been set down in Turkish in the palace of Sultan Sanjar; the *Salsal-Nāma;* the epic of Aḥmad Ḥarāmī; and the legend of Baṭṭāl Ghāzī held a great attraction for the Turks living in a wartime atmosphere in Anatolia. Finally, one of the principle works of Turkish epic literature having a less imaginary element was the *Dānishmend-Nāma,*[35] the heroic story of Dānishmend Aḥmad Ghāzī. It also contains an account of the heroic deeds against the Crusaders in central Anatolia by Chakan Beg (the *beg* of Izmir), Qılıch-Arslan I and Ḥasan Beg. This legend, which had apparently already been committed to writing in Anatolia in the twelfth century, was rearranged in 1244 upon the wish of ᶜIzz al-Dīn Kai-Kā'ūs II before it reached its final form in the reign of the Ottoman Sultan Murad II. The legend of the *bābā'ī shaikh* Sarı Saltuk was added to this as another product of Anatolian Turkish literature. It reached its final form during the time of Fatih {Mehmed II}. In addition, a great many works of a legendary nature {*menākib-nāmeler*} were written about such personalities as Bābā Ilyās, Ḥājjī Bektash Veli, Seyyid Maḥmūd Hayrānī, Ḥājjī Ibrāhīm Sultan, Ḥājjim Sultan, Akhī Ewrān, and Seyyid Hārūn, all of whom acquired great fame in thirteenth- and fourteenth-century Anatolia. These legendary stories were read with great affection by the people.

35. See I. Melikoff, *La Geste de Melik Dānişmend* (Paris, 1960), I.

Turkish *ṣūfī* poetry formed another genre of Anatolian Turkish literature. It began somewhat earlier under the influence of the religious poems and hymns of Aḥmad Yasawī and the Turkish poets inspired by him. Aḥmad Faqīh, who lived at the time of Mawlānā and was the author of a *ṣūfī* ethical work entitled *Charkh-Nāma;* and Shayyād Ḥamza, who followed him, were in the vanguard of this kind of poetry. If we leave aside the Turkish words and expressions found in the works of Mawlānā, which are anyway rare, and come to Sultan Veled, we find that he felt compelled to write Turkish poetry, even though he claimed that Turkish was inadequate for literary purposes, because of the gradually increasing pressure of Turkish culture. His verses are also the earliest examples of Anatolian *ṣūfī* literature. Sultan Veled undoubtedly prepared the way for such representatives of classic Turkish poetry as Gülshehrī and ʿĀshıq Pasha. But it can be said that Turkish reached its zenith in this field in the fourteenth century with the great Turkmen poet Yunus Emre (d. 1320). Yunus succeeded in speaking and writing Turkish with a skill that has been unrivaled by anyone throughout history for its ease and simplicity. He brought Turkish *ṣūfī* literature, which he never ceased to refine, to an incomparable level of maturity and channeled sincerity, rapture and ecstasy, like a powerful river, toward a future of endless centuries. On the one hand, his poetry became a source for troubador {*āshıq*} literature and, on the other, became a source for the famous classical school of poetry {*dīwān* literature} of the Ottoman period. Yunus consequently had a distinct influence on these two genres of Turkish literature. Anatolia, which the Seljuk sultans and commanders and Turkmen *beg*s took by the sword, was in fact conquered and became a real Turkish homeland thanks to the great representatives of the Turkish cultural struggle. We should mention that Āzarī literature, which was essentially based on the Oghuz-Turkmen dialect and later took a slightly different direction from Anatolian-Ottoman Turkish, was also one of the historical literary products brought about by Seljuk Turkishness.[36]

It is not possible to list here one by one the outstanding examples of architecture, miniatures, ceramics, carpets, kilims, inscriptions, calligraphy, gilding, decoration, and the like that reveal the craftsmanship and building activity of the Seljuk period and that are usually described as masterpieces. Animal designs, which were the product of the old steppe art, are found in abundance on the major sections of the walls of Diyārbakr, surviving from the reign of Malik-Shāh, and on the works in the other Turkmen *beylik*s. Moreover, thousands of palaces, cathedral mosques, local mosques, soup kitchens, *khāns,* public baths, hospitals, *madrasa*s, *ṣūfī* lodges {*khānqāhs*}, tombs {*türbe*s}, mausolea {*kümbet*s}, fountains {*çeşme*s}, public fountains {*sabīl*s}, caravansaries, fortresses, walls, *ribāṭ*s, and sarcophagi were built during the Seljuk era throughout the vast area stretching from the borders of China to the Mediterranean, Egypt, and the Bosphorus and from the steppes of the Oghuz and the Caucasus to the borders of India and Yemen. All our sources, including the accounts of a great many native and foreign travelers from Nāṣir-i Khusraw (d. 1061) until recent times, testify to this. The façades, doors, and frames of the windows of buildings were adorned with the most beautiful and colorful inscriptions, and inside they were embellished with fine decor. This period also provides the most beautiful examples of Turkish marble stone work, inlay work, and carving. This can be seen on the bases

36. Köprülü, *Türk edebiyatı tarihi* [The history of Turkish literature] (Istanbul, 1928), pp. 141–54, 178 f., 212–20, 226–32, 243–52, 281–322; idem, *Türk dili,* pp. 162–73; idem, "Anadolu Selçukluları tarihinin yerli kaynakları," pp. 386–89, 421–58; M. Şerefeddin, "Mevlānā'da türkçe kelimeler ve türkçe şiirler" [The Turkish words and Turkish poetry of Mawlānā], *TM* 4(1934):11–68; Gölpınarlı, *Melâmilik ve melâmiler;* idem, *Yunus Emre hayatı* [The life of Yunus Emre] (Istanbul, 1936); idem, *Yunus Emre dîvânı* [The poetry of Yunus Emre] (Istanbul, 1943); M. Mansuroğlu, "Anadolu metinleri: XIII. asır, Şeyyad Hamza, Dehhânî, İbtidâ-nâme" [Anatolian texts from the thirteenth century: Shayyād Ḥamza, Dehhānī, *Ibtidā'-Nāma*], *TM* 7–8(1942):95–104; Ş. Akkaya, *Kitabi-i Melik Danischmend Gâzî, Ein türkische historischer Heldenroman . . .* (Ankara, 1954).

of domes, which were sometimes covered with Turkish tiles, *minbar*s {pulpit}, *miḥrāb*s, ablution fountains, doors, and window shutters. The superiority of the Seljuk period can be seen in every respect. In our opinion, in order to get a good idea of these works, it suffices to take a look at just Anatolia, indeed only the city of Konya. The bibliography on this subject is very rich. For this reason we shall limit ourselves to a brief sketch of the Seljuk contributions to the world of art. Just as they stamped the centuries-old architectural tradition that they encountered when they came to the Iranian region with their own personality, the Seljuks also created new building forms. The architecture of the *madrasa*s, which spread in every direction at the end of the ninth century and took its initial form in three great Seljuk state *madrasa*s (the Niẓāmiyya *madrasa*s of Baghdad, Nīshāpūr, and Ṭūs), acquired a dominant position in the Turco-Islamic world as a new Turkish model for the building art. The construction of the *madrasa* mosque {*medrese cāmii*}, which was a new form of mosque having a large courtyard and enclosed within crenelated walls, was developed in Iran and Turkistan. This building form spread to Iraq, Syria, and Egypt. The basic plan of Malik-Shāh's Masjid al-Jāmiʿ {cathedral mosque}, part of the courtyard and dome of which still stand today in Iṣfahān, was applied to the great mosques in Iran, Turkistan, and Iraq. Thus Turkish architecture provided the form for the Iranian mosque. Furthermore, brick *kümbet*s, which bring to mind great pavilions, were another new building form that the Turks brought to the Islamic world. *Kümbet*s had conical or multi-sided roofs and were usually covered with tiles. These *kümbet*s, the tops of which had textilelike designs, were outstanding works of Seljuk architecture in Iran. In addition, the Turks also made changes in the construction of domed *türbe*s. By placing a second dome above the {main} dome by means of a cylindrical drum, they raised the height of the structure and thus made each *türbe* a monumental building that could be seen from a great distance (e.g., the *türbe* of Sultan Sanjar in Marv). Domes of this type spread to Transoxiana, Kirmān, Iran, Syria, and Egypt. Indeed, buildings inspired by this form are the major feature of Cairo. Finally, the cylindrical, sometimes grooved, high, thin minaret—in place of the old minaret in the shape of a square or polygonal tower—was also a gift of Turkish architecture to the Muslim world. Moreover, the Turks were not carried away by religious zealotry in art. This can be seen by the fact that when Toghrıl Beg put on the crown and girded himself with the sword in Baghdad, a gold medal depicting the sultan and his entourage was struck in commemoration of this ceremony. This medal was both an important historical document and a remarkable work of art.[37] Furthermore, reliefs of birds, bulls, dragons, double-headed eagles and the like were placed on Turkish buildings,[38] and the sultans of the Anatolian Seljuks coined money on which were human figures. Indeed, in this respect we have a rare surviving example of relief sculpture from the Seljuk period in the stucco panels portraying palace life in Rayy. In the Near East the Seljuks also contributed the form called "the bunch column" to the Greco-Roman and Byzantine columns and two other building forms called "stalagtite" and "diamond {*baklavalı*} shaped" to the earlier capitals of columns. There was a rich variation of these Turkish building forms in Anatolia. They especially show great development in the sixteenth century at the time of Mimar Sinan. In addition, the Seljuks developed the "pointed" arch in place of the "round" and "broken" arch found in early Islamic architecture. This new style was further refined by the Ottomans. The arrangement of windows in rows by floor in mosques and other buildings was a product of Turkish architecture and was not known in other Muslim countries. An important Seljuk innovation in dome construction was to secure the dome to the main walls with a transition zone of "triangular" areas. This form, which is called a "Turkish triangle" in the history of architecture, appeared in different styles and was further developed under the Ottomans. In *miḥrāb* construction in Islamic art, the Turkish form was rectangular or five-sided, the upper section ending with a stepped arch. Seljuk *miḥrāb*s usually had low ceilings, while those of the Ottomans were tall and narrow to parallel the grandeur of their mosques. As for *mimbar*s, Turkish art exhibited endless creative power by finding new areas to decorate, creating various designs and using different techniques. The styles of calligraphy for the Qur'ānic verses and prayers scattered about various places on Turkish architectural works in the Middle Ages also reveals Turkish tastes. In this way, "Seljuk *thulth*" and "Seljuk *naskh,*" which constitute the Seljuk {calligraphic} style, increased the grandeur and gracefulness of their monuments. Let me add here that a Seljuk school of book illumination and another for miniatures were established as a continuation of earlier Uighur-Turkish art. The architectural style and decoration which began in the Near East with the Seljuks was subsequently imitated in other Turco-Islamic states and acquired its most magnificent form, primarily by way of the *beyliks,* at the time of the Ottoman Empire. It eventually developed into one of the world's three original forms of architecture (Greek, Roman, and Turkish).[39]

37. See Artuk, "Abbasiler devrinde sikke" [Coinage from the ʿAbbāsid period], *Belleten* 24(1960):36–43.

38. See Önder, *Mevlānā şehri,* pp. 58–66.

The music of the Seljuk period was based on Oghuz music, which has been described as having a close relationship with Uighur-Turkish music.[40] Music from the time of the Seljuks was collected by the famous music theoretician Ṣafī 'l-Dīn ᶜAbd al-Mu'min (d. 1294), the author of *Kitāb al-Adwār*. A great many works have been written on the theory of this music, which later developed in three directions—Transoxiana, Āzarbāījān, and Anatolia—and spread to all the areas under Turkish influence.[41]

39. In general see J. Strzygowski, "Türkler ve Orta Asya san'atı meselesi" [The problem of the Turks and Central Asian art], *TM* 5(1935):1–80; H. Gluck, "Türk san'atının dünyadaki mevkii" [The place of Turkish art in the world], *TM* 5(1935):119–29; E. Diez, *Die Kunst der islamischen Völker* (Munich, 1915); E. Diez-O. Aslanapa, *Türk san'atı* [Turkish art] (Istanbul, 1955); S. K. Yetkin, *İslâm mimârîsi* [Islamic architecture] (Ankara, 1959); idem, *L'Architecture turque en Turquie* (Paris, 1962); Emel Esin, review of Basil Grey, *La Peinture persane*, in *Belleten* 26(1962):375–81; E. Kühnel, "Türkische und islamische Kunst," in *Halil Edhem hâtıra kitabı* [A presentation volume for Halil Edhem] (Ankara: TTK, 1947), I, 201–9.

40. See Mahmud Râgip Gâzîmihal, *Musikî sözlügü* [A music dictionary] (Istanbul, 1961), p. 285.

41. For details, see H. Sadeddin Arel, "Türk musikîsi kimindir?" [To whom does Turkish music belong?], *Türklük* [Turkism], no. 2(1939):150–55 and in later numbers.

9
The Seljuks and World History

The Seljuk Turks were of great importance in world history. In our description above, we have tried to show that they gave a new direction to the flow of Turkish history; opened a new age in the history of Islamic civilization; and for more than eight hundred years had a profound influence on the history of the Muslim peoples in such matters as the concept of the state, the idea of government, every aspect of organization, literature, and art. Not only did the Seljuks influence the Georgians and Armenians in language, literature, and various branches of fine arts, and even the Greek state of Nicaea in its organization[1] but they also had a direct effect on the Ilkhānid Mongols, who are known to have applied the laws of Malik-Shāh, especially during the reign of Ghāzān Khān,[2] and indirectly influenced the Turkish states of India and the Muslim states of North Africa.[3] The very Turkish foundation of public law in the latter places is noteworthy. But it appears that, by way of the Mongol states and the Golden Horde, the Seljuk influence on the Russians during the time of the Principality (*knezlik*) of Moscow was even more pervasive. It was found in the concept of sovereignty, the military system, the principles of taxation, the post, and other administrative matters.[4] The greatest impact of the Seljuks was on Europe. They played the major role in East-West relations owing to the Crusades, which were caused above all by the Seljuk appearance in Anatolia. Before the Crusades, medieval Europe was in a state of stagnation. Afterwards it became very familiar with the East, which was then enjoying a golden age under Seljuk rule. It consequently

1. See Barthold-Köprülü, *İslâm medeniyeti tarihi,* p. 176; Köprülü, "Ortazaman Türk hukukî müesseleleri," p. 410.

2. See Köprülü, "Anadolu Selçukluları tarihinin yerli kaynakları," pp. 407 f.

3. Köprülü, "Ortazaman Türk hukukî müesseseleri," pp. 408 f.

4. L. Rásonyi, "Contribution à l'histoire des premières cristallisations des Roumains," *Archivum Europae Centro- orientalis* 1(1936):242; Köprülü, "Ortazaman Türk hukukî müesseseleri," p. 416.

acquired great scientific, intellectual, commercial, and industrial benefits. In the West these benefits helped give birth to the Renaissance and later the worldwide European civilization.[5] Books on mathematics, astronomy, physics, chemistry, and the medical sciences as well as scientific discoveries were transferred from the East to Europe. The rise of such industries as perfume, glass, paper, ceramics and carpets—and the widespread use of these products—and the development of Gothic architecture took place in the West at the same time.[6] After contacts with the Turco-Islamic milieu, universities were established and Christian orders were founded in Europe. Peter Abelard (d. 1142), Roger Bacon (d. 1294), Duns Scotus (d. 1308), William of Ockham (d. 1347) and other outstanding personalities who played a role in the intellectual development of the West also transmitted Turco-Islamic thought and science to Europe. By way of Turco-Islamic scientists and intellectuals, Europe thus became aware of the scientific and intellectual life of the ancient Greeks, whose original sources it was later able to discover. Moreover, it was then that Europe began to develop with amazing speed and became aggressive in world trade. Before this time, there is no doubt that it had neither an industrial nor a commercial class. Indeed, it did not even traffic on the high seas.[7] The significant factor in the process of the development of Europe, the factor which provided the fortunate conditions for the speedy enrichment of the West and allowed it to surpass the contemporary stages of civilization, was Europe's knowledge of the Turco-Islamic world.[8] The economic wealth acquired by large-scale commercial activity and overseas voyages was the primary reason for the development that began with the collapse of the medieval feudal regime in Europe, {which in turn was} a consequence of the bourgeoise created by this wealth, and the foundation of modern state systems.[9] Finally, as a literary legacy parallel to this, we might mention that certain ideas that had been advanced by Muḥyī 'l-Dīn Ibn al-ʿArabī in his *al-Futūḥāt al-makkiyya* are found in the *Divine Comedy,* the well-known book by the famous Italian poet Dante.[10]

5. For details, see *The Legacy of Islam* (Oxford, 1952); S. Runciman, "Avrupa medeniyetinin gelişmesi üzerinde islâmî te'sirler" [The influence of Islam on the development of European civilization], *ŞM* 3(1959):1–12; Kafesoğlu, "Büyük Selçuklu imparatorluğunun dünya tarihindeki rolü" [The role of the Great Seljuk Empire in world history], *V. Türk tarihi kongresi zabıtları* [Communications of the Fifth Congress of Turkish History] (Ankara, 1960), pp. 267–78.

6. For details, see J. C. Risler, *La Civilisation Arabe* (Paris, 1955).

7. H. Pirenne, *Histoire de l'Europe des invasions au XVIe siècle* (Brussels, 1917), pp. 149 f.

8. See H. S. Nyberg, "Şark tetkikleri ve Avrupa medeniyeti" [Oriental studies and European civilization], Turkish trans. R. R. Arat, *TM* 12(1955):8.

9. See H. v. Loon, *Histoire de l'humanité* (Paris, 1949), pp. 138–63.

10. See *İlâhî Komedi* [*The Divine Comedy*], Turkish trans. Hamdi Varoğlu (Istanbul, 1938), *a'raf* {the place separating paradise from hell} section.

Part Three

The Controversy over Kafesoğlu's Article

10
Osman Turan and His Critique

As mentioned in the introduction, Osman Turan was one of Turkey's leading Seljuk scholars. He was born in 1914 in the village of Soğanlı in the province of Trebizond. He began his secondary education in Trebizond and completed it in Ankara. In 1935, he enrolled in the medieval history division of the Dil ve Tarih-Coğrafya Fakültesi of Ankara University, where he became a student of Fuad Köprülü, and graduated in 1940. He was among the first graduates of that faculty along with such Seljuk specialists as Mehmet Köymen and Kafesoğlu. Upon graduation, he became an assistant to Köprülü and in 1941 earned his doctorate with a thesis entitled "Oniki hayvanlı Türk takvimi" [The twelve-animal Turkish calendar]. It was published in Ankara in the same year. In 1944, he became an assistant professor at Ankara University and between 1948 and 1950 did research in England and France. In 1951, while still quite young, be became a full professor.

In 1954, during a very productive period of his academic life, his fellow townsmen urged him to run for Parliament. Like his teacher Köprülü, he subsequently joined the Democrat Party and was elected representative from Trebizond. Although Köprülü did not encourage him to enter politics, he did not try to stop him. While serving in Parliament, Turan continued his scholarly work. It was during this time that he wrote most of the articles in the *İA* on the Seljuk sultans of Anatolia and, on the same subject, published *Türkiye Selçukluları hakkında resmî vesikalar* [Official documents on the Seljuks of Turkey] (Ankara, 1958).

On 27 May 1960, when the Turkish military took control of the government, which was led by Adnan Menderes and the Democrat Party, Turan was arrested along with all Democratic members of Parliament and sent to Yassıada, where they were eventually tried for violating the constitution. After being imprisoned for more than 18 months, Turan was finally acquitted and released. An incident that he once related to Köymen about his initial detention at Yassıada does much to shed light on his character. As he described it, "When the commander of Yassıada appeared, everyone (the prisoners) rose to their feet and stood at attention. I did not get up. The commander asked me why I did not rise to my feet and stand at attention. I told him that I was not obliged to rise to my feet for him, much less stand at attention. He scolded me and came at me whereupon I slapped his face. The soldiers who were with him attacked me with bayonets, but he would not let them kill me. However, he threw me in an extremely damp cell that was full of mud up to my ankles. Before being taken to Yassıada I had had a serious operation and was still ill. I remained in that cell for days and was later taken out." Apparently, Turan's behavior eventually helped convince the commander to treat his prisoners leniently.

For an uncompromising and quick-tempered man like Turan, this entire affair was a very painful experience. Moreover, it was fatal to his academic career, for in the meantime various antagonisims and jealousies had arisen that made his attempt to return to university impossible. At Ankara University in particular, certain faculty members closed ranks to prevent him from regaining his position. Indeed, he was even expelled from the Turkish Historical Association. Consequently, Turan had no choice but to reenter politics and was again elected to Parliament as a representative from Trebizond, this time from the Justice Party, in 1965. Although he became assistant to the chairman of the party, he could not get along with party leaders. In 1969, he left politics for good and devoted himself to his intellectual pursuits.

It was after 1965, despite his renewed political activity, that Turan did his best scholarly work, primarily on the Seljuks. His major publications were *Selçuklular tarihi ve Türk-İslâm medeniyeti* [The history of the Seljuks and Turco-Islamic civilization] (Ankara, 1965), *Türk cihân hâkimiyeti mefkûresi tarihi* [The history of the Turkish concept of world dominion] (Istanbul, 1969), *Selçuklular zamanında Türkiye* [Turkey at the time of the Seljuks] (Istanbul, 1971), which is a massive book on pre-Ottoman Turkey with a rather different approach from Claude Cahen, and *Doğu Anadolu Türk devletleri tarihi* [The history of the Turkish states of eastern Anatolia] (Istanbul, 1973). Throughout his career, Turan wrote numerous articles on the Seljuks, some of which were later collected in a volume called *Selçuklular ve İslâmiyet* [The Seljuks and Islam] (Istanbul, 1980). It should be mentioned that he wrote a serious evaluation of Köprülü's work as the introduction to the *festschrift* for his teacher, *Fuad Köprülü armağanı* (Istanbul, 1953). He published a few articles in Western languages. The last was the chapter "Anatolia in the Period of the Seljuks and the *Beyliks*" in the *Cambridge History of Islam,* volume I, *The Central Islamic Lands,* edited by P. M. Holt et al. (Cambridge, 1970). This is almost a summary of his aforesaid book *Selçuklular zamanında Türkiye*. He was working on the economic history of medieval Turkey when he suddenly died from a brain hemorrhage on 17 January 1978. (For more details on his life, see the obituaries in *Türk Kültürü* [Turkish culture], March 1978, and *Turcica,* 11 [1979], and above all the long article on his life and work written by his former classmate Köymen as the introduction to the second edition of Turan's *Türk cihân hâkimiyeti mefkûresi tarihi* [ca. 1978], and reprinted in subsequent editions. Köymen has harsh words for the way Turan was treated by his colleagues in academia. There is also a very good discussion of Turan's life and work in Strohmeier, *Seldschukische Geschichte,* pp 151–63.)

Turan was without doubt among the most prolific writers on Seljuk history that Turkey has produced. After Köprülü, he was probably the best known Turkish authority in that field in the West. Köymen goes so far as to claim that Cahen, in his book *Pre-Ottoman Turkey,* "relied almost completely on the research of Osman Turan" (!). His most important work was unquestionably his *Selçuklular zamanında Türkiye*. But his most renowned work was perhaps his *Selçuklular tarihi ve Türk-İslâm medeniyeti,* which covered the history and civilization of the entire Seljuk period. It was this work that brought him into conflict with Kafesoğlu. The latter's article on the Seljuks in the *İA* appeared as parts of two fascicles in 1964 and 1965, about the same time that the *Selçuklular tarihi* was published. Turan had originally submitted the work that later became this book to the *İA* as the "article" on the Seljuks. For reasons that will be described below, the *İA* did not publish it. Instead, the encyclopaedia turned to Kafesoğlu. As soon as Turan saw the *İA* article on the Seljuks, he claimed that Kafesoğlu, in collusion with Ahmed Ateş, the head of the editorial committee of the *İA,* had not only plagiarized his work but had also made a shambles of Seljuk history. In a review article in *Belleten* 29(1965):639–60, entitled "Selçuklular hakkında yeni bir neşir münasebetiyle (*İslâm Ansiklopedisin*deki İ. Kafesoğlu'nun Selçuklular makalesi)" [Concerning a new publication on the Seljuks (İ. Kafesoğlu's article on the Seljuks in the *İslâm Ansiklopedisi*)], Turan launched what can only be described as one of the most vicious attacks on a colleague ever recorded in a scholarly journal.

What follows is a slightly edited translation of Turan's critique of Kafesoğlu's encyclopaedia article. Apart from certain redundancies, the text is complete. However, much of the venom and innuendo in the Turkish text could not easily be rendered into English. But enough is there to give one the flavor of the critique. For those who wish to compare Turan's work with that of Kafesoğlu, it should be mentioned that Turan, of course, cites the first edition (1965) of his book. The third edition, published in 1980, contains additions and revisions so the pages no longer match. Sometimes, he also somewhat annoyingly cites an offprint of the *İA* article, which is paginated differently from the way it is found in the encyclopaedia. The page numbers in brackets refer to the corresponding pages in the *Belleten* review.

* * *

[639] Because there is still very little and inadequate research on the Seljuks, who began a new period in the history of the Turkish and Islamic peoples and their civilizations, this great period continues to be obscure and not properly understood. Indeed, the chronology and important geneologies of the period have not even been described much less the major historical problems. In addition to the difficulties arising from studying a period that covers the history of various countries and peoples from the borders of China to the Mediterranean, one must take into account that the Seljuks opened a new period in the history of civilization, that they had close relations with Europe, and that the sources are in a great many languages. Thus, although one reason for the continuing obscurity of this period is the inadequacy of the research, another is the difficulty in carrying out that research. Consequently, the work that has been done to date cannot be considered sufficient to describe or evaluate various problems of the period.

Given the state of Seljuk studies, Professor İbrahim Kafesoğlu's sixty-four-page article the "Seljuks" in the *İslâm Ansiklopedisi* (parts 104–5, pp. 353–416) automatically attracts our attention. It is noteworthy that this article and my book *Selçuklular tarihi ve Türk-İslâm medeniyeti* (Ankara: Türk Kültürünü Araştırma Enstitüsü, 1965, xiii + 446) were published at the same time. In fact, when those who study Seljuk history read this article and my book, they will find a number of problems, interpretations, and discoveries common to both. Indeed, in both works they will see similarities in the way the material is organized and similar expressions and they will ask the reason for these remarkable coincidences. Therefore, I will explain here why the article on the Seljuks and my book have common characteristics. Before I begin my criticism [640] of this article, I will briefly describe how

I had originally written the Seljuk article for the *IA,* but because of a disagreement it could not be published there and thus appeared as the aforesaid book. It is a disagreeable story.

In an official message that I received that was signed by Professor Ahmed Ateş, the director of the editorial committee of *İA,* I was asked to write the Seljuk article and was told that it should not exceed 18–20 pages. Because of the importance of the period, the number of Seljuk states and their problems, and the fact that research on the Seljuks was still in its infancy, I explained that such a short article would be insufficient. Smaller and less important subjects in the *İA* ran 40, 60, 80, 120 ("mescid" {mosque}) and 160 ("İstanbul") pages. It was consequently agreed that the Seljuks warranted an article of 80–90 pages. I prepared an article of this estimated length and submitted it to the *İA* board. They agreed that what I submitted was about the right length. As the drafts were typed, they were sent to Ankara so I could prepare them for the press. They were corrected and returned. After several parts had been mailed, they realized that their original estimate of its length had been mistaken and that my article would be about two fascicles of the *İA*. The editorial director then immediately suggested that I reduce the parts that had been sent by half and return them. With regard to both time and the effect this would have had on the manuscript, I found this drastic suggestion to be unacceptable. Furthermore, from a scholarly point of view, it was even more difficult to accept his suggestion that I let the editorial committee cut the article. This was difficult enough for an author to do much less let his work go to waste at the hands of someone else. I explained that articles of equal length but less importance had been published, that an abridged article could not be prepared immediately, that an abridged article based on the work at hand would take on a different nature, and that therefore several more months would be needed. On the one hand Ateş, the editorial director, wanted to save time, but on the other he lost time by causing such a disagreement. Faced with this, I told him as a final suggestion that, if the civilization section was left out and only the political section was published, both his length and time constraints could be met. [641] In fact this part would be less than a fascicle. However, Professor Ateş, who seemed to relish causing difficulties, in agreement with Professor Kafesoğlu, who was eager to write the article, stressed the importance of the civilization section and maintained that they could not give it up. He forgot {both} the proposal for a twenty-page article and that such a long article had been out of the question. Furthermore, he did not think that such a comprehensive work was very unusual in the other articles. When this point also became difficult, he proposed that a short article be written by Kafesoğlu and because of time constraints that I permit him to use my work. Although this was an unusual proposal, I said I would agree on condition that my own ideas and rights be respected. But he stated that he did not know if the author would accept this stipulation. His decisions under these circumstances were incomprehensible to me. I told him that there was no choice but to publish it according to my conditions or return it. Without receiving any word in this regard, my work was kept at the *İA* office for another month. After being in their hands for almost three months all told, it was returned to me. However, when I came to Istanbul at the end of July 1964, I learned that they had kept the original typed sections (189 pages).

Anyway, after my Seljuk history underwent this experience and was returned to Ankara, it was given to the press on 20 September. The political section of this work (pp. 27–216) is the full text that was prepared for the *İA,* but with the references placed in footnotes. As for the civilization chapters, they were quickly expanded to the present form. The critical bibliography that had been placed at the end of the article was expanded and placed at the beginning of the book. It forms the introduction. The purpose for which this work was originally written affected the way it was organized. This led to certain peculiarities and some events were not in chronological order. These events have been properly arranged in my book. One of the reasons for briefly describing the genesis of my book is to place in perspective my criticism of Kafesoğlu's article and especially to show its close relationship with my work. Indeed, it seems that the adventure of my work is not finished, and certain rumors imply that there is more to come. After part of the Seljuk article was published in the 104th fascicle and before the rest of it appeared in the 105th fascicle, the whole thing was issued as an offprint (64 pp.). It was then clearly established that Kafesoğlu, in collusion with the editorial committee, had methodically abridged, broken apart, and plagiarized as he liked my work, which had been entrusted to the *İA*. [642] The Seljuk article thus appeared in this fashion while my book was in press.

Such blatantly dishonest behavior is truly rare and astonishing in the scholarly world. When it became clear that attempts to disguise this action were a complete failure and the material and scientific evidence to prove it were strong and plentiful, I made an official protest to Professor Ateş and, out of concern for protecting old friends and Turkish scholarship, asked if the *İA* director was responsible for this. I then called upon Kafesoğlu to turn away from error. I gave them the opportunity to straighten this out so they would not become victims of this action. It would have simply sufficed to say at the end of the article that use was made of the draft of my work. But my friends, who were slow to realize the solid evidence against them and the need to turn away from error, insisted on denying my allegations and ignored the evidence. The final suggestions that I made to my friends to close this case with such a statement, in light of the gravity of the consequences, were in vain. Kafesoğlu avoided an admission of guilt with a weak and conciliatory defense in his official reply, and Ateş stated his admiration for his friend's knowledge. Moreover, he felt the need to give a rather irritable, indeed, threatening, reply, thus showing his part in this affair. The main reason that impelled them to give such replies was their ignorance of the evidence at hand. In fact, despite my obvious claim, they have remained uninformed of the absolute proof. They suppose that I make my claim on the fact that my work was in their hands and they made critical notes on the margins of the draft, but they are wrong. After all my good intentions were in vain and, furthermore, I was subjected to threats and accusations, it has become necessary to show how the Seljuk article was plagiarized from my work. A serious criticism of this article is therefore in order, out of scholarly necessity and to protect Turkish scholarship from such incidents.

[643] The author of the Seljuk article, while plagiarizing my work, avoided an exact citation of the new interpretations and problems first advanced by me by skillfully and methodically breaking up my work, rearranging it, abridging it, and adding verbiage. But because of his inability to grasp properly the history of the period and its problems on the one hand, and because of his inability to find the time to digest properly and check the work on the other—since he was forced to squeeze into about two months a work that took me two years to prepare—he was not able to distinguish what were the new ideas and interpretations advanced by me in my book, and thought he would simply appropriate some of them to himself. The timidity that he showed at the beginning gradually decreased, a common psychological trait, while his boldness and appetite increased. Thanks to this, he provided much clearer and solid proof of his actions. Probably the first decision that was made in agreement with the editorial director was to act before the appearance of my book and immediately publish the article. In fact, inserting the name *Sencer* {i.e., *Senjer*} in the *İA* for the Seljuk Sultan whose name has always been written as *Sancar* {i.e., *Sanjar*} in the scholarly world, and even by Kafesoğlu in his writings to date, and postponing it until after the article on the Seljuks, were done in order to save time. This is the reason Kafesoğlu always uses the form *Senjer* in his article. {In the translation, however, the form *Sanjar* was used, which is the common Western spelling.}

A long time after studying Hungarology, Kafesoğlu began to work on the Seljuk period. He made a great effort because of the delay and change in specialization. As a result of his industriousness, he earned his doctorate with a monograph on Malik-Shāh and his assistant professorship with a work on the history of the Khwārazm-Shāhs. Since I was on the jury, I helped him by providing a report with some suggestions that he then used to improve his work for publication. Kafesoğlu thus gained a reputation for himself with this second book. In the introduction to my book, the evaluation that I gave of his work was favorable although very balanced. But despite his demonstrated efforts and work, Kafesoğlu has never been able to do very profound scientific research; he has not been able to show any real success in presenting and solving important historical problems, and has not been able to go much beyond being a narrator or compiler in the general sense of the term. Despite the lack of scholarly studies in Turkey, his work leaves no doubt in one's mind as to the scholarly propriety and correctness of this judgment. [644] The general and subjective conclusions in his writings reveal his worth. Instead of using primary sources and modern studies, he mixes late and valueless sources with each other—hence his lack of method and criticism—a point that has already been made (see Mehmet Köymen, *Belleten* 17[1953]: 557–604).

In fact, Kafesoğlu, who boasts of himself in his reply as a specialist in Seljuk history and is the object of admiration in Ateş's official message, unfortunately has a very superficial knowledge of this period. Indeed, he does not even have a general understanding of it. If he had had a higher general level of knowledge, he would not have sacrificed himself by plagiarizing someone else's work. A few examples will suffice to reveal his competence in Seljuk history. From the beginning, it is surprising that this specialist in Seljuk history indicates that the center of the Oghuz *yabghus,* the city of Yengi-Kent, was between the Aral and Caspian seas and that the Seljuks were also north of the Aral Sea. The truth is that he did not even bother to look at the maps of Turkistan and works by Barthold or Togan (see "Seljuks," pp. 354b, 355). Furthermore although our writer published an article called "Selçuk'un oğulları ve torunları" {[The sons and grandchildren of Seljuk], *TM* 13(1958): 117–30}, he was not even successful in doing simple research like determining and identifying these sons and grandchildren. He could only have learned, after using my work, that Seljuk's son Mūsā had the Turkish name İnanch, that Sanjar had the Muslim name Aḥmad, that Yınal is not a title but a name, and that prior to Ibrāhīm his father Yūsuf (a son of Seljuk) had a Turkish name. All this corrected the earlier mistakes in his article. Although Kafesoğlu did not adopt my view that Seljuk had a fifth son named Yūnus, by whom he had a grandson named Er-Basgan (El-Basan), he thought that he would appropriate everything else to himself. With the same idea in mind, he also arbitrarily spells the name of Seljuk's grandson, which he had written before as Er-Sıghın, here as Er-Sıghun ("Seljuks," pp. 367b, 369a; offprint, 466, family-tree; "Selçuk'un oğulları," pp. 120, 121, 129). Our specialist in Seljuk history also discovers in his article that there were Turkish cities on the banks of the Jaxartes {Turan is being facetious}, which was an old Oghuz homeland, and, by considering this to be proof of the Turkishness of Transoxiana, shows how he has changed the known to the unknown and the extent to which his judgments are built on air (offprint, p. 33a). He supposes that Toghrıl Beg and Chaghrı Beg were still around Jand (*Köprülü armağanı,* p. 259) when Arslan Yabgu migrated to the area around Bukhārā. This specialist in Seljuk history thus even lacks a general knowledge of the origins of the Seljuks and their homeland. [645] This reveals very clearly the extent of his specialization. It is not necessary to point out the great many other examples from his publications to confirm this. We can pass on to how he plagiarized my book for his article, the methods he used to do this, and the evidence he left behind. It is not possible to list here the enormous number of examples that I have encountered in this respect, so I will just point out the most striking evidence of his actions.

From the very beginning of the Seljuk article, our colleague found it necessary to follow my methods of classification and arrangement—even using my divisions and headings—and introduced into his article, with slight adaptations and modifications, the great many new ideas and problems raised in my book. In fact, he took, with certain changes, the information and sources that I gave on the pronunciation, origin, and meaning of the name *Seljuk* and appropriated to himself my final conclusion. Thanks to this, he thought at the very least that he would take possession of ready-made material (see my *Selçuklular,* pp. 27–28; "Seljuks," p. 353). On the coming of the Seljuks to the area around Bukhārā and the Oghuz migrations, Kafesoğlu also cites my book in a very abbreviated manner. Because he rejects the ideas of all the scholars who, to date, have said that this emigration occurred in 992, he is forced to reveal the author who was the source of that information {namely, Turan} and that he plagiarized his work, because he did not understand that the new interpretation that this event took place before that year belongs to me. Moreover, Kafesoğlu saw Barthold's name among my primary and secondary sources and, believing that this idea belonged to this writer, cites him and thus gives himself away. If this plagiarist writer had read Barthold, he would not have fallen into this mistake, as he has no doubt done in his other publications, and would not have given this example of childish behavior (cf. *Selçuklular,* p. 41, and "Seljuks," p. 356a).

The conclusion that the Oghuz participated in raids in Anatolia with the Khwārazmian *ghāzīs* before the Seljuks and that Chaghrı Beg's first raid in this direction is related to this precedent also belongs to me (*Selçuklular,* pp. 47–48). Our Seljuk historian colleague, who does not know to whom this idea belongs, encounters a serious failure in this regard and thanks to this provides us with clear proof of his plagiarism. Indeed, while omitting the chronicle of Ibn Miskawayh and the *Siyāsat-Nāma* from the sources that I gave, in order to hide the fact that he borrowed from me, he did not realize that he lost the primary references for this idea and gets caught ("Seljuks," p. 358b). [646] It is worthy of note that this information is lacking in his article on this subject in the *Köprülü armağanı.*

The problem of the Yabghulular {those with the title Yabghu or the followers of the Yabghu} has not been raised to date nor has the obscure form in which the sources report it—as *Nāvakiyya*—been understood. I presented and analyzed this in my work and explained their ethnic character and relationship with the Seljuks (*Selçuklular,* pp. 120–23). Kafesoğlu, by discovering with me a Yabghu name that had heretofore not been seen, gives another fine proof of his plagiarism ("Seljuks," p. 360a). I also presented in my book for the first time the historical personality and activity of Seljuk's grandson Er-Basgan (El-Basan), who was the *bey* of Qazvīn and helped Alp-Arslan ascend the throne (*Selçuklular,* p. 120). Kafesoğlu has the same analysis and interpretation, but to hide the fact that he took this from me, he resolves the problem by spelling the name "Er-Sıghun" and thus shows his cunning ("Seljuks," p. 367b). In the article that Kafesoğlu wrote on Chaghrı Beg's raid in Anatolia, he gave the date as 1016, taking it from Mükrimin Halil Yınanç. He now abandons this date and prefers my date of 1018. This shows that he no longer relies on himself or the earlier authority, or that while agreeing with me he has forgotten his previous article (*Selçuklular,* p. 48; "Seljuks," p. 358; *Köprülü armağanı,* p. 263).

The relationship and struggles between the Seljuks and the Oghuz *yabghus* of Yengi-Kent are as important as they are obscure, with regard to the beginning of Seljuk history. In my book, by making use of a few records that are reflected in the chronicles and epic (*Oğuz-Nāma*) tales, this stage of history has been rather well explained by me. I also explained that the Oghuz *yabghu* who drove the Seljuks from the Jand region and caused them to migrate to Transoxiana was a certain Baran, and his grandson Shāh-Malik settled in Jand as the merciless enemy of the Seljuks. Low and behold, our colleague summarizes these results, moves them about, and adds them to his article (*Selçuklular,* pp. 42–44; "Seljuks," p. 359).

I named the battle of Kaputru, which Ibrāhīm Yınal won against the Byzantines in 1048, the battle of Hasan-Kale in contrast to today's usage. By writing this name and place, which had heretofore not been seen, Kafesoğlu gives further proof that he plagiarized me (*Selçuklular,* pp. 76–77; "Seljuks," p. 365a). In addition Kafesoğlu, who wrote a separate work, and later an article {in the *İA*}, on Malik-Shāh, takes from me the information on Alp-Arslan's [647] appointment of Malik-Shāh as heir apparent and his appointment of his other sons to various provinces as *maliks*. He was not able to give this information in his previous works but does so in this article and thus immediately has comprehensive knowledge of this subject (*Selçuklular,* pp. 106–8; "Seljuks," 368b). Nevertheless, he dares to show his own work, which does not contain this information, as the authority (*Melikşah devri,* p. 14). While plagiarizing my analysis of Alp-Arslan's conquest of Ani, he simply replaces my *fetḥnāme* reference with *beyannāme* (?), a meaningless word (*Selçuklular,* p. 105; "Seljuks," p. 369). Moreover, while taking as his own the information that I gave on the war between the sultan of the Seljuks of Iraq, Masʿūd, and the caliph, he takes out the reference to ʿAbd al-Jalīl Qazvīnī and gives the page number of the translation of ʿImād al-Dīn al-Iṣfahānī, showing that he did not know the sources (*Selçuklular,* p. 184; "Seljuks," p. 376a). He used the same skill in his article to adopt my analysis of the relations between the Georgians and the Qıpchaqs, their relations by marriage, and their joint military operations against the Seljuks. He throws out some of the sources that he had never seen and in their place puts late and unnecessary sources. His treatment of this subject is thus completely misleading (*Selçuklular,* pp. 169–70; "Seljuks," p. 375a).

While using my analysis of the Seljuks of Turkey, a subject on which our writer has done no research, he deliberately repeats certain mistakes of Mükrimin Halil Yınanç that were corrected by me, thus revealing both his great lack of scholarly ethics and responsibility and his plagiaristic skill. In this respect it is fitting to give the reign of Sultan Masʿūd as an example. Indeed, apart from my study which I have not yet published, there is no research on this subject {Turan apparently never published a separate study on this sultan, but devoted considerable attention to him in his *Selçuklular zamanında Türkiye,* pp. 158–96.}. In my book I gave a synopsis of my research on him, but it was not possible to show the various sources (*Selçuklular,* pp. 205–08). Our colleague follows me here and, because he was not able to show the sources, naturally leaves them in darkness. Despite the ready-made information, our colleague is so foreign to the subject that he keeps

Dānishmend Gümüsh-Tegin Aḥmad Ghāzī, who died in 1104, alive until 1134 instead of his son Amīr Ghāzī. While abridging a period that he does not know or understand, he thus adds insult to injury ("Seljuks," p. 380). Despite the efforts of the late Mükrimin Halil Yınanç, the family tree of this dynasty and its early period had until recently remained confusing problems. [648] But with the research that I did in this respect, these problems have been completely solved and some of the results are given in my book. Despite certain important references that I gave in my book (see, e.g., pp. 19–22, 203–06), I invite Kafesoğlu to an examination to determine his ability to analyze this subject and to see if he can make sense of it. It is strange that our writer, after following me on this period and correctly citing the fact that Sultan Masʿūd was under the protection of the Dānishmend Amīr Ghāzī, loses control and confuses Gümüsh-Tegin with Amīr Ghāzī.

Even while abridging my ready-made analysis on political history, Kafesoğlu loses control and falls victim to mistakes. It would thus never occur to one that Kafesoğlu would attempt to write about the culture and history of a civilization that he has not understood to this day. But in his article it seems that he has suddenly been able to comprehend the social, cultural, and economic problems of the Seljuk period. The fact that what he wrote {on these subjects} is correct defies the laws of nature and makes one wonder about the source of these sections, which form about half the article. As is well-known, it is a common psychological trait for a plagiarizing writer to become embolden as he progresses. By plagiarizing my ideas and interpretations with greater facility, Kafesoğlu thus helps me to find full, solid proof of his actions. This can be seen from the awkwardness of these sections, his hurry to save time, and the redundant verbiage and insubstantial bibliography that he adds in order to hide what he has done. Noteworthy examples on the period of Malik-Shāh, to which he has devoted most of his studies, gain a special importance in this regard. We shall therefore begin with this section.

Throughout the entire Middle Ages, the Turks were bound to the ideal of world dominion. I had done research on this in articles entitled "Türkler ve İslâmiyet" [The Turks and Islam], *DTCF Dergisi* 4(1946), and "The Ideal of World Domination among the Medieval Turks," *SI* 4(1955). Afterwards, in my book, I presented new interpretations of this, especially with regard to the views of Malik-Shāh (*Selçuklular,* pp. 87–88, 137–38, 156, 306–12). Our bold plagiarizer, who has nothing to say about this in his book or recent article on Malik-Shāh, now has my ideas in his Seljuk article under the heading "The Seljuk Concept of Universal Dominion." He understood that Malik-Shāh "hoped for world dominion" and took my main ideas and captions in this respect along with even the comparison with Sultan Yavuz Selim (*Selçuklular,* p. 137). [649] This is very clear proof of his actions ("Seljuks," offprint, p. 40, article, pp. 373a, 377b). His description of Sultan Sanjar's view of world dominion was also taken from my book (*Selçuklular,* pp. 173–76). Although I considered Niẓām al-Mulk's expression "sultan ālemin efendisi ve sahibidir" {"the sultan is the master and possessor of the world"} to be a reflection of this idea and showed that it was a continuation of the early views that considered the old Turkish *qaghans* to be the fathers of the nation (*velāyet-i pederāne*), our writer did not understand this. Indeed, he did not understand the aforesaid expression which he took from me in the opposite sense ("Seljuks," offprint, pp. 35b, 45a).

While plagiarizing me, Kafesoğlu, as mentioned, did not even worry about copying my captions. For example, in my book there is the heading "Selçuklu devleti'nin bünyesi ve karakteri," which he plagiarized as "Selçuklu devletinin vasfı ve bünyesi." The content of this section in Kafesoğlu's article also derives in abridged form from my book (cf. *Selçuklular,* pp. 217–33 and "Seljuks," offprint, pp. 34, 45). What I wrote on the roles of women and *atabegs* in the Seljuk period and their influence on the political disintegration of the empire, was taken, along with the captions, for his article without hesitation (*Selçuklular,* pp. 221–23; "Seljuks," offprint, pp. 36b–37a, 45b). The sources for this are found in the political section of my book and are given over the course of the subject. Kafesoğlu more or less noted these references, added certain information of no interest, and then tried to appropriate this section to himself.

Because the Seljuks maintained the early Turkish concept of state and feudal political structure, their sultans never had absolute power, nor were they despots like the Sāsānid Iranian or Byzantine rulers. They were the representatives of the highest authority, but only over the aristocratic Turkish *begs*. I frequently mentioned this subject, which was first discussed by Köprülü, in my book and in my earlier research. I stated that from the time of the Gök-Turks and Qarakhānids to the Ottomans, the state continued to be considered the common property of the members of the dynasty. I explained in detail that the centralizing activity that began with Toghrıl Beg did not change the feudal structure, that the administration of *iqṭā's* was established according to this feudal structure, and that there was no feudalization among the Seljuks in Turkey only because the great military *iqṭā's* were not permitted (*Selçuklular,* pp. 62–63, 218). Kafesoğlu, who has done no work on this topic and does not have the ability to do so, collected the ready-made information here. [650] He borrowed from me the words that Ibrāhīm Yınal said while entering Nīshāpūr (cf. *Selçuklular,* p. 56, and "Seljuks," offprint, pp. 34a, 34). Kafesoğlu also took my analysis of the public feasts (*toy, sölen*) that the early Turkish *qaghans,* Qarakhānid rulers, and Seljuk sultans gave in their capacity as *velāyet-i pederāne,* and the custom of distributing the utensils from these feasts among the people (*khwān-ı yağmā*) (*Selçuklular,* pp. 138, 150–54, 180; "Seljuks," offprint, p. 37; Köprülü, *Türkiye tarihi* [Istanbul, 1923], p. 173).

One of the principle concerns of my research and my book was to describe the new period that began with the Seljuks, one that was a blend of Turkish and Islamic institutions and culture, and the extent to which the material power of Islamic civilization, as well as its spiritual elements and customs, progressed and reached a new phase. Heretofore our colleague and specialist in Seljuk history has shown absolutely no interest in these matters. He has not thought about it, nor has he studied it. Now, suddenly, he produces a study on it that parallels my work. This can only be the result of divination or plagiarizing my work (see "Seljuks," offprint, pp. 35, 37).

In my previous articles entitled "Türkler ve İslâmiyet" and "Les Souverains seldjoukides et leurs sujets non-musulmans," *SI* 1(1953), and in my book, I explained that the Turks behaved with tolerance and justice toward foreign religions and peoples in the Gök-Turk, Uighur, and Khazar periods as well as in Seljuk and Ottoman times, and by thus establishing their rule on a firm foundation, they gained widespread and lasting power (*Selçuklular,* pp. 230–32, 256–58). If Kafesoğlu had found the time and taken note of my earlier research, the results would have overshadowed what he plagiarized from my book. In the event, even this ready-made material was not enough and his general lack of knowledge caused him to confuse the widespread religious tolerance that was present among the Seljuks with the concept of "secularism" (?) ("Seljuks," offprint, p. 39). He shows the same clumsiness again while writing that the sultans Alp-Arslan and Malik-Shāh behaved in a "paternalistic manner" (?) toward non-Muslims and then says that this "manner" was only with regard to Christians. He thus comes to the opposite conclusion. By plagiarizing material on subjects that he does not understand he becomes confused ("Seljuks," offprint, p. 52).

He also benefited greatly from my research on the Seljuk policy of directing the Oghuz migrations toward Anatolia. [651] By plagiarizing my ideas on this matter, he clearly left his calling card. I described the importance of Michael the Syrian's reference to a Byzantine emperor's transfer of Christians to the Balkans during the Turkization of Anatolia. Kafesoğlu, who behaves as if he knew of this important question and had seen the source, cites it as well as me; but in place of the page numbers that I gave, he gives others and so is caught

(*Selçuklular,* p. 196; "Seljuks," offprint, p. 42b, see also *Selçuklular,* pp. 67–73, 195–98; "Seljuks," offprint, pp. 41–43). Our colleague did not overlook the discovery, in which he follows me, that the defeat of Sultan Sanjar, and later the appearance of the Mongols, were related to the beginning of new Turkish migrations into the Islamic world and Anatolia. His idea (?) about the "Turkmen migrations to which the Seljuk Empire began to apply a policy of emigration and settlement" belongs to me (*Selçuklular,* p. 69) but was presented in confusing Turkish. Another noteworthy proof of his plagiarism concerns the name *Turkey*. Indeed, I showed that since the Turkization of Anatolia in the twelfth century, Latin sources no longer referred to it as *Romania* ("Rūm," according to Muslim writers) but as *Turkia* (*Selçuklular,* p. 259). Our author cannot ignore this interesting information and, based on one or two late compilations, discovered that the name *Turkey* existed at the time of Qılıch-Arslan II (in fact his father Masᶜūd), although he plagiarized me in this respect ("Seljuks," offprint, pp. 42b–43a). He also summarized my work on the struggle for corporal rule that began between the sultans of Iraq and the caliphs, and added this to his article (*Selçuklular,* pp. 185–89; "Seljuks," offprint, p. 45).

By having access to my work before it was published, he also had a chance to make use of it with regard to economic questions. Our colleague has done nothing on this subject to date and has shown no energy or ability in this respect. Now he gives a mass of concise data, attributed to himself, on the economic and commercial activity in the period of the Great Seljuks—and especially on the Seljuks of Turkey—on the new economic system and institutions of the period, on monetary economics, industry, imports and exports, the cities, the accumulation of wealth, and social life. All this was taken from my research (*Selçuklular,* pp. 247, 257, 260 ff.). I calculated that the budget of the Great Seljuks during the reign of Malik-Shāh was 30 billion Turkish lira in today's money {1965}. Our brother Kafesoğlu, to show that he did not copy me, wanted to reduce this to 25 billion. But because he could not grasp such concepts, he hastily changed this amount to 225 billion. [652] He then found this figure to be unacceptable and arbitrarily increased it to the astronomical amount of 500 billion. This is one more example of his scholarly irresponsibility (cf. *Selçuklular,* p. 247, and "Seljuks," offprint, p. 49). He also did not want to credit me with my references to the monetary policy of Qāvurt, the Seljuk ruler of Kirmān (*Selçuklular,* p. 190; "Seljuks," offprint, p. 50)

As for the continuous economic and cultural development that began in Anatolia with the reign of Qılıch-Arslan II and the commercial policies of the sultans of Turkey and their military campaigns, which included the conquest of ports on the Mediterranean and Black Sea as part of their commercial policies, the necessary information was given in my book as well as in some of my previous publications. More fundamental information and interpretations will be given in the work I will publish entitled *Orta-çağda Türkiye iktisadî tarihi* [The economic history of Turkey in the Middle Ages] {never completed}. Kafesoğlu gives information that parallels mine in this field, but he cannot tell that he has fallen into a difficult position. Our brother Kafesoğlu adds to his article my description of the economic level of Anatolia and the fact that it was known for its "legendary" wealth in Europe. He thus immediately gets caught. Indeed, it was impossible for him to see or read the sources that I gave on this subject. In fact, he threw out these sources, which caused him trouble, and in their place put several well-known numismatic works. These works contain absolutely no information on the subject in question. This is further proof of his plagiarism and lack of scholarly scruples. Such misguided energy is bankrupt (cf. *Selçuklular,* pp. 274–76, and "Seljuks," offprint, pp. 50a–51a).

The writer of the Seljuk article also took note of the intellectual and artistic life of the period. He found readily availiable in my book the results of my research and that of Köprülü on the importance given to religious and philosophical questions and to freethinking in the reign of Qılıch-Arslan; on the stimulation given to the development of Ṣūfism by Seljuk religious tolerance; on the activity of Muḥyī 'l-Dīn Ibn al-ʿArabī and Mawlānā Jalāl al-Dīn al-Rūmī in this milieu; and finally on the incorporation of old shamanistic beliefs by the *ṣūfī* brotherhoods as part of this process. Thus he imagined that he "presented a moral and spiritual description of Anatolia." By coincidence, he also understood the religious and social movement of the Turkmen that began with Bābā Isḥāq (Bābā Rasūl) the same way I did (*Selçuklular,* pp. 257–59; "Seljuks," offprint, pp. 53a–53b). While attributing, with the same irresponsibility, to M. R. Gâzîmihal and S. Arel my views on the importance of music and *samāʿ* and the influence of shamanism on Ṣūfism, he could not comprehend that the basic ideas in this regard belonged not to me but to Köprülü, and the works that he cites contain nothing on this subject (*Selçuklular,* pp. 298–300; "Seljuks," offprint, pp. 52b, 60a, 60b).

[653] As for art and architecture, I was the first to describe the important reference in Harawī that there were marble statues in the Kamereddin garden in Konya during the reign of Qılıch-Arslan. Our writer also plagiarizes this information from me (*Selçuklular,* p. 291; "Seljuks," offprint, p. 52a). He made the great Masjid-i jumaᶜ that Malik-Shāh built in Iṣfahān the Masjid-i jāmiʿ; he also used my sources to take the historical material that I collected on the *türbe* of Sultan Sanjar (*Selçuklular,* p. 286; "Seljuks," offprint, pp. 59b, 60a). Here-

tofore, Kafesoğlu had never used the expression "Türkiye Selçukluları" and even made doubtful remarks concerning it on the margins of the draft I left at the *İA,* but it now appears in his article. By using this expression, he provided an excellent example of how accustomed he had become to using my work (*Selçuklular,* p. 259). Kafesoğlu also understood the importance of Seljuk caravansaries, which I had studied in a previous article and mentioned briefly in my book, but he does not state where this readily-available information came from (*Selçuklular,* pp. 262–64; "Seljuks," offprint, p. 50a).

Our colleague also makes public for the first time the existence of certain works that have not come down to us that were dedicated to Sultan Sanjar during his reign, namely, *Sanjar-Nāma, Siyar-u futūḥ sulṭān Sanjar,* and *Mafākhir al-atrāk,* but he omitted the sources that I gave for this information (*Selçuklular,* p. 2; "Seljuks," offprint, pp. 57b–58a). One cannot but be astonished at the coincidence or clairvoyance required to make this new discovery. I proposed for the first time a new interpretation of the importance of the cultural history of the Seljuk period which I had presented in my chapter "Selcuklular ve Avrupa medeniyetinin doğuşu" [The Seljuks and the birth of European civilization] (*Selçuklular,* pp. 321–22). Our plagiarizer was forced to take this interpretation into account, but he mixed unsound ideas with some of the ideas that he took from me and presented this under the heading "The Seljuks and World History" ("Seljuks," offprint, pp. 50b–61a).

By compensating merchants for their losses to brigands and pirates, the Seljuks initiated a kind of state insurance. This institution was one of their forward-looking measures that encouraged commerce [654] and first appeared as a legal contract in Italy in the fifteenth century. I described all this and how the latter derived from the Seljuk precedent in my earlier publication and in my book (*Selçuklular,* pp. 234–325 {sic}). On the one hand Kafesoğlu, who tried to take these ideas of mine for his own, forgot my earlier publications, or more correctly he did not know about them or quickly became confused, and on the other there is no information in this respect in the references that he gives. By paying no attention to the fact that the numismatic catalogues that he cites are of no use in this regard, he goes astray and betrays all his secrets ("Seljuks," offprint, pp. 49, 50, 61a).

Kafesoğlu provides further proof of his plagiarism by taking what I presented on the special tent-bath of the nomadic Turks. In fact, this tent-bath (*çerge*), which was used by the nomads, passed to the Byzantines by way of the shamanistic Turks in the Balkans and was taken on campaign by the emperors. We know this from the work of Byzantinists. I presented to the scholarly world for the first time the fact that the tent-bath was brought to Anatolia by the Oghuz, that it was used on campaign by ʿAlāʾ al-Dīn Kai-Qubād and called *hamām-i seferī,* and that the Khwārazm-Shāhs preserved the old Turkish word *çerge* (*Selçuklular,* p. 254). Kafesoğlu plagiarized this information without citing my sources. By saying nothing about where he got this information, he helps us confirm his plagiarism. The tent-hospital which appeared in the Seljuk armies also became a Turkish institution. Kafesoğlu adds this to his article (offprint, p. 48b). Furthermore, after he discovered that there were Turkish cities along the Jaxartes, which was an old Turkish homeland, he added this attractive evidence (?) to my research on the Turkization of Transoxiana ("Seljuks," offprint, pp. 33b, 44a). Using the same method of plagiarism, Kafesoğlu cites, according to me, the words of the Arab thinker al-Jāḥiẓ on the relations of the Turks with Khurāsān, and describes, according to me as well, the commercial importance of this country (*Selçuklular,* pp. 349–50; "Seljuks," offprint, 33b–34a).

It is as difficult to plagiarize new interpretations and problems as it is easy to plagiarize ready-made political history and events. Thus it is more difficult to find in this respect the kinds of proof I gave above. Nevertheless, Kafesoğlu even risked exposing himself in this regard while appropriating to himself my work on political history. Here, he tried to hide his efforts by removing some of the sources in my book and sometimes replacing them with late or unnecessary sources. [655] However, sometimes he gives himself away when he removes the sources for the text that he plagiarizes. In my book I frequently used Ibn al-Athīr and each time gave the page number. It would arouse suspicion if he were to cite the same edition and page numbers that I gave, and it would take a lot of time and effort to substitute the page numbers of another edition. After all, Kafesoğlu had to finish quickly his article before my book appeared. Finding himself in a difficult position, he substituted the years in which events occurred for page numbers. He ignored the fact that this method is only used for manuscripts without page or folio numbers and did not think that this would be questioned.

The political section of my Seljuk history, especially the Toghrıl Beg and Alp-Arslan periods, which are very obscure and require detailed study, was simply abridged and plagiarized. In fact, while having recourse to the research of Mehmet Köymen for the early history of the Seljuks, Kafesoğlu tried to hide the material that belongs to me but he did not succeed in the other periods. While making clear that he did not follow me on the question of Christianity among the Oghuz, he zealously disregarded the work of Z. V. Togan, which was my only source here. This question and its resolution are thus left in suspense.

When he plagiarized me on the Oghuz' adoption of Islam, he needed to find a reference for this. He attributed it to an article by Faruk Sümer, where there is nothing on this subject, and again exceeds the bounds of scholarly ethics (*Selçuklular,* pp. 35–36; "Seljuks," p. 355a).

It would take a long time to identify and analyze all the evidence that shows that the Seljuk article in the *İA* was taken from my book. This would have to be done elsewhere. Nevertheless, the scientific and material evidence that I have presented above is so strong and undeniable that just one piece of it suffices to prove Kafesoğlu's plagiarism. The fact that my work was available to Kafesoğlu and Ateş, who were both on the editorial committee, for three months—and a copy is still at the *İA*—contributes to these questions. [656] But despite this ready-made work, Kafesoğlu could not master the history and problems of the Seljuk period. He could not digest in two months a work that took two years to produce. His attempts to add or delete material simply brought confusion to the Seljuk article. It is therefore an article that satisfies neither scholars nor intellectuals. Even if this article were clearly not a work of plagiarism, the author would have gained nothing from it. This is obviously a worrysome example of how great a spiritual crisis there is in Turkey and Turkish scholarship, and of how a serious publishing institution like the *İA* can be shaken. This behavior of our friends, who have taken over the administration of this institution with great ambition and infighting, and consequently have alienated a great number of serious scholars because of their temperament, has gained neither them nor the *İA* anything.

Despite all the absolute proof as to how the Seljuk article was written, Ateş, in his official reply states, "the Seljuk article was written before my very eyes." He thus astonishingly presents himself as an unwitting witness to this affair. In addition to this amazing testimony, he says, "Professor Kafesoğlu is a scholar with a very thorough knowledge of the entire Seljuk period and its problems." He thus felt the need to identify him with a new specialization and ability. He cannot understand that such testimony would not be materially acceptable in the first instance or scientifically acceptable in the second. However, my first problem is not with Kafesoğlu's scholarly ability, but with the method he used to write this article and his source. In his reply, Kafesoğlu expressed his feelings of appreciation to me on the one hand and, with hesitation, considered me to be "a specialist on the Seljuks of Anatolia" on the other. Thus his statement that "the difficulty that I faced in embracing the entire breadth of Seljuk history prevented me from completing the article in time," is a superb measure and example of his scholarly depth and authority. This statement is nothing but an admission of guilt. The veracity of this judgment is based on the fact that my book took two years to write while his article took two months and was the product not of a scholarly but of an elementary mentality. It also remains an unanswered question why this article was originally requested from me and not from Kafesoğlu, if he had had the competence and had won the admiration of our brother Ahmed Ateş. [657] While stating in one place in his answer that "it would be proper for the Seljuk article to be given to Osman Turan," he both contradicts himself and denies the truth. For, after I had written much of my article, Kafesoğlu stated in the *İA* office that he wanted to write the Seljuk entry with me and had a file brought out in order to confirm that the proposal to write it had been made to me. As a compromise I had wanted to leave a section to him. A message was sent to the editor to ask if he knew about this change and would be responsible for it. Ateş gave an angry reply and, by mentioning the principle of "not giving the printed drafts of articles even to their authors," gave a strange reason for hiding the typescript and made one feel that he behaved graciously because he returned my draft. We should not forget that after this event, the editor, who had previously stressed haste and avoiding delays, and originally suggested that the Seljuk article be eighteen to twenty pages, allowed it to increase to sixty-four pages. This also raises questions.

As mentioned in his aforesaid reply, Kafesoğlu takes a mild and conciliatory approach, although there are some awkward passages and he contradicts himself. With regard to plagiarism, he believes that I based "the evidence for this on the notes that he made on the draft" and completely disregarded the scientific proof that I presented. After seeing the analysis and examples that I have given, he will finally understand the situation and see that his error has been discovered and his ability has been exposed. However, in order to cover again any suspicion, he says that "in articles that make use of the same sources it is natural to find similarities and connections." This appears to place Kafesoğlu in an awkward or embarrassing situation. For it is known to everyone that serious scholars make various discoveries with the same materials and sources while weak scholars cannot advance beyond being simple compilers. This is the case in both the physical and social sciences. While stating that my inability to meet the deadline for the article was obvious proof that I could not comprehend the totality of Seljuk history, he says that he had the ability to do so in two months "by writing the article in the hot summer months." This is an excellent example of his understanding of scholarly work as well as an implied confession. The required criticism here of the aforesaid, recently published Seljuk article has thus unfortunately taken the form of an unsavory story. [658] Nevertheless, despite its nature, there was a scientific obligation to subject this article to criticism. Although it greatly worries me that our colleagues have stooped to this behavior, I should go on record and be excused for presenting the truth in light of persistent and adverse actions. It should be stated here that, although man has the ability to discover the secrets of the universe, he cannot hide the truth about his own character. One must believe that this is divine wisdom.

It is worthy of note that after he plagiarized my book and this matter became widely known among colleagues, Kafesoğlu was not discouraged. He continued to behave in the same manner with regard to my other work. In fact, his article on Qılıch-Arslan II (*Hayat Tarih Mecmuası* [Life, the history magazine], July, 1965, pp. 13–17) was taken completely from my article in the *İA*. My ideas reveal this and make clear that he has acquired the habit of taking what is available.

11
Ahmed Ateş and His Rebuttal of Turan

Ahmed Ateş was born in 1917 in the village of Ağcaköy near the town of Birecik on the Syrian border. The son of a railroad contractor, he completed his elementary education in Marash and his secondary education in Konya. In 1935, he entered the Edebiyat Fakültesi (Faculty of Literature) of Istanbul University as a student in the Advanced Teachers' School. Among his professors were Fuad Köprülü and M. Şerefeddin Yaltkaya. He received solid training in Turkology and Arabic and Persian philology and, after graduation in 1939, he joined the same faculty as an assistant of Helmut Ritter. From then until his death, he completely devoted himself to his academic interests.

In 1943, Ateş became an assistant professor with a thesis called "An-Nâbiga az-Zubyânî, hayatı ve eseri hakkında araştırmalar" [Research on the life and work of al-Nābigha al-Zubyānī]. This later appeared in the first three volumes of *ŞM* (1956, 1958, 1959), which he was instrumental in founding. In 1953, he became a full professor. He helped organize Arabic and Persian philological studies in the Edebiyat Fakültesi and gained official status there for the Şarkiyat Enstitüsü (Oriental Institute), which had been founded earlier by Ritter. Between 1954 and 1957, he was its director. A driving force in Oriental studies, Ateş represented Turkey a number of times at the International Congress of Orientalists: Paris in 1948, Cambridge in 1954, Munich in 1955, and Moscow in 1960.

As a philologist, Ateş' major works were editions and Turkish translations of important Arabic and Persian texts. With respect to Seljuk studies, he translated Rāvandī's *Rāḥat al-ṣudūr* (Ankara, 1957–60), and edited the sections of volume 2 of Rashīd al-Dīn's *Jāmiʿ al-tawārīkh* on Maḥmūd of Ghazna and the Seljuks (Ankara, 1957 and 1960 respectively). These two Persian works are primary sources for the history of the Great Seljuks. In recognition of his many contributions to Persian philology, the Iranian government bestowed upon him a medal of merit in 1957.

Ateş was associated with the *İA* from its very beginning. From 1942 to 1966, he wrote more than sixty articles for this publication. Long a member of its editorial committee, he became its director in 1962. Except for two articles in French, none of his work appeared in a Western language. Ateş was a dynamic man who worked at a feverish pace until his life was cut short by a heart attack on 20 October 1966. (For more details on his life and a list of his publications, see *Türk Kültürü,* December 1966, and *ŞM* 7[1972]: 1–24, see also *Türk Edebiyatı Ansiklopedisi* [The encyclopaedia of Turkish literature], I, 155.)

As for Osman Turan's "critique" in *Belleten,* Ateş took exception to his allegations against the editorial committee of the *İA,* and himself in particular. In a rebuttal in the same journal, 30(1966): 459–66, entitled "Prof. Dr. Osman Turan'ın yazısı dolayısı ile bir açıklama" [An explanation in response to Prof. Dr. Osman Turan's article], he refuted Turan's charges and made his own pointed criticism of Turan's "irresponsibility" and "poor scholarship."

* * *

[459] In Osman Turan's article entitled "Selçuklular hakkında yeni bir neşir münasebetiyle" in *Belleten,* he claims that the Seljuk article in the *İA* was plagiarized from his book *Selçuklular tarihi ve Türk-İslâm medeniyeti* and, to use his terms, "indeed, such blatantly dishonest behavior is truly rare in the scholarly world." The writer of the aforesaid article will reply to his allegations. Turan, furthermore, has accused the *İA* editorial committee, especially its director, whose name he has frequently mentioned, of assisting in this or of criminal complicity. In order to do so he has distorted the facts, beginning with the request for the Seljuk article from him, and has related the story with certain embelishments. As he very well knows, all the facts in question have been documented in the *İA* office—my correspondence and the originals of his letters—and upon his urging an investigation committee of the National Ministry of Education looked into the matter and found no irregularities. But it appears that he has forgotten all of this, otherwise one could only be horrified at the conscious recklessness required by one making such claims. Despite everything, it would not really be necessary to respond to his allegations and relate the real story here, but because this concerns the *İA,* which has been appearing for a quarter

century, thanks to the common devotion of a generation of scholars, and has rightfully earned the respect of the scholarly world, the story needs to be retold and Turan needs to be reminded of certain things.

Although this is known to readers, and I appologize right from the start for having to mention it again, the matter in question is the Seljuk article that appeared in the *İA*. This encyclopaedia is published in fascicles which, as far as possible, appear periodically in a certain size. It is necessary for the articles appearing therein to be prepared more or less at a certain time and in a certain length. It is clear that the timing and size of the article in question were very important in this case.

Turan, omitting the dates, begins his story in the following manner, "In an official message that I received signed by Professor Ahmed Ateş, the director of the *İA* editorial committee, I was asked to write the Seljuk article and was told that it should not exceed eighteen to twenty pages. Because of the importance of the period . . . and the fact that research on the Seljuks was still in its infancy, I explained that such a short article would be insufficient . . . it was consequently agreed that the Seljuks warranted an article of eighty to ninty pages." [460] The truth of the matter is this: In May 1963, Turan came to the *İA* office. The nature of the Seljuk article, who would write it, and its length were discussed with him, and together a set of principles was established. In my first official message, number 84, dated 31 May 1963, the original of which was sent to Turan and a copy of which is in the *İA* office, the following was stated: "With regard to the previous discussion of the Seljuk article in our office, it was agreed that the article on the Seljuks of Anatolia would be written by you, but in three encyclopaedia pages because of the considerable detail you have given in the articles on the rulers of the Anatolian Seljuks. If you wish to write the article on the Seljuks as a whole, the editorial committee would be agreeable to its being written by you on condition that it not exceed eighteen to twenty encyclopaedia pages. Please send us this article within four months or let us know whether or not this will be possible."

On 12 June 1963, Turan answered as follows: "I believe a more extensive article should be written on the Seljuks and wanted to ask how we should cooperate on this. I also thought I would write only on the Seljuks of Turkey. Given the special articles that have been written, you have decided that this article should be written in a very general manner. If so, it would therefore be better to consider having it written by a single author. Because this coincides with the summer months, perhaps the time will not be enough. At any rate, there will be a chance to speak with you soon. Therefore, I will try to write according to the size that you have outlined."

It will be seen that there was agreement on all aspects of this article including its size. His own letter gives the lie to his contrary claims. In the event, there was only a difference regarding the time. In message number 93, dated 12 June 1963, I stated, "only an additional month can be given to the time for the Seljuk article. I hope we can discuss further details on this matter when you are in Istanbul."

After Turan took this article upon himself and the time allotted for it had passed (October 1963), he wrote to say that the article would be one fascicle (80 encyclopaedia pages). The following was written to him in response on 19 February 1964—again long after the extension that was given to him— because he insisted on discussions and they wasted time: "You have stated that the Seljuk article, which the *İA* editorial committee agreed to have you write, will constitute a fascicle. Because the *İA* editorial committee wishes to complete the encyclopaedia as soon as possible, and taking into consideration the fact that there are separate articles on virtually all the important Seljuk rulers, and articles on those who are missing will appear in later sections in the supplement, it will not be possible to have an article of the length that you mentioned. At most, we will agree to an article of 25 to 30 pages. Thus, please write an article of this length or, if it is of the size you mentioned and could be published as a rather large book by Türk Tarih Kurumu [Turkish Historical Association], please send the encyclopaedia a condensed version of it." However, after considerable correspondence that is not necessary to describe here, the deadline passed. In order to avoid holding up the publication of the encyclopaedia, we nevertheless agreed to accept an article of 80 encyclopaedia pages. [461] In message number 53, dated 18 April 1964, six months after the end of the extension, the Seljuk article was requested from him. Finally, after putting us off, at the beginning of June 1964, eight months after the extension, Professor Turan personally brought the article, which he said would be 80 pages, to our office. Believing it to be the length agreed upon, we turned it over to Doç. Dr. Şükrü Akkaya, who was then in charge of reviewing articles. After a section was reviewed, it was typed by another office. After 50 pages were typed, it was clear that the draft amounted to 500 pages of typescript (160–170 encyclopaedia pages). The section that was typed was sent to Turan for review and abridgement along with a message from us, number 105, dated 1 July 1964. In it we said, "Because your draft cannot be accurately estimated in its present state, we hope you will immediately read the typescript, shorten it and return it to us. Otherwise there is a danger that the encyclopaedia will get behind schedule and the typesetter will be idle." On 16 July 1964, a second 50-page section was sent to him with the same request. Because of his long delay, Professor Turan brought the administration of the encyclopaedia to a standstill. Instead of immediately making the requested abridgment, he said in a letter dated 4 July 1964, "I would like to state that I am sorry but it would be materially and morally impossible for me to make the abridgment . . . efforts to conform to the encyclopaedia specifications have sufficiently tired me." Consequently, fifteen months after the article was requested, and ten months after the extension, in my message number 109, dated 8 July 1964, I proposed the following to Turan in order to rescue the encyclopaedia, which had been completely idle, and his own work: "After taking into consideration the fact that the history of the Seljuks was of very great importance with regard to Turkish history and our national history, the editorial committee unanimously decided that this article could not be accepted in its present size. Because it seems that you will not be able to condense the article, we would request, under these circumstances, that you leave this matter to our office. Afterwards, if you wish, on condition that you retain the copyright and be immediately compensated, the initials T. H. (i.e., Tahrir Heyeti {Editorial Commmittee}) could be placed {at the end of the article}." The intent of this proposal was obvious—by paying the author for the full value of his article, we would take upon ourselves the responsibility for it and save him from the trouble of doing something that he did not wish to do himself. Meanwhile I visited him in Ankara and suggested the following:

1. that he himself abridge the article as soon as possible,
2. that we do it, in which case,
   a. if he wished, we could sign his name or,
   b. if not, give him all rights and sign with the initials T.H., and
3. that we propose to the National Ministry of Education that his work be published in its entirety and that an abridgement be published in the *İA,* stating that it was an abridgement of a book to be published by Osman Turan.

In our discussion, Turan rejected all this and did the same in a letter dated 13 July 1964, while again stressing the importance of the history of the Seljuks. In the same letter he said that it would not be possible for us to abridge his work, stating, "this was the moral equivalent of proposing to the writer of a work that he kill it with his own hands." [462] Telling the members of the editorial committee, all of whom were professors, that there was no one who had the ability to abridge a historical article was tantamount to insult. In the same letter, he also said, "one must show a certain responsibility and consideration for someone who has been made to work for a year." There appears to be no difference between the actions of Professor Dr. Osman Turan, who speaks of consideration for rights and responsibility, and the unjust behavior of someone from whom a two-meter table is ordered within five months and then fifteen months later he shows up with a twenty-meter table, tries to place it in one's house by destroying the walls, and then has the temerity to claim his rights.

In the same letter, he finally said, "there is no choice but to request that the work be returned immediately and to allow you to have your wish (?!)." Under these circumstances, there was no alternative but to accede to his request, return the manuscript that he had submitted for the Seljuk article—which when published would have reached the great length of some four hundred pages—and have another author write the aforesaid article. This was done.

Such was the fate of Turan's article until it was returned to him, as evidenced by his letters. When this is taken into account, it will be easier to understand that what he later maintained has no substance to it. In one place (p. 640) he says, "Faced with this, I told him {Ateş} as a final suggestion that if the civilization section was left out and only the political section was published, both his length and time constraints could be met. In fact, this part would be less than a fascicle." This is completely false. This is obvious from his own letters and our replies. Such a suggestion has no basis in fact. At the same time, this claim does not conform with what transpired, for when we spoke with him—as frequently repeated in our letters cited above—it was agreed that the articles on the Seljuk rulers were very long and consequently political and military events should be passed over as briefly as possible and much more attention should be given to general problems and questions of civilization and culture. This was repeated by Turan himself in his first letter. In like manner, for him to say that "Professor A. Ateş, . . . in agreement with Professor İ. Kafesoğlu, who was eager to write the article, stressed the importance of the civilization section and maintained that they could not give it up," is a vulgar and ugly allegation that contradicts the series of events described above and the text of his own letter. A bit further he says, "he {Ateş} even proposed that a short article be written by Kafesoğlu and, because of time constraints, that I permit him to use my work." No such suggestion was ever made to him. This assertion is completely baseless. This is clear from our various letters and proposals.

Turan, who tries to see or present everything in an atmosphere of intrigue, also says that his one 189-page typescript was kept at the encyclopaedia office. He knows very well that this is normal procedure, that drafts of articles being published are never removed from that office. For just as the encyclopaedia has a responsibility, so too do the authors. Moreover, these articles can each serve as documents to resolve a great many problems. Indeed, his own writings will serve to settle a number of issues.

[463] It should also be added here that the 189-page manuscript that was typed and kept for a time in our office only covered Seljuk history up to the battle of Malazgird and all specialists know that the history of the Seljuks to this point is outside Turan's main area of expertise.

Professor Turan, no matter what he tries to imagine about this affair, nevertheless provides the evidence that easily confirms that his claims are baseless. In fact, he himself says, "Indeed, it seems that the adventure of my work is not finished and certain rumors imply that there is more to come (p. 641)." His purpose is clear. Whereas it never occurred to him that, if someone decided to plagiarize a work, he would naturally keep it secret. It would therefore be impossible for certain rumors to begin before such a work is published. This being the case, it is obvious that Turan is aware of the fact that these things exist only in his imagination and that the rumors he heard and all that he has written are figments of that imagination.

This affair between the *İA* and Turan did not end here. He had recourse to the National Ministry of Education. The head of its investigation committee came to Istanbul, looked into the matter, and was completely amazed {at Turan's behavior}, especially at the amount of time involved. One can easly imagine that, if the editorial committee had to spend this much time with every article, the *İA* would never get published.

When the Seljuk article, which he thought could not be written, was written and the first part was published, Turan, as he himself says, believed the conjecture about it that he perceived and protested to me as the delegated director of the *İA*. In the reply given to him, it was shown that his allegations were based completely on mistaken and silly assumptions. To remind him: "İbrahim Kafesoğlu is a scholar who has studied Seljuk history continuously for years and has taught it at university. . . . You must realize that it would be impossible for Kafesoğlu to commit the crime for which you blame him, the name of which I cannot write here, indeed impossible that he would deign to do such a thing. Moreover, it would be futile for you to imagine that my friends and I would willfully tolerate this. Given the work and publications that you and he have done to date, it would be easy to prove such an allegation is nothing more that calumny." I saw nothing in Turan's article in *Belleten* to change my mind.

In this article, which is based on his own imagined, unfounded suspicions, he also says, "Probably the first action that was attempted according to the agreement with the editorial director was to act before the appearance of my book and immediately publish the article." While making this judgment, which again is an expression of his faulty reasoning, the historian Turan forgets dates. A work that appears at regular intervals receives from him in June 1964 a manuscript that was requested no later than 1 October 1963 and one month later has to be returned to him. This means that by even the most conservative estimate, the *İA* was delayed at least eight to nine months because of him. Consequently, I want to make it very clear that, although the Seljuk article {Kafesoğlu's} was immediately typed as it came in, part by part, sent to the press and printed, it was impossible to make up for the delay for which he was responsible.

[464] Professor Turan, who wants to see everything with the same glasses, explains with the same reasoning how the article on the Seljuk ruler whom he calls Sultan Sanjar was replaced by *Senjer* {i.e., *Sencer*}. But one should naturally not be surprised. Let me say right away that he is wrong. If he had read the article on Senjer in the *İA,* he would have seen there that the original form of the word is related to the root *sanç,* that the true form must be *Sanchar,* but that this was softened by the effect of the ç and pronounced in Turkey—and even at the time of Senjer, if one looks at how it was written in Arabic—with a softer sound. Turan would thus have seen why the article on this sultan was placed under *Senjer*. With such material proof it is easy to understand that all this is a figment of his imagination. The typesetting and printing of this seven-page article took one week, so it is clear how serious a fifteen-month loss in time has been.

Turan also says the following with the same reasoning: "our friends, who have taken over the administration of this institution with great ambition and infighting, and consequently have alienated a great number of serious scholars because of their temperament." It is very sad to see our friend Turan make such public statements to describe a dispute the details and nature of which he knows very well.

Let me say this above all: while writing the words "to the alienation of a great number of serious scholars," it is obvious that Osman Turan was so careless that he did not even feel the need to examine the pages of the *İA* that were right before his eyes. Otherwise, instead of one missing signature {Turan's}, he would have seen at least ten signatures that have not yet appeared in the encyclopaedia. As for some writers who have not appeared, even if I personally respect an author and his knowledge, if it appears that the scholarly level of the *İA* might be lowered by his work, then unfortunately there will be a difference between us. Furthermore, when it was proposed that I be placed in charge of the administration of the *İA,* I discussed this with him before anyone else, for I was anxious to avoid the possibility of any misunderstanding between us. At the very least, Turan, although he knows the situation, is making a vicious statement.

Turan also says, "It also remains an unanswered question why this article was originally requested from me and not from Kafesoğlu, if he had . . . won the admiration of our brother Ahmed Ateş." The answer to this question must be found in the depths of our brother Osman Turan's conscience.

* * *

The *İA* editorial committee, despite everything, is sorry that it has not been able to reach an understanding with him for some time. It has had the best intentions. When it was suggested that his book be published by Türk Kültürünü Araştırma Enstitüsü, we voted in favor of doing so although we had not read it. However, when his book appeared, it was obvious that we were very fortunate in deciding not to publish his work in the *İA*. For Turan's book, despite the allegations made in his article in *Belleten* and his endless confidence in himself, is full of major, basic, and terrible mistakes. [465] In order to get an idea about some of them, see for now the following reviews:

A. Ateş, "Yabgulular meselesi" [The problem of the Yabghulular], *Belleten,* 29(1965):517-25.

İ. Kafesoğlu, *Tarih Dergisi* [The journal of history], 15(1965):171–88.

A. Ateş, *ŞM,* 6(1966):162–73.

In these reviews, it has been shown that Professor Dr. Osman Turan, who wants "to protect Turkish scholarship from such incidents" (p. 642) and expose "the extent of the crisis of values in which our universities find themselves" (p. 640), is able to reveal the ignorance of other scholars without knowing the basic rules of philology and grammar, and make discoveries in every field without understanding the texts that he reads. Some will think that these words are exaggerated, but one can give examples in various places to show how much he misunderstands things and then makes discoveries based on such misunderstandings. One example is the following: In Ibn Bībī (TTK ed., [Ankara, 1956], p. 272, lines 6–7), there is found this sentence:

سلطان در علائیه از قلعه عزم « شکر خانهٔ » که در صحرا ساخته است فرمود کمال‌الدین
در خدمت سوار گشت . . .

Turan saw this and immediately says, "Ibn Bībī states that there was a *şekerhane* {sugar factory} in the countryside near ʿAlā'iyya and that it was built by ʿAlā' al-Dīn Kai-Qubād. Consequently, it is possible that there was sugarcane as well as lemons and oranges on the coast at that time (*Selçuklular,* p. 267, lines 24 f.)." While describing the misfortune of Kamāl al-Dīn Qāmyār, Ibn Bībī mentions a شکر خانه in the countryside, that is, far from the city, to which the sultan went with friends. It is obvious that it would make no sense to build a factory, above all a sugar factory, in the countryside. This alone should lead one to deduce that this word must have another meaning. The same word is found, for example, in one of {Afḍal al-Dīn Ibrāhīm} Khāqānī's letters (Shehid Ali Pasha Library, MS nr. 2796, fol. 145b):

و یوز را از شکر خانهٔ خاص بیرون فرمرد افکندن
دیگر نگذاشت که آن یوز را بشکارگاه آورند ...

If we were to accept Turan's interpretation, we would have to read Khāqānī's sentence as "He ordered the leopard to be thrown outside the special 'sugar factory' and did not allow the leopard to be brought again to the hunting area." It is not necessary to look in a large dictionary. If we simply look at *Burhān-i qāṭiʿ*, we will find that *şiker* {perhaps more properly *shikār*} (reading the word as *şeker* is mistaken) means "prey, hunting, something torn to pieces" and that in Persian there are the expressions *can-şiker* (hunter of living game), *dil-şiker* (hunter of hearts, beloved), and *düşmen-şiker* (hunter of enemies). It is therefore easy to see that *şiker-hane* means "hunting hut" or "hunting lodge." The meaning of Ibn Bībī's sentence is thus, "The Sultan, who was at ʿAlā'iyya, deigned to go from the citadel to the hunting lodge that he built in the countryside. Kamāl al-Dīn also rode with him." There is nothing unusual in meaning in this sentence and there is no room to imagine a sugar factory. And whereas it was known that rulers built hunting lodges and huts in the countryside, we know of no sugar factory or any other kind of factory built in such a place.

In the same manner, Turan, who reads *yuġannūna* as *yaġinūn,* although the words *muganni* and *teganni* are found in Turkish, even says in his aforesaid article (p. 653) that *Masjid al-jāmiʿ* is a mistake. [466] He says it should be *Masjid-i jumʿa*. He thus tries to correct the words and expressions of a language that he does not know. While there is no such compound as *masjid al-jumʿa* in classical Arabic, the compound *masjid al-jāmiʿ* is very common, as seen in numerous grammar books (see, e.g., Ibn Yaʿīsh, *Shārḥ al-Mufaṣṣal li'l-Zamakhsharī,* ed. G. Jahn [Leipzig, 1882], 2:330 f.; W. Wright, *A Grammar of the Arabic Language,* 3d ed. [Cambridge, 1896–98], 2:232). The expression *masjid al-jāmiʿ* was always used in historical and geographical works for the great mosques in the large cities. It would require 120–30 pages of *Belleten* to point out all of Turan's mistakes. Let me add that, if Osman Turan would not say that I am threatening him (cf. his aforesaid article, p. 642), and if sufficient space were provided, I am prepared to do this for the sake of scholarship.

If we had read the work that Turan had submitted to us, naturally we would not have included it in the *İA*. We would also have had to withdraw, with some embarrassment, the proposal that we promised to make to the ministry for its complete publication. I personally want to thank him for insisting on the length that he wanted, for he saved us from such a fate.

12
Kafesoğlu's Refutation of Turan

Kafesoğlu, of course, had even more reason to respond to Turan's critique than Ateş. In the same issue of *Belleten* (30[1966]:467–79), in an article entitled "Prof. Osman Turan'ın tenkid yazısı dolayısiyle Selçuklu tarihi meselelerine toplu bir bakış" [A concise view of Seljuk historical problems in response to Professor Osman Turan's critical article], he refuted point by point Turan's criticism of his article on the Seljuks and made a blistering attack of his own on the quality of Turan's work. In the translation that follows, it should be mentioned that Kafesoğlu does not always quote Turan exactly. And sometimes he uses quotation marks only for emphasis. The information in Kafesoğlu's few footnotes, where not already found in Ateş' rebuttal, has been incorporated in the body of the text.

* * *

[467] I am compelled to respond to the article published by Osman Turan entitled "Selçuklular hakkında yeni bir neşir münasebetiyle (*İslâm Ansiklopedisi*ndeki İ. Kafesoğlu'nun Selçuklular makalesi") because of his incredible opinion concerning my integrity and the scholarly level of my work. This response is not only meant as a defense of myself against unjust and unseemly accusations for, by bringing to light numerous facts on the Seljuks, I also hope to take a step towards saving certain historians who do not have a good knowledge of the primary sources and general literature of this most important phase of

Turkish history and who have not been very effective in grappling with historical questions from the misfortune of having to change identity.

Osman Turan's article, in which historical subjects and his personal remarks aimed at me are all mixed together, can be divided into three main sections: (1) his allegations against the *İA*, (2) general and preconceived ideas about Seljuk history, and (3) his claim that my article is a plagiarization.

1. With reference to the time in which an attempt was made to resolve the dispute that occurred after Osman Turan prepared the Seljuk article and submitted it to the *İA*, his statement that the *İA* director "proposed that a short article be written by Kafesoğlu and, because of time constraints, that I permit him to use my work (p. 641)" is a nonsensical claim. Furthermore, his statement that "although this was an unusual proposal, I said I would agree on condition that my own ideas and rights be respected (same page)" is equally without validity and baseless. After the draft of Turan's article was returned to him, I had to write the Seljuk article because of the short time. When half the text of what I had written (on political history) was published in fascicle 104 of the *İA*, Turan was of the opinion that this was surely plagiarized from his draft and sent a notarized protest to the administration of the encyclopaedia. [468] I replied to this protest. He describes my reply in a rather obscure manner saying, "Kafesoğlu avoided an admission of guilt with a weak and conciliatory defense in his official reply (pp. 642, 656)." (This reply in fact was addressed to the directorate of the *İA*.) In addition, he says, "Kafesoğlu stated in the *İA* office that he wanted to write the Seljuk article with me and had a file brought out in order to confirm that the proposal to write it had been made to me (p. 657)." All this is a masterpiece of mind-boggling falsehood. Because the Seljuk article was given to him, Turan wants to make the claim that I lost the chance to write it, but such action is further proof of the weakness of his case because, as a member of the editorial committee, I can write an article for the encyclopaedia whenever I wish. This cannot be denied, not even by Turan. With my personal insistence, despite the urging of certain members of the editorial committee, the Seljuk article was assigned to Turan with whom I thought I had very close relations. Moreover, at that time Turan was in difficult straits which was a major factor in assigning the article to him. As Professor Ateş says above, "Osman Turan must find the reason why the article was given to him in the depths of his conscience." Naturally, to the sympathy that was felt toward Turan was added the thought that he could write an appropriate article on the Seljuks for the *İA*, which has an international scholarly reputation. But this friend

who, in an unexpected manner, debased, to use his own expression, "the former friendship (p. 641 {*sic*})," showed in the section of his book which would have formed the basis of the Seljuk article (see *Selçuklular tarihi,* pp. 27–216) that he could not write an article of the serious scholarly level required by the *İA*. We therefore must express our feelings of relief that the draft of his article, which I had not read, was returned to him. According to his own statement, the *Selçuklular tarihi* was originally 216 pages but was expanded to 400 pages and was published by the Türk Kültürünü Araştırma Enstitüsü. It should be mentioned that, although Turan succeeded in hiding his thoughts and intentions towards me for a long time, I recommended his work to this Institute. (Both Professor Ateş and I are members of the Institute's scientific committee. Before Turan's book could be published, we had to review it. Nevertheless, we did not object to having this task assigned to two friends who were not close to the subject, and we accepted their very short report. However, much later, as the publication of the book reached the index stage, we learned the content of the work and submitted our reports with scholarly critiques in order to stop the publication. We fulfilled our obligation to the Insitute and could not accept any future responsibility for this book.)

2. [469] As for Osman Turan's general and preconceived ideas about Seljuk history, the following sentences are worthy of note to show how well he knows this subject, on which many Turkish and foreign scholars have fastidiously worked for perhaps a quarter century: "Because research that has been done on the Seljuks . . . is still very little and inadequate, this great period continues to be obscure and not properly understood, . . . one reason for the continuing obscurity of this period is the inadequacy of the research, another is the difficulty in carrying out that research (p. 639) . . . . {Because of} the importance of the period, . . . {and the fact that} research on the Seljuks was still in its infancy" (p. 640).

Because Turan believes that everything he saw in the sources on the Seljuks was something he discovered, he lost sight of reality. Thus Turan, who as will be seen below, presented everything he wrote as new ideas, original interpretations, original revelations, or guideposts to Seljuk history, was astounded to find in my article that I discussed almost the same problems of Seljuk history as he did. As a result of this situation, "which he could not stomach" (the expression is his {but Turan seems to use the verb "*hazmetmek*" with a slightly different meaning in his critique}), he came to the conclusion that, because his draft remained for a time at the *İA* office, Ateş and I secretly conspired against him (pp. 642, 643, 656). The link was easily made with plagiarism, and on the basis of this imagined plagiarism he set to work looking for parallels between my article and his book. Ignoring the major differences between the two and discovering similarities that were unavoidable because of common sources, special names, the names of years and months, and the like, he characterized me as a compulsive, blatant plagiarizer. Reserving the right of judgment to himself he claims: "Kafesoğlu methodically abridged, broke apart and plagiarized as he liked my work which had been entrusted to the *İA* (pp. 641–42) . . . . He rearranged and added verbiage to the new interpretations and problems first advanced by me while plagiarizing them . . . he thought he would appropriate some of them to himself (p. 643) . . . he had a great lack of scholarly ethics and responsibility (p. 647). . . . By plagiarizing material on subjects that he does not understand he becomes confused (p. 650) . . . . He mixed unsound ideas with some of the ideas that he took from me (p. 653)." He thus tries to undermine my reputation. As if he were the only competent authority, he accuses me of "being superficial, lacking a general knowledge of this period, being unable to go beyond compiling, and of having no methodology or critical sense (pp. 644, 646, 651, 656 f.)." He alleges that I have been "apprehended," that he has "provided firm evidence to reveal plagiarism," and that I made "misleading appropriations" of his work. Only on the long subject concerning the civilization and cultural life of the Seljuk period, where he could not find parallels to my extensive and clear explanations, which were provided with a rich biblography that is found in neither his book nor any other work, is he forced to say, "Kafesoğlu appears to speak authoritatively on the social, cultural and economic problems of the Seljuk period, subjects which to date he has not understood. In fact he has *defied the laws of nature* (p. 648)." He adds, "these sections of his article make one wonder about the source (ibid.)."

Osman Turan is a person of whom one must be careful because he gets carried away by his emotions. This must be taken into consideration when he makes his accusations. [470] Moreover, Turan cannot understand how I was able to write a praiseworthy, sixty-four-page article on the Seljuks for the *İA* in a short time, saying, "He squeezed into about two months a work that took me two years to prepare (p. 643)." In addition to the fact that he was not able to find any parallels in the civilization section between my article and his book, he must have forgotten his own statement concerning the fact that this section did not exist in the draft that he sent to the *İA,* namely, "The political history section of this work (pp. 27–216) is the full text that was prepared for the *İA,* but with the references placed in the footnotes (p. 641)."

Let me say from the very first that I did not write the Seljuk article in two months, but in a month and a half (1 August–15 September 1964). Having recourse to thousands of note cards, notes concerning the political and cultural history of the Seljuks, a subject on which I have worked for years, and my two-volume book entitled *Umumî Türk tarih ve kültürü,* which is being prepared for publication {apparently his *Türk tarih ve kültürü* (Ankara, 1976)}, I wrote this article by working through many nights during the heat of the summer in order not to disrupt the encyclopaedia's schedule. Although this was a grueling job, I must admit that I did it as a kind of atonement for the fact that Turan, who, by attempting to have a book-sized article published after a twelve-month delay, did not do what the editorial committee, which he likes to belittle, asked and because he used to dishonorable purpose the good intentions that we previously had shown by having the article assigned to him. I was successful and consequently prevented his plan of putting us in a position in which we would have to publish his work, and thus maintained the scholarly standards of the *İA*. By the way, let me repeat that if I had read Turan's article at that time as a member of the editorial committee, I would have considered its immediate rejection to be a duty on both scientific and conscientious grounds.

3. After explaining the full truth of the matter, I now come to my main subject. As previously mentioned, Turan, who believes that everything he sees in the sources is new and proposes that every idea that first comes into his head is an original discovery, compared his book with my article line by line. He was not content to say that the infrequent similarities were plagiarized from his own work, but in addition to the "similarities," which total perhaps 5 percent of my article, he claims ownership of everything else. Indeed, by skillful means of illusion, he attempts to lay claim to the entire Seljuk article. With regard to the "similarities," in the section that follows it will be seen that we have a very different appreciation of common sources, that there are great differences with respect to the direction of our research, and that we are far apart in the understanding of historical events and problems. [471] The facts will show that my article is completely different from Turan's book in quality and content. I have carefully counted the items that Turan claims were "stolen" in his critique. In order to save space, I will reply to each one briefly. At the same time, I believe that this will provide a concise view of the problems of Seljuk history.

1. P. 643: The transliteration of the name of the famous Seljuk sultan Sanjar as *Senjer* {i.e., *Sencer*} in the *İA* rather than as *Sanjar,* as it is usually written in scholarly works, is the direct result of scholarly

reflection. This is explained in the *Senjer* article. To insist on this as a mistake based strictly on an accusation reveals the weakness of one's scientific approach.

2. P. 644: Citing an article by M. A. Köymen to say that I lacked any methodology and sense of criticism by mixing late, valueless sources and modern works with each other instead of using primary sources and important modern works is no proof. To the contrary, it accuses the accuser. In that article Köymen described the *'Iqd al-jumān* as a late source for Sultan Malik-Shāh. But I later showed in detail that this source contained material for the period in question ("Selçuklu tarihinin meseleleri," *Belleten* 19[1955]:466 f.), and Köymen agreed with me. To use my accuser's terms, it would require "scholarly honesty" to take note of my response to Köymen while criticizing my work. Indeed, I rather doubt that Turan saw my response. Moreover, by taking issue with *'Iqd al-jumān,* he reveals that he did not know one of our primary sources very well, which is a reflection of his own lack of methodology and criticism.

3. P. 644: On the question of the location of the Oghuz city of Yengi-Kent, although I mentioned V. Barthold's book and clearly cited what he says (*Orta Asya Türk tarihi hakkında dersler* [Istanbul, 1927], p. 53; cf. "Seljuks," *İA,* p. 355b), this full reference was accidently omitted. It is simply incorrect for Turan to make a connection between this and his book for, "if I had plagiarized it," I would not have had the chance to make this mistake!

4. P. 644: There is naturally no basis to his claim that I took advantage of his book to adopt titles like *Inanch* and *Yınal,* which were borne by the sons and grandsons of Seljuk, as genuine names and wrote them as such (see "Seljuks," *İA,* p. 357a; also see Kafesoğlu, *Tarih Dergisi* 15, no. 14 [1965]:175, on this gross error by Turan). Those who think that these are real names, like Turan, do not know the Seljuk administration and political organization very well.

5. P. 644: Seljuk had four, not five sons. The name *Yūnus,* which Turan gives as the fifth son, appears in a late source as a copiest's error for *Yūsuf,* one of the four sons (for details, see Kafesoğlu, "Selçuk'un oğulları ve torunları," *TM* 13[1958]:117–30; cf. "Seljuks," *İA,* p. 357a). As for Er-Sıghun, he was the brother of the famous Ibrāhīm Yınal, the son of Yūsuf, not Yūnus, who never existed (*TM,* op. cit., p. 129).

6. P. 644: *Er-Sıghun* or *Er-Sıghın* are my suggestions for the way to read the name of this Seljuk prince, a name which is written many different ways in the sources. [472] In the article "Malazgirt muhārebesi" [The battle of Malazgird], which I wrote for the *İA* in 1956,

this name appeared as *Er-Saghun* because of a typing error, but this was corrected in the offprint ("Malazgirt meydan muhārebesi" [The pitched battle of Malazgird], *İA*, offprint from fascicle 72, Istanbul, 1956, p. 6). One must be happy that Turan, who takes every opportunity to be the first to discover something—because he is unaware of the research of others—did not see this mistake in the *İA*, for there is no doubt that he would also have said that it was "plagiarized" or "secretly corrected."

7. P. 644: As for the existence of old Oghuz cities on the banks of the Jaxartes, this is not one of his new discoveries as he thinks, but has been previously known from historical materials (see Barthold, *Dersler*, p. 53; O. Pritsak, "Der Untergang des Reiches des Oğuzischen Yabğu," *Köprülü armağnı*, pp. 399 f.).

8. P. 645: The bibliography that I gave on the pronunciation of the word *Selchuk*, is richer and more concise than Turan's and my scholarly presentation is more convincing and clearer. Turan tries to establish a connection with his own work saying, "Kafesoğlu avoided taking for himself my final conclusion," but this can only be an illusion. Indeed, his view of the pronunciation of the name *Selchuk* cannot be considered correct. It suffices to point out that the first syllable of this name as written in the Arabic script is not *sal* but *sel* (cf. the name *Sencer;* see also Ateş, *ŞM* 6[1965]:164 f.).

9. P. 645: The story of the coming of the Seljuks to Transoxiana is given in my article (p. 360a). The reference in question here is obviously not to Barthold's book, but to the eleventh-century author al-ʿUtbī.

10. P. 645: The authors that I mentioned (Ibn Funduq, Ibn al-Athīr) concerning the coming of certain volunteers from Khurāsān to Armenia before the Seljuks are more reliable and respected than the others. Ibn al-Athīr's *al-Kāmil* in particular is at the top of the list of the most acceptable sources in the scholarly world. It would be necessary to refute these two sources in order to claim the opposite. It is ludicrous to refer to a study I made fourteen years ago.

11. P. 646: I put the word *Yabghulu* next to the word *Nawbakī* {*Nāvakī*}, which appears in the sources concerning the Seljuks, with a question mark. This was suggested in a discussion held in Istanbul with Z. V. Togan and Ali Sevim. This proves that I could not have relied on Turan's identification of *Nāvakī* with *Yabghu,* which he says I plagiarized. In fact, this point, which he tries to explain at great length in his book as a "scientific discovery," is baseless, for it appears to be the result of Turan's mistaken reading of the old texts (see Ateş, "Yabgulular meselesi," *Belleten* 29[1965]:517–25).

12. P. 646: Our source, which states that Er-Sıghun together with Erdem had Alp-Arslan's name read in the *khuṭba* in Qazvīn, is recorded in Ibn al-Athīr (*al-Kāmil* [Cairo, 1357]:8:95, year 455). Naturally, strange expressions that Turan invented and need to be explained, like "Kazvīn Beyi," do not appear in my article.

13. P. 646: With regard to Chaghrı Beg's raid in eastern Anatolia, I made it clear in my article that the second date given (1018) was the year in which the Seljuk forces were seen around Lake Van (p. 358b). [473] It is worthy of note that this important point, the historical significance of which I previously described in detail, was appropriated by Turan to himself.

14. P. 646: Turan did not understand very well the name *Baran,* which he considers to be one of his "discoveries." This word is not a first name, but the name of a Turkish tribe and means "sheep" (Kafesoğlu, *Tarih Dergisi,* p. 174, no. 10).

15. P. 646: Turan claims that he mentions for the first time the victory of the Seljuks at Hasan-Kale, but this is unquestionably wrong. The names *Pasinler* and *Hasan-Kale* were mentioned long ago in 1944 by M. H. Yınanç with regard to the wars of Ibrāhīm Yınal in that area (see his *Selçuklular devri,* vol. I, *Anadolu'nun fethi* [Istanbul, 1944], pp. 44 f.). Yınanç called the place of the battle *Kapetre,* which was corrected to *Kaputru* by V. Minorsky who, in 1953, gave the date of this battle for the first time (18 September 1048), albeit with a question mark (*Studies in Caucasian History* [London, 1953], p. 61n. 2; cf. "Seljuks," *İA,* pp. 355a–b, and idem, *Tarih Dergisi,* p. 175, no. 15). I called this battle the victory of Pasinler, not the victory of Hasan-Kale. In his zeal to make "discoveries," Turan attempts to veil the efforts of other scholars on this subject in an air of mystery, but he cannot hide the facts.

16. P. 646: In my book *Sultan Melikşah,* published in 1953, considerable detail was given to Alp-Arslan's appointment of Malik-Shāh as his heir apparent and the appointments of the other princes (pp. 9–17, 16n. 16). The positions of the latter during the reign of Malik-Shāh were also narrated in order.

17. P. 647: As concerns Alp-Arslan's conquest of Ani, Turan rashly claims that I replaced the word *fetḥnāme* in his book with *beyannāme.* Let me remind him that in my article both words were used with very specific meanings (p. 368b). *Fetḥnāmes* were written by the sultan while *beyannāmes* were "issued" by the caliph (Yınanç, *Anadolu'nun fethi,* p. 95). In his book, Turan passes over the decrees of the caliph with the simple word *letters* and does not appreciate what a *beyannāme* is.

18. P. 647: The reference to the war between the Seljuk sultan of Iraq, Masʿūd, and the caliph is translated from the source in our possession and is correct. However, I have not seen the work by a certain ʿAbd al-Jalīl Qazvīnī.

19. P. 647: On the subject of Georgian-Qıpchak relations in the Seljuk period, my major source was Brosset's book, which can be found in the Istanbul Municipal Library. The information in it was cited in 1953 by F. Kırzıoğlu long before Turan "discovered" it (Kırzıoğlu, *Kars tarihi,* vol. I [Istanbul, 1953], pp. 373–76). One must use Turan's own expression, "a misleading attempt at appropriation," to describe his own work for ignoring a researcher who had done considerable work on this subject before him.

20. P. 647: [474] On the question of the establishment of the Seljuks in Turkey, Turan's judgments with regard to "scholarly ethics" are among the points that arouse suspicions about his own critique. First, he claims both "plagiarism" and then says "that I preferred someone else." Second, "the fact that Turan presented for the first time" the subject of the establishment of the Anatolian Seljuks is wrong. Indeed, he has difficulty grasping this subject on which he has worked for so many years. This subject, on which Yınanç has given very valuable information, was described in detail and in proper order in my article (*Tarih Dergisi,* pp. 182 f.).

21. P. 647: There is no monograph on the Anatolian Seljuk sultan Masʿūd. Meanwhile there have been serious disputes about the Dānishmendids. Altogether this question is rather confused. In my article, I relied on the entries in the *İA,* since sorting error from fact falls upon the authors of these entries. It is worth noting here Turan's invitation to me to take an "examination," the nature of which I have not been able to understand very well. If his purpose is to evaluate historical sources, then his own work is the best measure in this regard. If his intention is to meet before a general committee on a broad subject like Seljuk history, then I am ready to offer my work to any logical, erudite, fair judge. Common sense will prevail.

22. P. 648: With regard to the civilization of the Seljuk period, I devoted thirty-two pages to this in my article in the *İA*. In a comprehensive manner reflecting the balance required for an *İA* article, I discussed the administrative, military, financial, judicial, and cultural organization as well as social, economic, commercial, scientific, literary, and religious life. This bewildered Turan, who has great difficulty trying to show parallels between these subjects and his book. Consequently, his statement that my work "defies the laws of nature" is an expression of frustration born of the inability to hide from the truth.

Although in general I mentioned the sources and modern studies in the proper places, he says my article is full of "redundant verbiage" and has an "insubstantial bibliography"—by saying this he wants to avoid the heart of the matter. This is nothing but an admission of his own weakness. If the problem is so simple, one could propose to Turan that he write such a study of the same quality.

23. P. 648: As for the idea of universal rule among the Turks, as usual Turan believes that he has come up with "new ideas and interpretations." His statement that I was not aware of this problem is simpleminded, and his statement that I did not mention it in my book on Malik-Shāh is untrue. In this book, published in 1953, I said that Malik-Shāh shared such a view (pp. 101, 116). I mentioned Sultan Yavuz Selim in my article because the famous words of this sovereign, which typify this view, were supposedly said with respect to Pīri Reis' map of the world (see A. A. Adıvar, *Osmanlı Türklerinde ilim* [Science among the Ottomans] [Istanbul, 1943], p. 58, n. 1). Furthermore, let me add that there are aspects of the idea of universal dominion among the Turks on which I cannot agree with Turan. [475] While he limits this concept to the "medieval Turks" (the expression is his), I am of the opinion that this idea was prevalent throughout Tukish history in light of the historical facts ("Seljuks," *İA*, p. 392a; see also Kafesoğlu, *Tarih Dergisi*, pp. 178 f., 183).

24. P. 649: As was pointed out in my article, Senjer's ideas on the subject of universal dominion had already been reported by Köymen in 1954 (*Büyük Selçuklu imparatorluğu tarihi II* [Ankara, 1954], pp. 219, 222). Turan claims that I took this material from his book. If he did not know of Köymen's work, then he was not a very good researcher. If he did know, then his remarks about "scholarly ethics" are a charade.

25. P. 649: Turan considers the words of Niẓām al-Mulk to be a reflection of the old Turkish view of dominion. Apparently he cannot distinguish the view of Islamic dominion as understood in Iran from the Turkish state practice and view of dominion. I noted this difference in passing in my article (pp. 387a–b, see also Kafesoğlu, *Tarih Dergisi*, p. 178).

26. P. 649: His claim that I even took the subject titles from his draft is baseless. This is clear from the fact that the pages in question given in his book were not found in the draft that he sent to the *İA* office. There are also differences in the two works concerning the roles of women and *atabegs* in the Seljuk state, as can easily be seen by comparing the texts.

27. P. 649: The problem of the "feudal political structure" that

Turan unconvincingly tries to apply to the Seljuk Turks is unreasonable speculation that has no connection with the facts. I mentioned this point in my article as well as in my review of his book ("Seljuks," *İA*, p. 387b; idem., *Tarih Dergisi*, pp. 179–81; Ateş, *ŞM*, 6[1966]:166).

28. P. 650: The words that Ibrāhīm Yınal, the Seljuk prince, spoke in Nīshāpūr, which Turan believes I "borrowed" from his work were previously cited in 1957 in full detail by Köymen ("Büyük Selçuklu imparatorluğu'nun kuruluşu," *DTCF Dergisi* 15[1957]:95 f.). Turan was either trying to hide this or was not aware of it, whereas I gave Köymen full credit in my article.

29. P. 650: The questions of *toy, khwān-ı yağmā,* and so forth, among the Turks, as well as their origins, are subjects too general to require comment. Full references are found in the bibliography of my article. Furthermore, this was all discussed in my book on Malik-Shāh, published in 1953 (p. 137 and n. 3).

30. P. 650: Turan is generally confused about cultural problems, and this applies to the difference between secularism and religious tolerance. Thus he cannot find the right approach to study the concept of secularism in Turkish history. This subject is so far beyond him that he believes that this concept came to the Seljuks from the Būyids (cf. "Seljuks," *İA*, p. 391a, and *Tarih Dergisi*, p. 183). He therefore came to a dead end on the establishment of the state of the Anatolian Seljuks (see *Tarih Dergisi*, pp. 182 f.). This view was naturally not written down in the law, but it was the continuation of an old Turkish custom. [476] This was first pointed out by Barthold (see *Sultan Melikşah*, p. 153, n. 42).

31. P. 650: Is it necessary to say that, if the Seljuk sultans acted in a fatherly manner towards non-Muslims, they could behave in no other manner towards Muslims?

32. P. 651: I believe that I described very well in my article how, as a major goal of Seljuk state policy, the sultans encouraged the Turkmen to come and settle in Anatolia (pp. 392b–96b, and *Tarih Dergisi*, pp. 180 f.). It is clear that this problem, which I presented, has no bearing on his book. In 1956 I had already described in my article "Malazgirt muhārebesi" in the *İA* the reasons for the coming of the Turkmen and their settlement and the great importance of this for Turkish history. It appears that Turan, who says that the page numbers were changed here, has revealed the false basis of his own book. Things like this shake one's confidence in his work. Although it is not known if Turan gives the right page numbers for the works he uses, it is certain that he did not give a proper bibliography in his articles. This can be seen above all in his *İA* articles which are methodologically

unacceptable because they are so hard to check {see, e.g., Leiser's English trans. of Turan's *İA* article "Kaykhusraw II" in the *Journal of the Pakistan Historical Society* 33(1985)}.

33. P. 651: References to Anatolia as *Turkia* in foreign sources in Seljuk times had been cited in various studies long before Turan made it one of his many "discoveries." Indeed, there is one reference that is more than two hundred years old (Joseph De Guignes, Turkish trans. by H. Cahid as *Hunların, Türklerin Moğolların ve daha sair Tatarların tarih-i umumīsi* [Istanbul, 1924], IV, 9 {in Ottoman}. This work was written between 1756 and 1758). G. Moravcsik's monumental work is a bibliographical source, not a compilation (*Byzantinoturcica* [Budapest, 1943], 2:269, where it can be seen in Byzantine sources as well which territory, including Anatolia, was called *Turkia*).

34. P. 651: Another thing that our friend claims to have "discovered" was the struggle between the caliph and sultan. Turan reveals himself to be an amateur historian in such subjects. Let me remind him that Köymen was the historian who presented the "problem" of these struggles in Seljuk history (*Büyük Selçuklu imparatorluğu tarihi II,* pp. 91–113, 255–300). I later investigated those aspects of these struggles concerning the Khwārazm-Shāhs (*Harezmşahlar devleti tarihi* [Ankara, 1956], index). The information in my article is supported by other sources related to the Seljuks of Iraq.

35. P. 651: Turan, who makes a habit of allotting to himself every line of my article, notices a "similarity" in estimating the value of the Seljuk revenue while ignoring how this figure was reached, namely, by a quantitative method, and thus thinks that he has discovered another point of support for his allegations. If my estimate is wrong, it would be better for Turan to try to correct it.

36. P. 652: Turan says, "Kafesoğlu did not credit me with my references to the monetary policy of Qāvurt, the Seljuk ruler of Kirmān." But he only gives six words on this subject in his book! He therefore admits here that he did not know the publications on this subject for, in my article on "Kavurd" in the *İA* in 1953, I described the value of the money of this ruler—which became famous as *naqd-i Qāvurdī*—and cited my source. [477] Let me mention that in the section of Turan's book on the Seljuks of Kirmān, a subject that he summarizes in two and a half pages, he does not mention a single source. In the same manner, apart from two insufficient articles in the *Encyclopaedia of Islam* {1st ed.}, he does not bother to give a bibliography on the subject of the Seljuks of Syria, to which he devotes one and a half pages. It is possible to see all this as proof that Turan did not really comprehend Seljuk history even after working on it for two years.

37. P. 652: I cited the *İA* articles not only for the period of Qılıch-Arslan II but also for other matters related to the Anatolian Seljuks. The questions of *efsanevī zenginlik, heykel* (p. 653), *sigorta* (p. 654), and *çerge* (p. 654) were based on these *İA* articles. As I stated above, the authors of these articles are responsible for their accuracy.

38. P. 652: One of the things that reveals Turan's lack of historical method is his ideas about coinage. Coins are the most reliable of historical sources because there is no likelihood that they have been falsified. Turan, who talks about "bankrupt, misleading efforts," considers himself well-versed in numismatic research, but this is an example of his boundless ignorance. He writes that Qılıch-Arslan II struck silver coins (see the *İA* article "Kılıç Arslan II."). Instead of touching on this mistake in my article, I simply showed, and gave a bibliography, that this sultan minted gold coins. Doubts must be raised about one who claims to be a historian but does not distinguish the difference between gold and silver in the economic life of a state. {Qılıch-Arslan II minted both silver and gold coins, see İbrahim and Cevriye Artuk, *İstanbul arkeoloji müzeleri teşhirdeki İslâmî sikkeler kataloğu* [A catalog of the Islamic coins on exhibit in the Istanbul archeology museums] (Istanbul, 1970–74), 1:350.}

39. P. 652: I stick to my opinion that I presented a description of the moral and spiritual life of Anatolia in my article. I repeat that I presented very clearly, with a rich bibliography, a description of the moral and spiritual life not only of Anatolia—including Ibn al-ʿArabī, Mawlānā, and Bābā Isḥāq—but also of Iran, Iraq, Syria, Āzarbāījān, Central Asia, and other Turkish states in the Seljuk period. Turan claims that I found the subject of Seljuk culture in Anatolia ready-made in his book. Given the fact that it requires a very sharp mind to delve into a subject like Seljuk civilization, one cannot help but notice that Turan cannot even determine why works on music were mentioned in my article.

40. P. 653: The correct form of the name of the mosque that Malik-Shāh had built in Iṣfahān is not *Masjid-i jumaʿ* but *Masjid al-jāmiʿ* (see Ateş above). The historian who criticizes the concise information and extensive bibliography that I gave in my article is one who cannot go beyond the amateur level on cultural problems.

41. P. 653: While it is known that Anatolia was called *Türkiye* in the Seljuk period, Turan takes possession of the phrase *Türkiye Selçukluları* and insists that the notes on his draft that was sent to the *İA* are mine. Such a thing is beyond my psychological comprehension. [478] If I had read his draft and written any notes, they would have no doubt stated, "This article is unacceptable to the *İA*."

42. P. 653: There are some lost works concerning the Seljuk period

that Turan claims I brought to light "with him at the same time." Let me list these lost works and the sources in which they are mentioned: *Sanjar-Nāma* in *Ta'rīkh-i Ṭabaristān,* II, ed. ʿA. Iqbal, p. 54; *Kitāb Mafākhir al-atrʿāk* by Ibn Funduq in *Ta'rīkh-i Baihaq,* ed. A. Bahmanyār, 1317 *sh.*, p. 241; *Siyar-u futūḥ sulṭān Sanjar* in *Mujmal al-tawārīkh wa'l-qiṣaṣ,* ed. M. Bahār, 1318 *sh.*, p. 412; M. M. Qazvīnī, *Bīst maqāla,* II, 1332 *sh.*, p. 231. These are not all the works on the Seljuk period that are currently not in our possession, but I found it necessary to mention them in my article.

43. P. 653: As for the history of the civilization of the Seljuk period that Turan believes he presented for the first time, this has been the focus of major studies for about a half century and there is considerable literature on it. Because Turan is a novice in such subjects, he naturally could not have known of the research that I mentioned in my article ("Seljuks," pp. 412b–13b; idem, *Tarih Dergisi,* p. 177; idem, "Ortaçağ Türk-İslâm dünyasında ilim ve garbe tesirleri," *Türk Yurdu* [The Turkish homeland], 50[1960]:17–21).

44. P. 654: It is impossible to work on Turkish history and culture and not know al-Jāḥiẓ. C. E. Bosworth, for example, knows this Arab author very well and cites in his work the references to al-Jāḥiẓ that I mentioned in my article. One would therefore also expect Turan to attack Bosworth as another "plagiarizer." This would be particularly appropriate for his critique, which is already a comedy of the first order.

45. P. 655: Why did I cite Ibn al-Athīr by year and not by volume and page number? Turan bases one of his strangest accusations on this. Let me explain. There are many editions of *al-Kāmil* and they may not be available to everyone. This makes it difficult to check the text by giving just the page numbers. My goal is always to make it easy to check what I have written. For a long time I have therefore preferred to give the year in which events took place. This has been the case in the publication of much research and many sources.

46. P. 655: I have always relied on the research of Köyman for the periods of Seljuk history that are "obscure and require detailed study," because he writes well and keeps his references clear. As for the question of religion among the Oghuz, I gave the necessary information, as well as useful bibliography, in my article.

Summary: Up to this point, I have replied to Turan's allegations, which have recklessly exceeded the bounds of "scholarly honesty" and "scholarly ethics" (the expressions are his). Finally, let me regretfully state that I am obliged to record that Turan, who cannot even correctly write the name of the period on which he claims to be a specialist (e.g., *Selçuk devleti,* p. 640; *Selçuk sultanı,* p. 643; *Selçuk tarihi,* pp.

644, 645; *Selçuk kervansarayları,* p. 653, and so forth, where in each case the first word should be *Selçuklu*) and then says (e.g., p. 651) that my Turkish is confusing (!), has, thanks to his "new interpretations, new ideas and discoveries" in his book and this indictment of his, brought utter chaos to Seljuk history, both political and cultural, which he believes had "remained in darkness" because he has been unaware of the research and publications that have been made up to now in this field. In my review of his book, from which he alleged that I had plagiarized material for my *İA* article, I mentioned subjects which show an astounding degree of weakness in his knowledge, especially of research and sources, and cited various passages and made comparisons to show that this specialist (!) cannot properly follow or make sense of {historical} events, cannot grasp the organization and structure of the Seljuk state, and moreover, mistakenly explains events because he tries to see everything from the Islamic point of view {*koyu bir islāmcı kafa ile çalıştığı için*} (see above n. 6). Professor Ateş has provided evidence to prove that this work also has no value with regard to Arabic and Persian philology, and that it paves the way to erroneous conclusions (see above n. 6). Both of our reviews as well as the present response reveal that the famous specialist, who considers himself to have great historiographical ability, would by no means be able to comprehend the article that I wrote on the Seljuks for the *İslâm Ansiklopedisi,* which was the product of years of continuous study.

Translator's Comments

As mentioned in the preface, I have made no attempt to confirm Kafesoğlu's statements or references, nor do I have any intention of trying to substantiate all the points raised by Turan in his critique or by Ateş and Kafesoğlu in their responses. Furthermore, with respect to the controversy, no Turkish scholar, to my knowledge, has ventured to resolve the matter. Köymen, for example, has only stated that he does not believe that the Seljuk article could have been written in a month and a half. Nevertheless, a number of comments from the perspective of the translator would seem to be in order. First, Kafesoğlu's article is not easy to read in Turkish. He frequently tries to pack an enormous amount of information, not always well-connected, into long, cumbersome sentences. This often leads to ambiguities that are especially confusing to anyone who is not familiar with the subject. In short, Kafesoğlu presumes to much on the part of his readers. This may be one consequence of hurried writing, to which he admits. One unquestioned consequence of this is the apparent haphazardness of certain sentences and paragraphs. Second, encyclopaedia articles, above all those surveying broad subjects, are indeed usually derivative in nature. Thus, as Kafesoğlu states, the fact that he mentions the same topics and references with respect to the Seljuks as Turan is not necessarily proof of plagiarism. Third, both Kafesoğlu and Turan overstate their cases in their attacks on each other. Turan in particular makes many allegations based on extremely convoluted logic. Moreover he appears to attack Kafesoğlu not only for plagiarizing his work, but also for *not* plagiarizing it. Fourth, the intensity of the dispute no doubt resulted to a certain extent from the not inconsiderable prestige that was at stake in being asked to write the *İA* article on the Seljuks. Professional jealousy is clearly a factor in the strident, uncompromising, and often exaggerated positions taken by both men. Fifth, this episode in Turkish Seljuk historiography needs to be placed in the context of Turan's experience as a member of the Democrat Party during the time and after the military took control of the government in 1960, and then of his attempt to reenter academia. And finally, it must be emphasized that although Kafesoğlu and Turan differ on numerous points, their interpretations of Seljuk history, at least concerning the Seljuk article, are in fact quite similar. This, of course, is at the heart of Turan's accusation of plagiarism. On the other hand, one could simply argue that Turan and Kafesoğlu both ascribe to the same interpretation of Seljuk history.

Appendix

Glossary of Technical Terms

Bibliography

Appendix

Modern Turkish and Arabic Equivalents of the Medieval Names of Cities and Rivers*

(r. = river)
Akshehir : Philomelium
Ala-Shehir : Philadelphia
Amasya : Amasea
Antalya : Attalia
Aras : Araxes
Aydın : Tralleis
Balıkesir : Palaeocastro/Achyraus
Bergama : Pergamum
Denizli : Laodicea
Dragos : Dracon (r.)
Dulūk : Teloukh
Edirne : Adrianople
Edremid : Adramyttium
Efes : Ephesus
Ereghli (Ereğli) : Heraclea
Eskishehir : Dorylaeum
Gök-Su : Calycadnus (r.)
Harput : Kharput, Khartpert
Ḥiṣn Kaifā : Castrum Cepha
Izmir : Smyrna
Izmit : Nicomedia
Iznik : Nicaea
Jeyhān : Pyramus (r.)
Kayseri : Caesarea
Kemah : Kāmākh
Khunas : Chonae
Konya : Iconium
Kütahya : Cotyaeum
Lādhiqiyya : Laodicea
Manisa : Magnesia
Marash : Germanicea
Niksar : Neocaesarea
Oltu : Ukht'ik'
Pasin : Phasiane
Qaramān : Laranda
Qızıl Irmak : Halys (r.)
Sakarya : Sangarius (r.)
Shaizar : Larissa
Shebin-Qaraḥiṣār : Colonia
Sheki : Shakki
Silifke : Seleucia
Niksar : Neocaesarea
Sivas : Sebastea
Siverek : Sevaverak
Suwaidiyya : St. Simeon
Ulu-Borlu : Sozopolis
Üsküdar : Chrysopolis
Zamantı : Karamalas (r.)

* Medieval names are based primarily on the spellings in *The Cambridge Medieval History*, volume 4, *The Byzantine Empire*, ed. J. M. Hussey (Cambridge, 1966).

Glossary of Technical Terms

ʿAmīd	Title of administrative officials of high rank.
Atabeg	Majordomo, title of a high dignitary under the Seljuks and their successors.
Bāṭinī	Name given to those who rejected the literal meaning of sacred texts and stressed the "inward" meaning, especially the Ismāʿīlīs.
Baş-buğ	Commander, chief, leader.
Beg	Title of a prince, ruler, chief, notable.
Beylik	Principality, a region ruled by a *beg*.
Dāʿī	Propagandist, especially for the Ismāʿīlīs.
Dars	Lesson, especially in Islamic law.
Derebey	Local potentate or despot. This name was used in Ottoman times.
Dhikr	Session or seance of a *ṣūfī* brotherhood.
Dihqān	Member of the lesser feudal nobility in Sasānid Persia, village headman.
Dīwān	Government ministry or bureau. Anthology of poetry.
Ferman	Government edict.
Fetḥnāme	Official announcement of a military victory.
Ghāzī	Warrior for the faith.
Ḥadīth	Tradition of an alleged saying or practice of the Prophet.
Imām	Prayer leader, head of the Islamic community.
Iqṭāʿ	Grant of state lands or revenues by a Muslim ruler in exchange for service, usually military.
Jihād	Holy war against non-Muslims.
Khān	Title usually used for subordinate rulers, not to be confused with the same word meaning inn or warehouse.
Kharāj	Tax, land tax.
Khuṭba	Sermon given at the Friday congregational prayer in a mosque.
Kümbet	Tower tomb, usually with conical roof.
Kunya	Patronymic, surname.

Laqab	Byname.
Madhhab	Any one of the four legal systems recognized as orthodox by Sunnī Muslims.
Madrasa	Islamic "college" of law.
Malik	King, sovereign.
Manshūr	Patent of office.
Miḥrāb	Niche in the wall of a mosque indicating the direction of Mecca.
Mimbar	Pulpit in a mosque from which the *khuṭba* is delivered.
Mithqāl	Standard of weight.
Nā'ib	Representative, deputy, substitute.
Naqīb	Leader, headman.
Qāḍī	Judge.
Rāfiḍī	Apostate, heretic, renegade, Shīʿī.
Ra'īs	Chief, leader.
Ribāṭ	Fortified Muslim, usually *ṣūfī*, monastery.
Samāʿ	Music, singing, and dancing that takes place during a *ṣūfī dhikr*.
Shāh	King, sovereign.
Shaikh	Elder, chief.
Sharīʿa	Revealed holy law of Islam.
Shiḥna	Police, police chief, security forces.
Sü-başı	Army commander.
Tuğra/Tughra	Monogram, signature.
Türbe	Tomb, mausoleum.
Yabghu	Title of the Oghuz ruler.

Bibliography

A great amount of research has been done on Seljuk history. This work has been mentioned in the relevant sections of the narrative given above and so will not be mentioned here. The bibliography that follows is therefore limited to the primary sources for the history of the Seljuks.

Collections of Documents

Bahā' al-Dīn Muḥammad b. Mu'ayyad al-Baghdādī. *Al-Tawassul ilā 'l-tarassul*. Edited by Aḥmad Bahmanyār. Tehran, 1315/1936–37.

Juvainī, Muntajab al-Dīn Badīʿ al-Kātib. *ʿAtabat al-kataba*. Edited by ʿAbbās Iqbāl. Tehran, 1329/1950.

Köymen, Mehmet. "Selçuklu devri kaynaklarına dâir araştırmalar, I. Büyük Selçuklu devrine âit münşeât mecmuaları" [Research on the sources of the Seljuk period: I Secretarial handbooks from the Great Seljuk period]. *DTCF Dergisi* 8(1951):537–634. On the Leningrad collection of documents.

Vaṭvāṭ, Rashīd al-Dīn. *Abkār al-afkār fī 'l-rasā'il va 'l-ashʿār*. Istanbul University Library MS FY 424.

General Chronicles, Special Histories, and Local Histories

Afḍal al-Dīn Kirmānī. *Badā'iʿ al-azmān fī ta'rīkh* {or *waqā'iʿ*} *Kirmān*. Edited by Mahdi Bayānī. Tehran, 1326/1947.

———. *ʿIqd al-ʿūlā li 'l-mawāqif al-aʿlā'*. Edited by ʿAlī Muḥammad ʿĀmirī. Tehran, 1311/1932–33.

Al-ʿAinī, Badr al-Dīn. *ʿIqd al-jumān*. Veliyüddin Efendi Library MS 2374–2396. Turkish translation, Topkapı, Baghdad *köşk* MS 278.

Anonymous. *Ta'rīkh-i āl-i Saljūq*. Photocopy edition and Turkish translation by F.N. Uzluk. Ankara, 1952.

Anonymous. *Ta'rīkh-i Sīstān*. Edited by Malik al-Shuʿarā' Bahār. Tehran, 1314/1935.

Al-Aqsarāyī, Karīm al-Dīn. *Musāmarat al-akhbār*. Edited by Osman Turan. Ankara: TTK, 1944.

Al-ʿAẓīmī. "La Chronique Abrégée d'Al-ʿAẓīmī." Edited by Cl. Cahen. *JA* 230(1938):353–448.

Baihaqī, Abū 'l-Faḍl. *Ta'rīkh-i Baihaq*. Edited by Q. Ghanī and ʿA. Fayyād. Tehran, 1324/1945.

Baybars al-Manṣūrī. *Zubdat al-fikra*. Feyzullah Efendi Library MS. 1459.

Al-Dhahabī, Shams al-Dīn Muḥammad. *Ta'rīkh duwal al-islām*. Köprülü Library MS 1079.

Fakhr al-Dīn al-Rāzī. *Jawāmiʿ al-ʿulūm*. Nuruosmaniye Library MS. 3760.

Gardīzī. *Zain al-akhbār*. Edited by Mīrzā Muḥammad Qazvīnī. Tehran, 1315 *sh*.

Ḥāfiẓ-i Ābrū. *Zubdat al-tawārīkh*. Süleymaniye, Damad İbrahim Paşa Library MS. 919.

Ibn al-ʿAdīm. *Zubdat al-ḥalab fī ta'rīkh Ḥalab*. Edited by Sāmī al-Dahhān. Vols. 1–2. Damascus, 1951–54.

———. *Bughyat al-ṭalab fī ta'rīkh Ḥalab*. Topkapı, Sultan Ahmet III Library MS 2925, vol. 3.

Ibn al-ʿAmīd. *Al-Majmūʿ al-mubārak*. Süleymaniye, Laleli Library MS. 2002.

Ibn al-Athīr. *Al-Kāmil fī 'l-ta'rīkh*. Vols. 8–9. Cairo, 1357/1938–39.

Ibn al-Azraq. *Ta'rīkh Mayyāfāriqīn*. British Museum Or. MS 5803.

Ibn Bībī. *Al-Awāmir al-ʿalā'iyya*. Vol 1. Ankara, 1957. Photocopy edition, Ankara: TTK, 1956. German translation by H. W. Duda as *Die Seltschukengeschichte des Ibn Bībī*. Copenhagen, 1959.

Ibn Funduq. *Ta'rīkh-i Baihaq*. Edited by Aḥmad Bahmanyār. Tehran, 1317/1938.

Ibn Ḥassūl. *Tafḍīl al-atrāk*. Edited with Turkish translation by Şerefeddin Yaltkaya. *Belleten* 4(1940):1–51, 235–66.

Ibn Isfandiyār. *Ta'rīkh-i Ṭabaristān*. Edited by ʿAbbās Iqbāl. Vols. 1–2. Tehran, 1320 *sh*.

Ibn al-Jawzī. *Al-Muntaẓam*. Vols. 8–9. Hyderabad, 1359/1941.

Ibn Muyassar. *Akhbār Miṣr*. Edited by H. Massé as *Annales d'Égypte*. Cairo, 1919.

Ibn Niẓām al-Ḥusainī, Muḥammad. *Al-ʿUrāḍa fī 'l-ḥikāyat al-saljūqiyya*. Edited by K. Süssheim. Cairo, 1326/1908.

Ibn al-Qalānisī. *Dhail Ta'rīkh Dimashq*. Edited by H. F. Amedroz. Leiden, 1908.

Ibn al-Sāʿī. *Jāmiʿ al-mukhtaṣar*. Edited by M. Djawad and F. Anastase-Marie. Baghdad, 1934.

Ibn al-Ṭiqṭaqa. *Munyat al-fuḍalā'* (*Kitāb al-Fakhrī*). French translation by É. Amar as "Al-Fakhrī, histoire des dynasties musulmans depuis la mort de Mahomet jusqu'à la chute du khalifat ʿAbbâside de Baghdad (11–656 de l'hégire = 632–1258 de J.-C.)." *Archives Morocaines,* 16(1910): i–xlv, 1–628.

Ibn Wāṣil. *Mufarrij al-kurūb*. Edited by Jamāl al-Dīn al-Shayyāl. Vol. 1. Cairo, 1953.

ʿImād al-Dīn al-Iṣfahānī. *Zubdat al-nuṣra*. Turkish translation by Kıvâmüddin Burslan as *Irak ve Horasan Selçukluları tarihi*. Istanbul: TTK, 1943.

Juvainī, ʿAlāʾ al-Dīn ʿAṭāʾ Malik. *Taʾrīkh-i Jahān-Gushā*. Edited by Mīrzā Muḥammad Qazvīnī. 3 vols. *GMS*, vol. 16. London, 1912–37.

Jūzjānī. *Ṭabaqāt-i Nāṣirī*. Edited by ʿAbd al-Ḥayy Ḥabībī Qandahārī. Vol. 1. Kabul, 1963.

Khwāndamīr. *Ḥabīb al-siyar*. Vols. 2–3. Tehran, 1333 *sh*.

Marvazī, Sharaf al-Zamān. *Ṭabāʾiʿ al-ḥayavān*. Edited and translated by V. Minorsky as *On China, the Turks, and India*. London, 1942.

Mīrkhwānd. *Rawḍat al-ṣafāʾ*. Bombay, 1270 and Lucknow, 1308.

Muḥammad b. Ibrāhīm. *Taʾrīkh-i Saljūqiyyān-i Kirmān*. Edited by M. Th. Houtsma in *Recueil des textes relatifs à l'histoire des Seldjoucides*. Vol. 1. Leiden, 1886.

Müneccim-başı. *Jāmiʿ al-duwal*. Turkish translation as *Ṣaḥāʾif al-akhbār* by Ahmed Nedim, first part, Istanbul, 1285/1868–69. Recent translation of the section on the Seljuks of Anatolia by H. F. Turgal, Istanbul, 1939, and of the section on the Qarakhānids by N. Lugal, Istanbul, 1940.

Al-Narshakhī. *Taʾrīkh-i Bukhārā*. Edited by Ch. Schefer. Paris, 1892.

Al-Nasawī. *Sīrat al-Sulṭān Jalāl al-Dīn*. Edited with French translation by O. Houdas. 2 vols. Paris, 1981–95.

Nāṣir al-Dīn Munshiʾ Kirmānī. *Simṭ al-ʿulā li ʾl-haḍra tal-ʿulyā*. Edited by ʿAbbās Iqbāl. Tehran, 1328/1949.

Qāḍī Aḥmad of Niğde. *Al-Walad al-shafīq*. Fâtih Library MS 4519.

Qāḍī Burhān al-Dīn al-Anawī. *Anīs al-qulūb*. Edited by M. F. Köprülü. *Belleten* 7(1943):475–501.

Qazvīnī, Ḥamd Allāh Mustawfī. *Taʾrīkh-i Guzīda*. *GMS*, vol. 14. London, 1910.

———. *Nuzhat al-qulūb*. Edited by G. Le Strange. *GMS*, vol. 23. London, 1915.

Rāvandī. *Rāḥat al-ṣudūr*. Edited by M. Iqbāl. *GMS*, n.s., vol. 2. London, 1921. Turkish translation by A. Ateş. Ankara: TTK, 1957–60.

Rashīd al-Dīn, Faḍl Allāh. *Jāmiʿ al-tawārīkh*. Seljuk section edited by A. Ateş. Ankara: TTK, 1960.

Ṣadr al-Dīn ʿAlī al-Ḥusainī. *Akhbār al-dawla al-saljūqiyya*. Turkish translation by N. Lugal. Ankara: TTK, 1943.

Sibṭ b. al-Jawzī. *Mirʾāt al-zamān*. Topkapı MS 2907, vol. 12. Partial facsimile edition by J. Jewett. Chicago, 1907. Al-Yunīnī's copy under the same title, Türk-İslam Eserleri Müzesi MS T. 2135, vol. 12.

Al-ʿUtbī. *Al-Taʾrīkh al-Yamīnī*. Cairo, 1286/1869.

Yazdī, Ḥasan. *Jāmiʿ al-tawārīkh-i Ḥasanī*. Fâtih Library MS 4507.

Yazıcıoğlu. *Tawārīkh-i āl-i Saljūq*. Topkapı, Revan *köşk* MS 1391.

Ẓahīr al-Dīn al-Marʿashī. *Taʾrīkh-i Ṭabaristān va Rūyān va Māzandarān*. Edited by B. Dorn. St. Petersburg, 1850.

Ẓahīr al-Dīn Nīshāpūrī. *Saljūq-Nāma*. Edited together with Abū Ḥāmid Muḥammad b. Ibrāhīm's *Dhail-i Saljūq-Nāma* by Ismā'īl Khān Afshar. Tehran, 1332/1954.

Latin Sources

Histoire anonyme de la Première Croisade. Edited with a French translation by L. Bréhier. Paris, 1924.

Recueil des Historiens des Croisades. Historiens Occidentaux. Publ. Académie des Inscriptions et Belles Lettres. 5 vols. Paris, 1844–95. Contains the works of Albert of Aix, Fulcher of Chartres, William of Tyre, and others.

Byzantine Sources

Anna Comnena. *Alexiad*. French translation by B. Leib. 2 vols. Paris, 1937–40. French translation by Cousin in *Histoire de Constantinople*. Vol. 4. Paris, 1685.

Bryennius, Nicephorus. *Historia*. French translation by Cousin in *Histoire de Constantinople*. Vol. 3. Paris, 1685.

Lehmann, B. *Die Nachrichten des Niketas Choniates, Georgios Akropolites und Pachymeres über Selčuqen in der Zeit von 1180 bis 1280*. Leipzig, 1939.

Moravcsik, G. *Byzantinoturcica*. Vol. 1. Budapest, 1942–43. For G. Cedrenus/Skylitzes, M. Attaliates, J. Cinnamus, N. Choniates, Michael Glycas, Eustratius, Cecaumenus, Constantine Manasses, Nicephorus Gregoras, and the *Epistolae Turcicae*.

Psellus, Michael. *Chronographie ou Histoire d'un siècle de Byzance (976–1077)*. Edited with French translation by É. Renauld. 2 vols. Paris, 1926–28.

Zonaras, Joannes. *Chronique ou annales de Jean Zonare*. French translation by M. de S. Amour. Lyon, 1560.

Armenian Sources

Aristaces of Lastivert. *Histoire d'Arménie, comprenant la fin du Royaume d'Ani et le commencement des invasions des Seljoucides*. French translation by Ev. Prud'homme. Paris, 1864.

Gregory of Akner. *Moğol tarihi* [The history of the Mongols]. Turkish translation by H. D. Andreasyan. Istanbul, 1954.

Kirakos of Gantzag. *History*. Venice, 1863.

Matthew of Edessa. *Chronique de Mattieu d'Edesse*. French translation by E. Dulaurier. Paris, 1858. Turkish translation by H. D. Andreasyan as *Urfalı Mateos vekayinâmesi* (with the continuation by Gregory the Priest). Ankara: TTK, 1962.

Samuel of Ani. *Chronological Tables*. French translation by M. Brosset in *Collection d'historiens arméniens*. Vol. 2. St. Petersburg, 1876.

Stephen Orbelian. *Histoire de la Siouni*. French translation by M. Brosset. St. Petersburg, 1864.

Vartan the Great. *History*. Turkish translation by H. D. Andreasyan as "Türk fütûhât tarihi 889–1269." *İstanbul Üniversitesi Edebiyat Fakültesi Tarihi Semineri Dergisi*, 1(1937), 153–244.

Syriac Sources

Barhebraeus, Gregory Abū 'l-Faraj. *Abū 'l-Farac tarihi*. Turkish translation by Ö.R. Doğrul. 2 vols. Ankara: TTK, 1945–50.

Michael the Syrian. *Chronique de Michel le Syrien*. French translation by J.-B. Chabot. Vol. 3. Paris, 1905.

Georgian Sources

See M. Brosset, *Histoire de la Géorgie* (St. Petersburg, 1849–58), vols. 1–5.

Travelers' Accounts and Memoirs

Czeglédy, K. "Zur Meschheder Handschrift von Ibn Faḍlān's Reisebericht." *Acta Orientalia Hungarica*, 1(1950–51), 217–43.

Ibn Faḍlān. *Al-Riḥla*. Edited with a German translation by A. Zeki Velidi Togan as *Ibn Faḍlān's Reisebericht*. Leipzig, 1939.

Jamāl Qarshī. *Mulḥaqāt al-ṣurāḥ*. Edited by V. Barthold in *Turkestan Down to the Mongol Invasion* (in Russian). Vol. 1. St. Petersburg, 1900.

Nāṣir-i Khusraw. *Safar-Nāma*. Edited by M. Ghanīzāde. Berlin, 1341. Turkish translation by Abdülvahab Tarzı in the series *Şark-islâm klâsikleri*, {Eastern Islamic classics} no. 22. Istanbul, 1950. {English translation by W. M. Thackston. Albany, New York, 1986.}

Al-Qazwīnī, Zakariyyā'. *Āthār al-bilād*. Edited by F. Wüstenfeld. Göttingen, 1848.

Yāqūt. *Mu'jam al-buldān*. Edited by F. Wüstenfeld. 2d ed. Leipzig, 1924.

Works on Government and Social Life

Aflākī, Shams al-Dīn Aḥmad. *Manāqib al-'ārifīn*. Edited by Tahsin Yazıcı. 2 vols. Ankara: TTK, 1959–61. Turkish translation by Tahsin Yazıcı as *Âriflerin menkibeleri* in the series *Şark- islâm klâsikleri*, number 26. 2 vols. Istanbul, 1953–54.

Anonymous. *Mujmal al-tawārīkh wa 'l-qiṣaṣ*. Edited by Malik al-Shu'arā' Bahār. Tehran, 1318/1939.

Anonymous. *Oğuz Kağan destanı*. Edited and translated by W. Bang and G.R. Rahmeti Arat. Istanbul, 1936.

Ibn al-Bannā', Abū ʿAlī. See George Makdisi, "Autograph Diary of an Eleventh-Century Historian of Baghdad." *BSOAS* 19(1957):13–48, 281–303, 426–43.

Kāshgharī, Maḥmūd. *Dīwān Lughāt al-Turk*. Edited by Besim Atalay. 4 vols. Ankara: TDK, 1939–43.

Muḥammad b. al-Munawwar. *Asrār al-tawḥīd fī maqāmāt al-shaikh Abī Saʿīd*. Edited by Dhānīḥ Allāh Ṣafā. Tehran, 1332/1953–54.

Niẓām al-Mulk. *Siyāsat-Nāma*. Edited with French translation by Ch. Schefer. 2 vols. Paris, 1891–93. Also edited by ʿA. Khalkhālī. Tehran, 1310 *sh*.

Orhun, H. N. *Eski türk yazıtları*. 4 vols. Istanbul: TDK, 1936–41.

Al-Qalqashandī. *Ṣubḥ al-aʿshā*. Vol. 6. Cairo, 1915.

Yūsuf Khāṣṣ Ḥājib. *Kutadgu Bilig*. Turkish translation by G. R. Rahmeti Arat. Ankara: TTK, 1959. {English translation by Robert Dankoff. Chicago, 1983.}

Biographical Works

Amīn Aḥmad Rāzī. *Haft iqlīm*. Calcutta, 1918.

ʿAwfī, Muḥammad. *Lubāb al-albāb*. Vol. 2 edited by E. G. Brown. Leiden, 1903. Vol. 1 edited by Brown and Mīrzā Muḥammad Qazvīnī. Leiden, 1906.

———. *Jawāmiʿ al-ḥikāyāt*. Istanbul University Library MS FY 595. Summary in M. Nizāmuddin's English translation *Introduction to the Jawāmiʿ u'l-Ḥikāyāt*. *GMS,* vol. 7. London, 1929.

Dawlatshāh. *Tadhkirat al-shuʿarā'*. Edited by E. G. Brown. Leiden, 1901.

Ibn Abī Uṣaibiʿa. *ʿUyūn al-anbā' fī ṭabaqāt al-aṭibbā'*. Cairo, 1299/1881–82.

Ibn Hindūshāh Nakhshivānī, Muḥammad. *Tajārib al-salaf*. Edited by ʿAbbās Iqbāl. Tehran, 1314 *sh*.

Ibn al-ʿImād, Abū 'l-Ḥayy. *Shadharāt al-dhahab*. 10 vols. Cairo, 1345/1926–27.

Ibn Khallikān. *Wafayāt al-aʿyān*. Vols. 1–3. Cairo, 1299/1881–82.

Ibn Shākir al-Kutubī. *Fawāt al-Wafayāt*. 2 vols. Cairo, 1299/1881–82.

Ibn Zarkūb Shīrāzī. *Shīrāz-Nāma*. Edited by Bahmān Karīmī. Tehran, 1310 *sh*.

Khwāndamīr. *Dastūr al-wuzarā'*. Edited by S. Nafīsī. Tehran, 1317 *sh*.

Niẓāmī ʿArūḍī. *Chahār maqāla*. Edited by Mīrzā Muḥammad Qazvīnī. *GMS,* vol. 11. London, 1910.

Al-Qurashī, ʿAbd al-Qādir. *Al-Jawāhir al-muḍīʿa fī ṭabaqāt al-ḥanafiyya*. Süleymaniye, Turhan Sultan Library MS 232.

Al-Subkī, Tāj al-Dīn. *Ṭabaqāt al-shāfiʿiyya al-kubrā*. Vol. 3. Cairo, 1299/1881–82.

Inscriptions and Numismatic and Archeological Works

Artuk, İbrahim. "Selçuklu sultanı Mahmud bin Melik Şah'a âit bir dinar." *İstanbul Üniversitesi Edebiyat Fakültesi Tarih Dergisi* 6(1954): 141–44.

———. "Abbasi ve Anadolu Selçukîlerine ait iki eşsiz dinar." *İstanbul Arkeoloji Müzeleri Yıllığı* 8(1958):44–46, 86–87.

———. "Abbasiler devrinde sikke." *Belleten* 24(1960):25–43.

Butak, Behzad. *XI. XII. ve XIII. yüzyıllarda resimli Türk paraları*. Supplements 1–2. Istanbul, 1950.

———. *Ġiyās al-Dīn Kayhusrav II.'in görülmemiş iki sikkesi*. Istanbul, 1950.

Combe, Ét., et al. *Répertoire chronologique d'épigraphie arab*. Vols. 7–9. Cairo, 1936–37.

Erel, Şerafeddin. *Nâdir bir kaç sikke*. Istanbul, 1963.

Gabriel, A. *Monuments turcs d'Anatolie*. 2 vols. Paris, 1931–34.

———. *Voyages archéologiques dans la Turquie orientale*. Paris, 1940. With inscriptions prepared by J. Sauvaget.

Lane-Poole, S. *Catalogue of Oriental Coins in the British Museum*. Vols. 3 and 9. London, 1875 and 1890.

Miles, G. C. *The Numismatic History of Rayy*. *ANSNS*, vol. 2. New York, 1938.

Monnaies antiques et orientales (private collections). Amsterdam, 1913.

Sourdel, D. *Inventaire des monnaies musulmanes anciennes du Musée de Caboul*. Damascus, 1953.

Tevhîd, Ahmed. *Meskûkât-i kadîme-i islâmiye kataloğu*. Pt. 4. Istanbul, 1321.

Uzunçarşılı, İsmail Hakkı. *Anadolu Türk tarihi vesikalarından: Kitâbeler*. 2 vols. Istanbul, 1927–29.

Ziya, Ahmed. *Meskûkât-i islâmiye takvîmi* [A catalogue of Islamic coins]. Istanbul, 1328/1910.

Genealogical Charts of the Seljuks

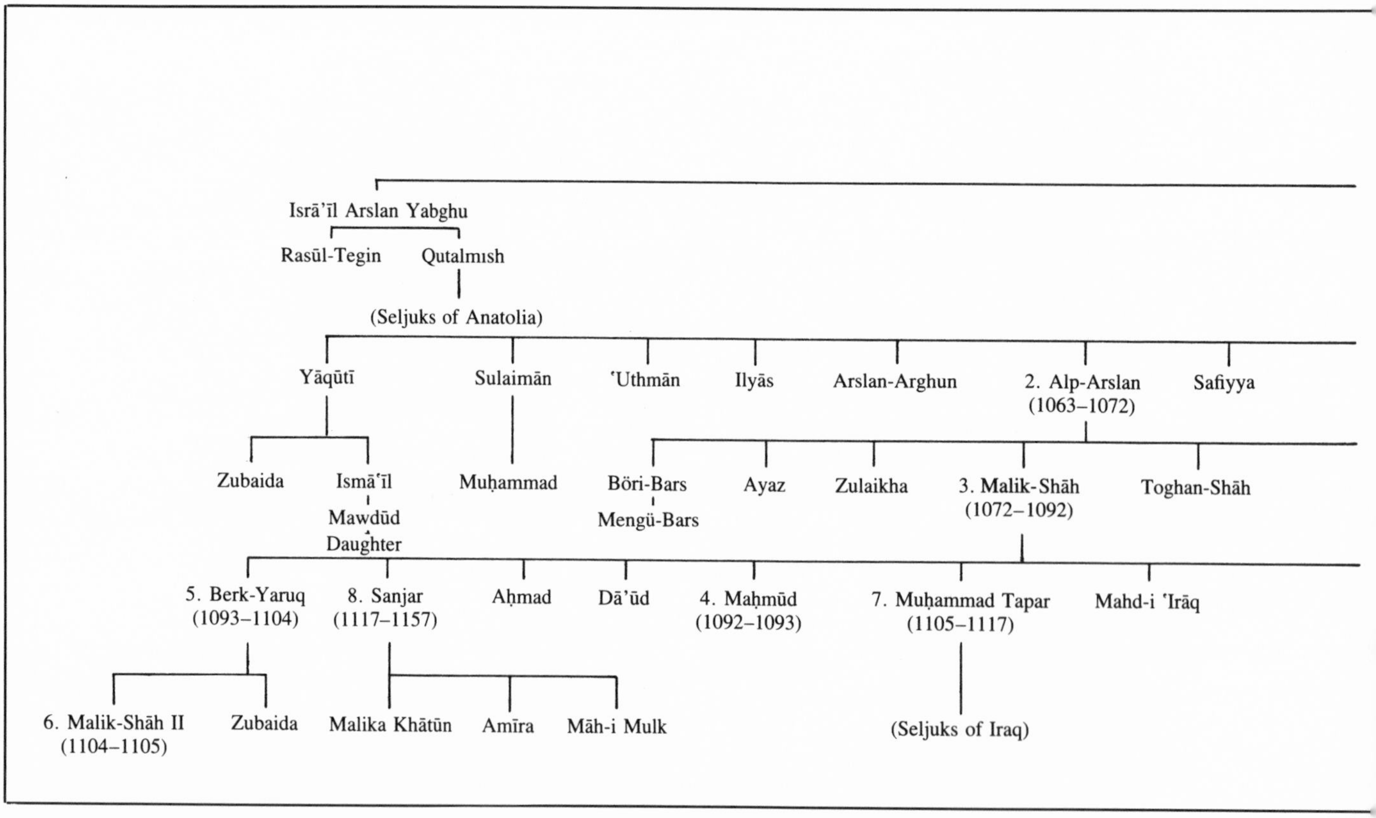
Isrā'īl Arslan Yabghu
Rasūl-Tegin
Qutalmısh
(Seljuks of Anatolia)
Yāqūtī
Sulaimān
'Uthmān
Ilyās
Arslan-Arghun
2. Alp-Arslan
(1063–1072)
Safiyya
Zubaida
Ismā'īl
Mawdūd
Daughter
Muḥammad
Böri-Bars
Mengü-Bars
Ayaz
Zulaikha
3. Malik-Shāh
(1072–1092)
Toghan-Shāh
5. Berk-Yaruq
(1093–1104)
8. Sanjar
(1117–1157)
Aḥmad
Dā'ūd
4. Maḥmūd
(1092–1093)
7. Muḥammad Tapar
(1105–1117)
Mahd-i 'Irāq
6. Malik-Shāh II
(1104–1105)
Zubaida
Malika Khātūn
Amīra
Māh-i Mulk
(Seljuks of Iraq)

THE GREAT SELJUKS

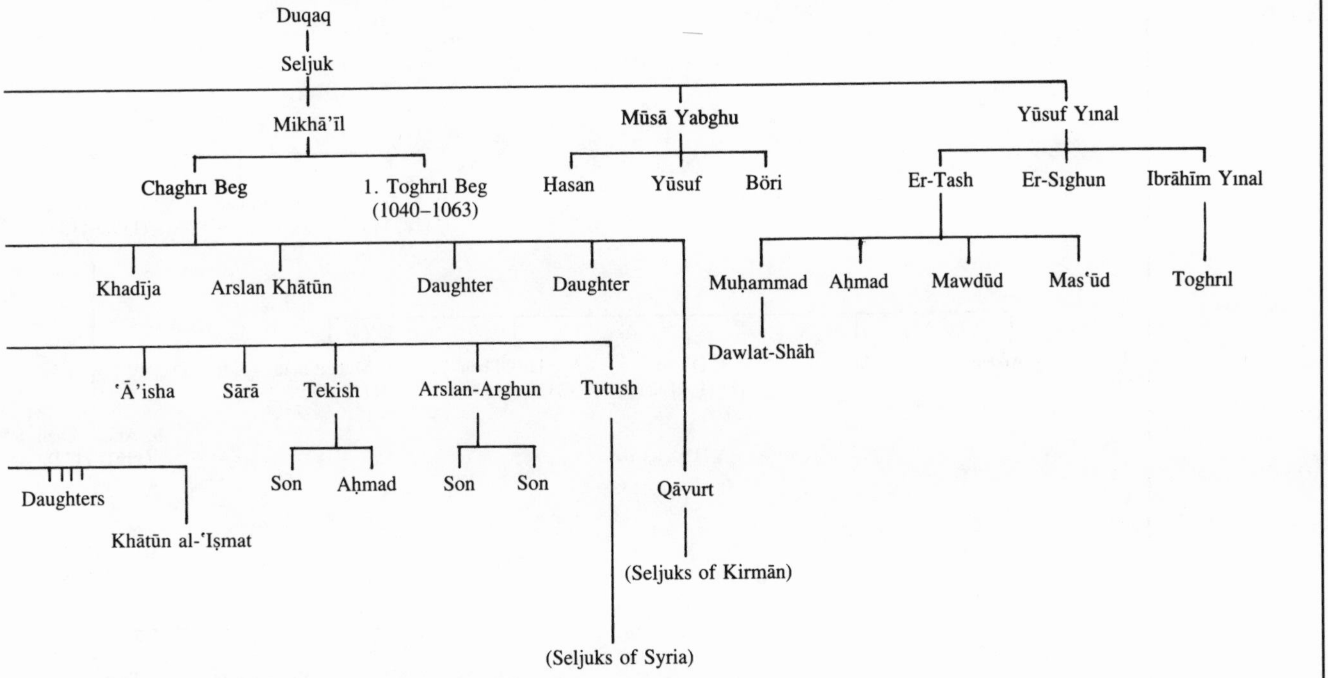

Note: Kafesoğlu's genealogical data on the Seljuks in the *İA* has been revised to incorporate the corrections found in Mehmet Altay Köymen, *Büyük Selçuklu imparatorluğu tarihi,* vol. 1, *Kuruluş devri* (Ankara, 1979); Erdoğan Merçil, *Kirman Selçukluları* (Istanbul, 1980); and Ali Sevim, *Suriye ve Filistin Selçukluları tarihi* (Ankara, 1983).

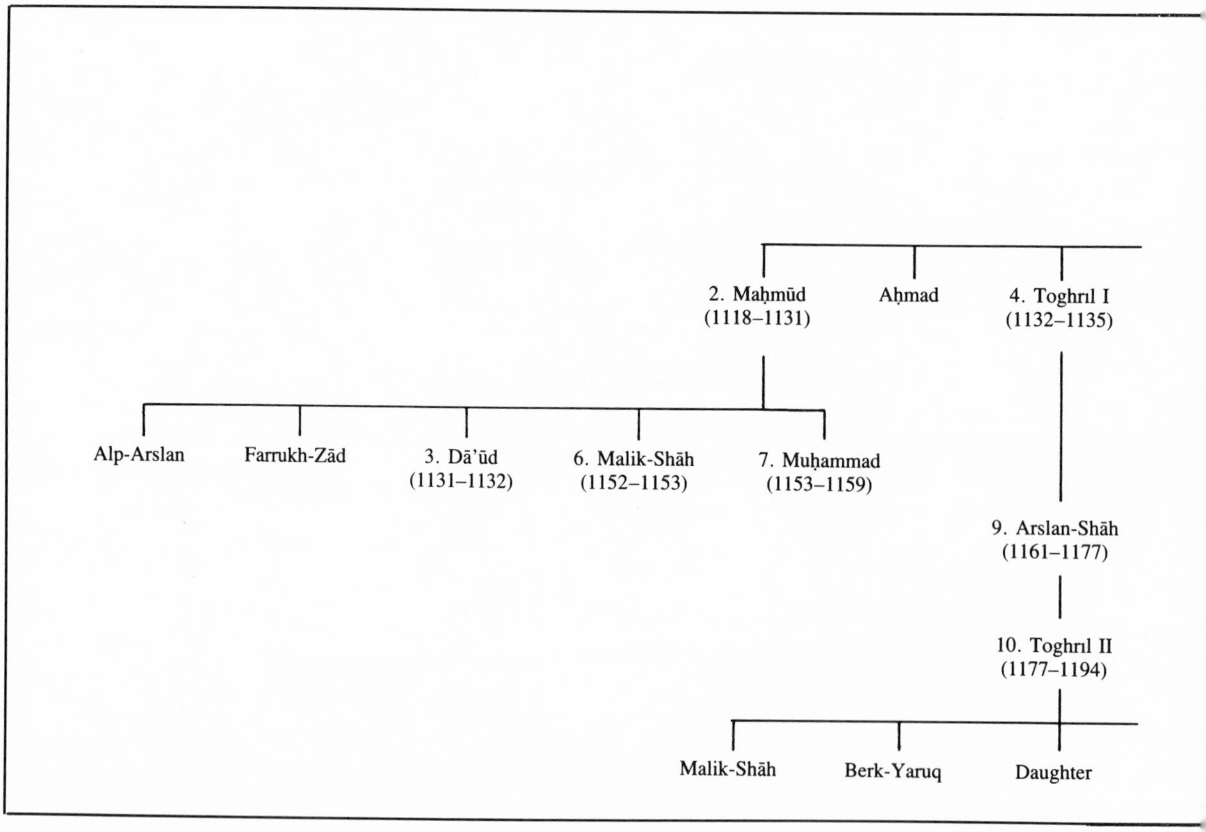
2. Maḥmūd
(1118–1131)
Aḥmad
4. Toghrıl I
(1132–1135)
Alp-Arslan
Farrukh-Zād
3. Dā'ūd
(1131–1132)
6. Malik-Shāh
(1152–1153)
7. Muḥammad
(1153–1159)
9. Arslan-Shāh
(1161–1177)
10. Toghrıl II
(1177–1194)
Malik-Shāh
Berk-Yaruq
Daughter

THE SELJUKS OF IRAQ

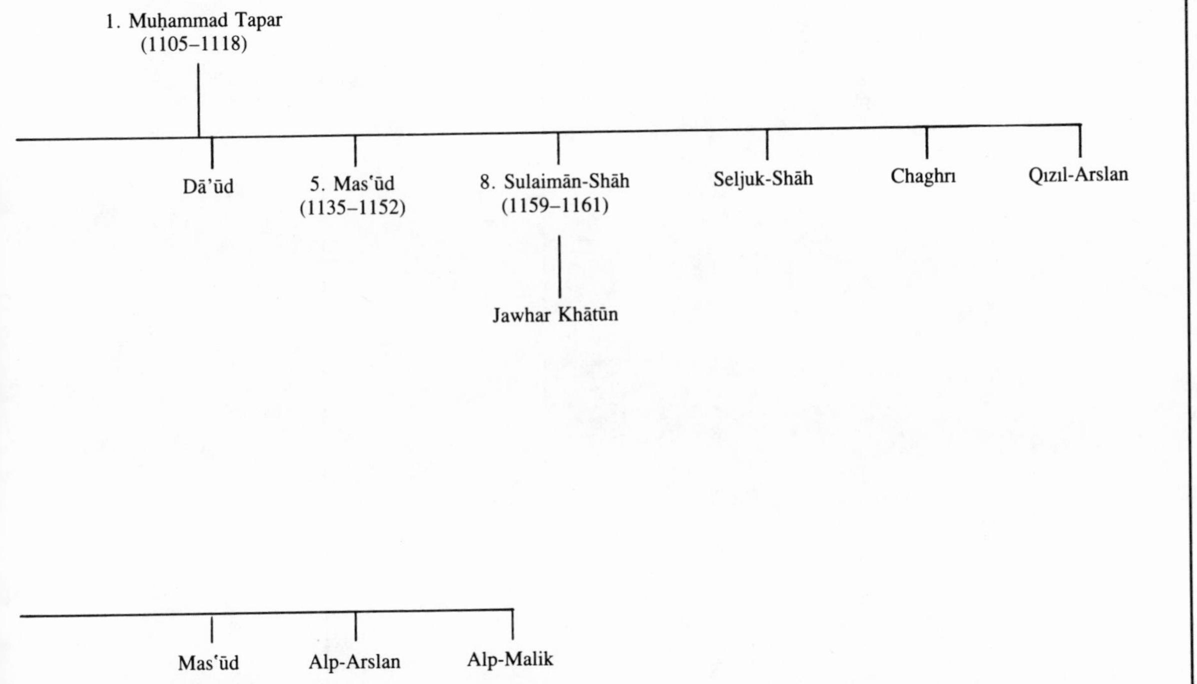

THE SELJUKS OF KIRMĀN

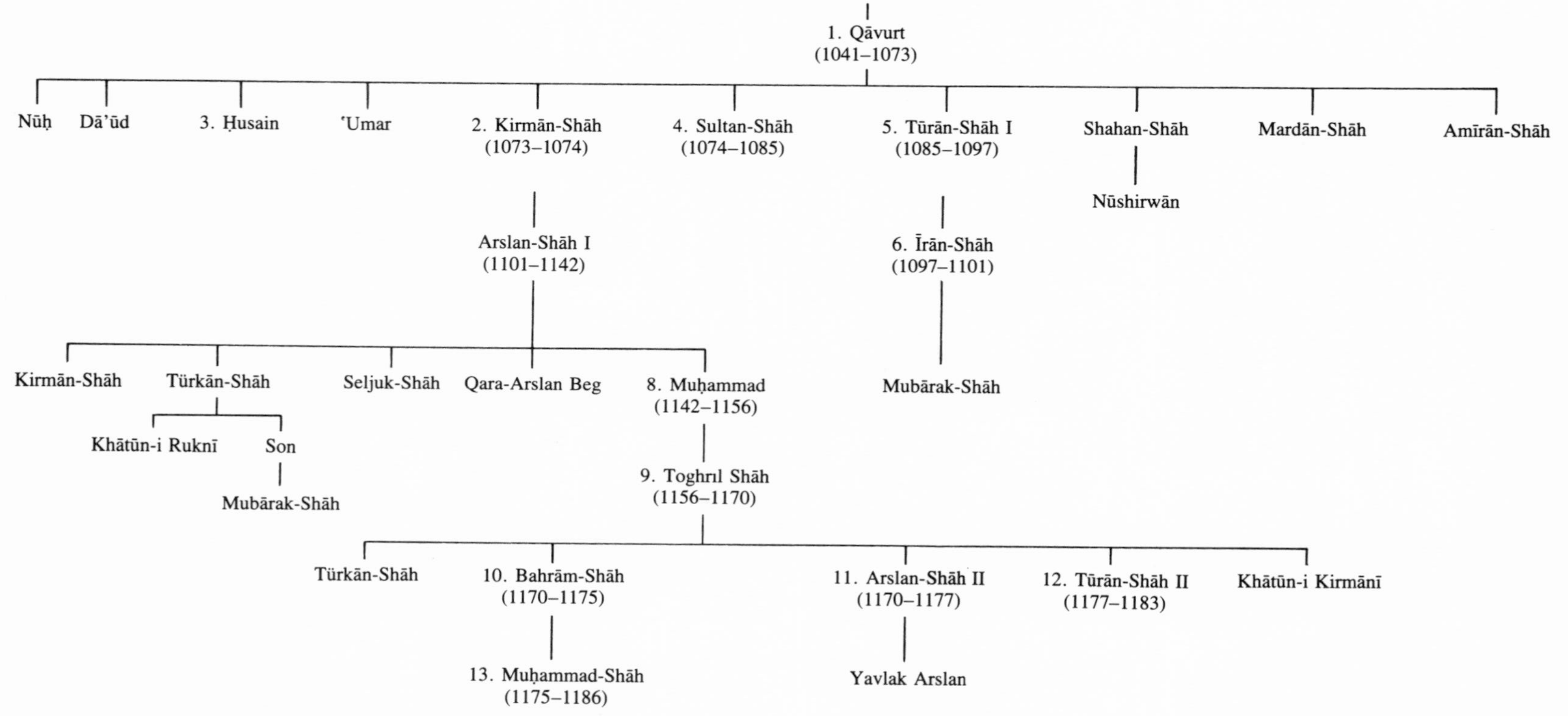

THE SELJUKS OF SYRIA

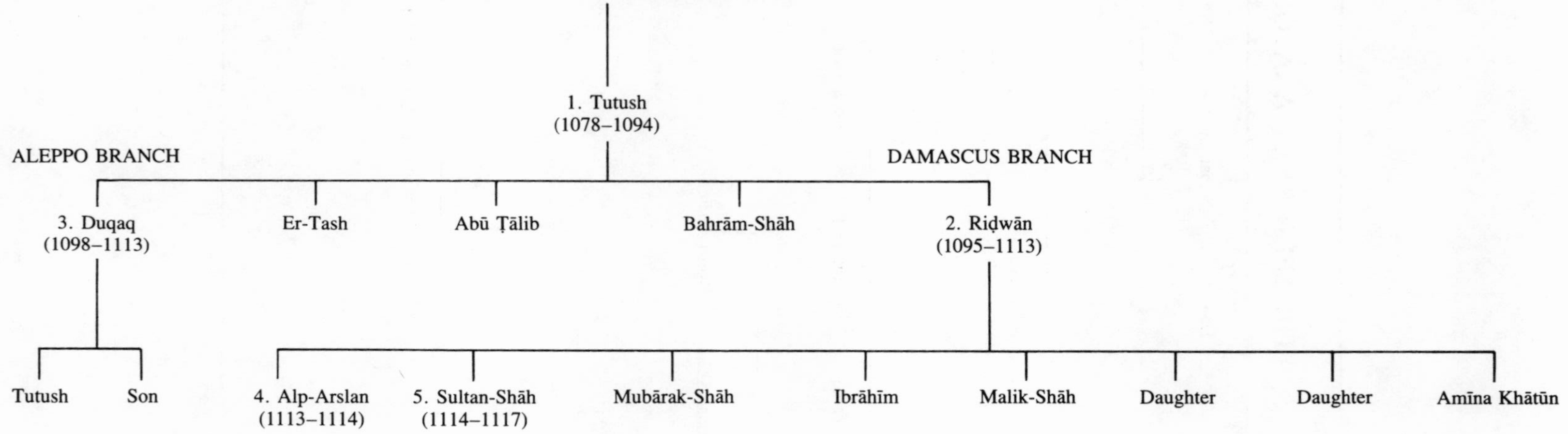

1. Tutush
(1078–1094)
ALEPPO BRANCH
DAMASCUS BRANCH
3. Duqaq
(1098–1113)
Er-Tash
Abū Ṭālib
Bahrām-Shāh
2. Riḍwān
(1095–1113)
Tutush
Son
4. Alp-Arslan
(1113–1114)
5. Sultan-Shāh
(1114–1117)
Mubārak-Shāh
Ibrāhīm
Malik-Shāh
Daughter
Daughter
Amīna Khātūn

THE SELJUKS OF ANATOLIA

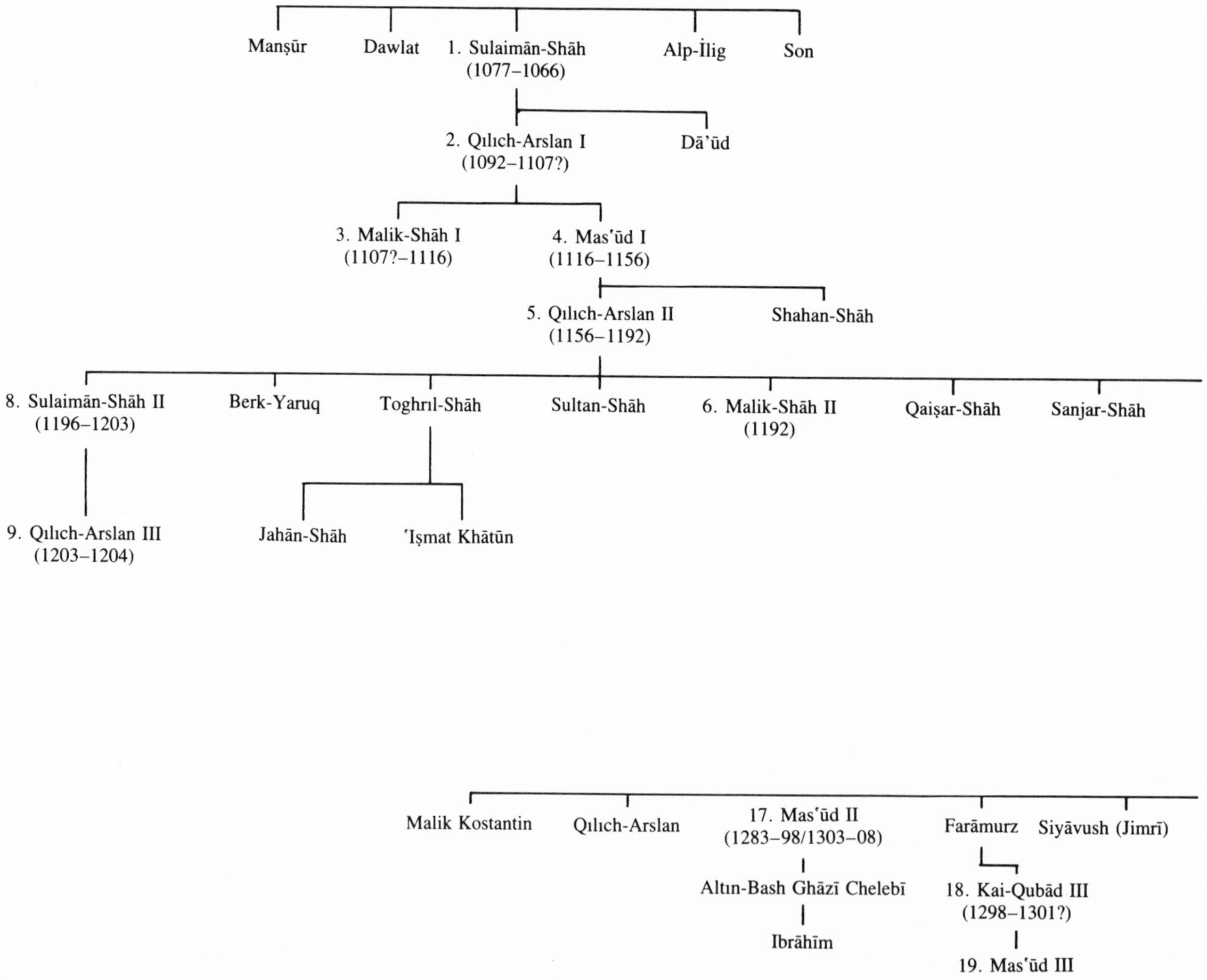

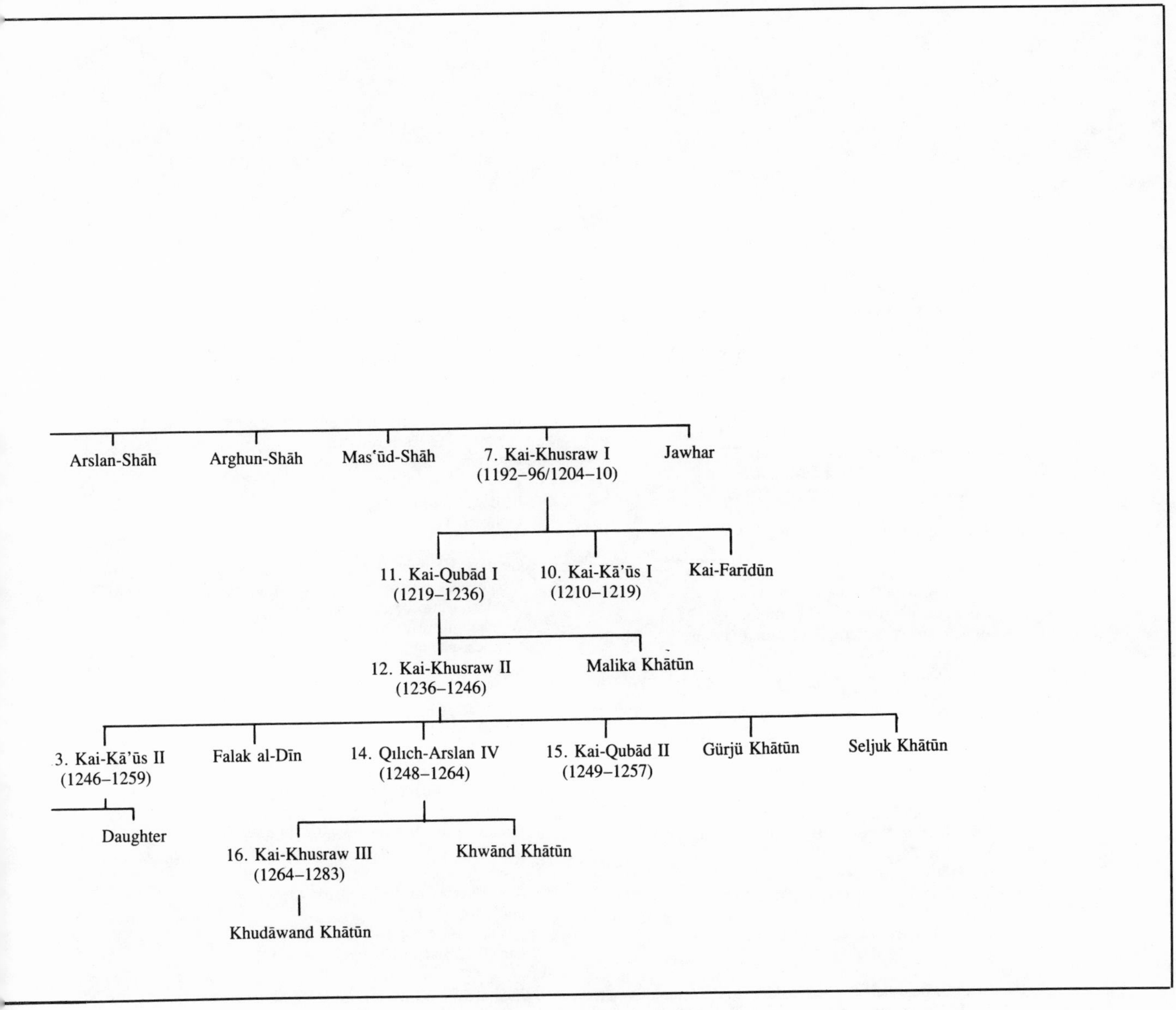

Arslan-Shāh
Arghun-Shāh
Mas'ūd-Shāh
7. Kai-Khusraw I (1192–96/1204–10)
Jawhar
11. Kai-Qubād I (1219–1236)
10. Kai-Kā'ūs I (1210–1219)
Kai-Farīdūn
12. Kai-Khusraw II (1236–1246)
Malika Khātūn
.3. Kai-Kā'ūs II (1246–1259)
Falak al-Dīn
14. Qılıch-Arslan IV (1248–1264)
15. Kai-Qubād II (1249–1257)
Gürjü Khātūn
Seljuk Khātūn
Daughter
16. Kai-Khusraw III (1264–1283)
Khwānd Khātūn
Khudāwand Khātūn

Index

Gary Leiser grew up in the Willamette valley in Oregon. In 1964 he enrolled in Portland State University where he majored in anthropology and Middle East studies. During the academic year 1966-67, he was a student at the British Middle East Center for Arabic Studies, Shemlan, Lebanon, and in June 1967, was among those evacuated in the midst of the "Six-Day War." After receiving a B.A. from PSU in 1969, he entered the University of Pennsylvania as a National Defense Foreign Language Fellow. At Penn, he specialized in medieval Islamic history, Arabic, and Turkish, earning both an M.A. (1973) and Ph.D. (1976). While taking a holiday from dissertation research in Egypt, he and his wife visited northern Cyprus and were caught in the fighting in the summer of 1974. Upon completing graduate school, he taught briefly at the University of Utah and worked as a Middle East consultant. He then served for four years as a language and area specialist for the Department of Defense in a liaison office with the Turkish General Staff in Ankara. He is currently the historian for Headquarters, The U.S. Logistics Group (U.S. Air Forces in Europe), Ankara. He has published numerous articles and translations on Middle East history.

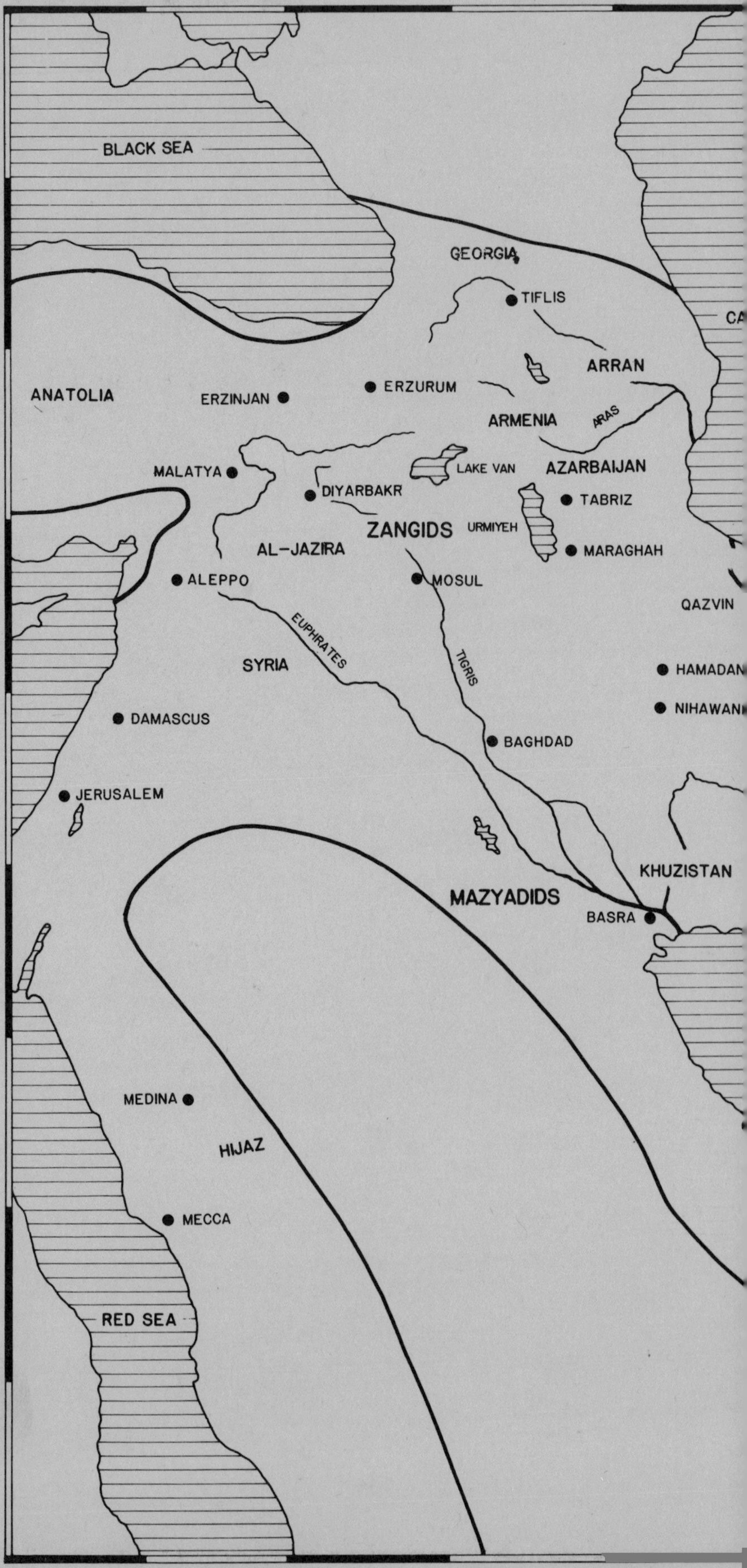

BLACK SEA
GEORGIA
TIFLIS
CA
ARRAN
ANATOLIA
ERZINJAN
ERZURUM
ARMENIA
ARAS
MALATYA
LAKE VAN
AZARBAIJAN
DIYARBAKR
TABRIZ
AL-JAZIRA
ZANGIDS
URMIYEH
MARAGHAH
ALEPPO
MOSUL
QAZVIN
EUPHRATES
SYRIA
TIGRIS
HAMADAN
NIHAWAN
DAMASCUS
BAGHDAD
JERUSALEM
KHUZISTAN
MAZYADIDS
BASRA
MEDINA
HIJAZ
MECCA
RED SEA